INTERNATIONAL POLITICAL ECONOMY SERIES
General Editor: Timothy M. Shaw, Professor of Political Science and
International Development Studies, Dalhousie University, Nova Scotia

The global political economy is in a profound crisis at levels of both production and
policy. This series provides overviews and case-studies of states and sectors, classes
and companies in the new international division of labour. These embrace political
economy as both focus and mode of analysis; they advance radical scholarship and
scenarios.

The series treats polity-economy dialectics at global, regional and national levels
and examines novel contradictions and coalitions between and within each. There
is a special emphasis on national bourgeoisies and capitalisms, on newly industrial
or influential countries, and on novel strategies and technologies. The concentration
throughout is on uneven patterns of power and production, authority and distribution, hegemony and reaction. Attention will be paid to redefinitions of class and
security, basic needs and self-reliance and the range of critical analysis will include
gender, population, resources, environment, militarization, food and finance. This
series constitutes a timely and distinctive response to the continuing intellectual and
existential world crisis.

Recent titles:

Robert Boardman
PESTICIDES IN WORLD AGRICULTURE

Inga Brandell (*editor*)
WORKERS IN THIRD-WORLD INDUSTRIALIZATION

Bonnie K. Campbell (*editor*)
POLITICAL DIMENSIONS OF THE INTERNATIONAL DEBT CRISIS

Bonnie K. Campbell and John Loxley (*editors*)
STRUCTURAL ADJUSTMENT IN AFRICA

Jerker Carlsson and Timothy M. Shaw (*editors*)
NEWLY INDUSTRIALIZING COUNTRIES AND THE POLITICAL
ECONOMY OF SOUTH-SOUTH RELATIONS

David P. Forsythe (*editor*)
HUMAN RIGHTS AND DEVELOPMENT
THE UNITED NATIONS IN THE WORLD POLITICAL ECONOMY

David Glover and Ken Kusterer
SMALL FARMERS, BIG BUSINESS

Steven Kendall Holloway
THE ALUMINIUM MULTINATIONALS AND THE BAUXITE CARTEL

Matthew Martin
THE CRUMBLING FAÇADE OF AFRICAN DEBT NEGOTIATIONS

James H. Mittelman
OUT FROM UNDERDEVELOPMENT

Dennis C. Pirages and Christine Sylvester (*editors*)
TRANSFORMATIONS IN THE GLOBAL POLITICAL ECONOMY

Garry Rodan
THE POLITICAL ECONOMY OF SINGAPORE'S INDUSTRIALIZATION

Jorge Rodríguez Beruff, J. Peter Figueroa and J. Edward Greene (*editors*)
CONFLICT, PEACE AND DEVELOPMENT IN THE CARIBBEAN

Patricia Ruffin
CAPITALISM AND SOCIALISM IN CUBA

Roger Southall (*editor*)
LABOUR AND UNIONS IN ASIA AND AFRICA

Peter Utting
ECONOMIC REFORM AND THIRD-WORLD SOCIALISM

Fiona Wilson
SWEATERS: GENDER, CLASS AND WORKSHOP-BASED INDUSTRY
IN MEXICO

David Wurfel and Bruce Burton (*editors*)
THE POLITICAL ECONOMY OF FOREIGN POLICY IN SOUTHEAST ASIA

Economic Reform and Third-World Socialism

A Political Economy of Food Policy in Post-Revolutionary Societies

Peter Utting
Research Consultant
United Nations Research Institute
for Social Development, Geneva

St. Martin's Press   New York

First published in the United States of America in 1992

Printed in Hong Kong

ISBN 0–312–06807–7

Library of Congress Cataloging-in-Publication Data
Utting, Peter.
Economic reform and third-world socialism: a political economy of
food policy in post-revolutionary societies/Peter Utting.
p.   cm.—(International political economy series)
Includes bibliographical references and index.
ISBN 0–312–06807–7
1. Food supply—Government policy—Developing countries.
2. Agriculture and state—Developing countries.   3. Land reform–
–Developing countries.   4. Developing countries—Economic policy.
5. Socialism—Developing countries.   6. Communism—Developing
countries.   I. Title.   II. Series.
HD9018.D44U88   1992
338.1'91724—dc20   91–24939
                                                                    CIP

Contents

List of Tables and Maps

Tables

Maps

Acknowledgements

This book is based on research, carried out during 1988 and 1989, which formed part of a doctoral programme at the University of Essex and a project co-ordinated by the United Nations Research Institute for Social Development (UNRISD) on 'Food Policy and the World Recession'.

I am greatly indebted to Maxine Molyneux, Valpy Fitzgerald and Cynthia Hewitt de Alcántara for their continuous support and valuable advice throughout that time – in particular, their prompt willingness to read drafts and provide detailed comments. I also benefited from the insightful comments and criticisms of David Kaimowitz, Max Spoor, Tony Woodiwiss, Harold Wolpe and Marc Wuyts.

Special thanks go to Brenda Corti and Mary Girling at the Sociology Department of Essex University, as well as Françoise Jaffré, Rhonda Gibbes, Irene Ruíz, Wendy Salvo and Josephine Yates at UNRISD, for their highly efficient logistical support and cheerful attitude towards life; Solon Barraclough and Dharam Ghai for their encouragement and example regarding research and writing; and Orlando Nuñez, then director of the Centre for Research and Studies of the Agrarian Reform (CIERA) in Managua both for his intellectual support and for adopting a healthy, unbureaucratic attitude toward my requests for leave.

The fact that this text was ever finished owes much to the emotional support of loved ones. To my compañera, Amalia Chamorro; parents, Christina and Trevor Utting; and sister, Lesley Micheletti – thanks for helping me weather the storm.

Finally I would like to thank the following institutions for their financial support: the International Development Research Centre (IDRC) of Canada; UNRISD; the British Government's Overseas Research Scholarship (ORS) Awards Scheme; and the Sociology Department of the University of Essex.

PETER UTTING

Abbreviations

GENERAL

Institutional

CMEA	Council for Mutual Economic Assistance
ECLAC	Economic Commission for Latin America and the Caribbean
EEC	European Economic Community
FAO	United Nations Food and Agricultural Organization
IADB	Inter-American Development Bank
IDRC	International Development Research Centre
IFAD	International Fund for Agricultural Development
IMF	International Monetary Fund
OECD	Organization for Economic Co-operation and Development
UNRISD	United Nations Research Institute for Social Development
USAID	United States Agency for International Development

Technical

EAP	Economically Active Population
FI	Fixed Investment
FYP	Five-year Plan
GDP	Gross Domestic Product
GI	Gross Investment
GMP	Gross Material Product
GSP	Gross Social Product
Ha	Hectare (2.47 acres)
Gm	Gramme
Kcal	Kilocalorie
Kg	Kilogramme (2.205 lb.)
Lb	Pound (454 grams)
Mz	Manzana (0.7 ha.)
NEP	New Economic Policy

PSA	Primitive Socialist Accumulation
QQ	Quintal (100 lb.)
ST	Short ton (2000 lb.)

References

CW	*Collected Works*
FEER	*Far Eastern Economic Review*
FT	*Financial Times*
GWR	*Granma Weekly Review*
YICA	*Yearbook on International Communist Affairs*

COUNTRY

Mozambique

ERP	Economic Recovery (or Rehabilitation) Programme
FRELIMO	Frente de Libertação de Moçambique: Front for the Liberation of Mozambique
RENAMO	Resistência Nacional Moçambicana: Mozambican National Resistance (MNR)

Vietnam

DRV	Democratic Republic of Vietnam
SRV	Socialist Republic of Vietnam
VNCP	Vietnamese Communist Party

Cuba

ANAP	Asociación Nacional de Agricultores Pequeños: National Association of Small Farmers
CDR	Comité de Defensa de la Revolución: Committee for the Defence of the Revolution
JUCEPLAN	Central Planning Board
SDPE	El Sistema de Dirección y Planificación de la Economía: Economic Management and Planning System

Nicaragua

AMNLAE	Asociación de Mujeres Nicaragüenses Luisa Amanda Espinoza: Luisa Amanda Espinoza Association of Nicaraguan Women
ANS	Asociación de Niños Sandinistas: Sandinista Children's Association
APP	Area Propiedad del Pueblo: Area of People's Property
ATC	Asociación de Trabajadores del Campo: Association of Rural Workers
BND	Banco Nacional de Desarrollo: National Development Bank
CAT	Centro de Abastecimiento de los Trabajadores: Workers' Supply Centre
CAS	Cooperativa Agrícola Sandinista: Sandinista Agricultural Co-operative
CCS	Cooperativa de Crédito y Servicios: Credit and Service Co-operative
CDC	Centro de Desarrollo Campesino: Peasant Development Centre
CDS	Comité de Defensa Sandinista: Sandinista Defence Committee
CIERA	Centro de Investigación y Estudios de la Reforma Agraria: Centre for Research and Studies of the Agrarian Reform
CRIES	Coordinadora Regional de Investigaciones Económicas y Sociales: Regional Office for Economic and Social Research
CST	Central Sandinista de Trabajadores: Sandinista Workers' Federation
CT	Colectivo de Trabajo: Work Co-operative
DGRA	Dirección General de Reforma Agraria: General Division of the Agrarian Reform
DGFCDC	Dirección General de Fomento Campesino y Desarrollo Cooperativo: General Division of Peasant and Cooperative Development
ENABAS	Empresa Nicaragüense de Alimentos Básicos: Nicaraguan Basic Foodstuffs Company
FDN	Fuerzas Democráticas Nicaragüenses: Nicaraguan Democratic Forces ("Contras")

FER	Frente Estudiantíl Revolucionario: Revolutionary Students' Front
FSLN	Frente Sandinista de Liberación Nacional: Sandinista National Liberation Front
IHCA	Instituto Histórico Centroamericano: Central American Historical Institute
INCEI	Instituto Nicaragüense de Comercio Exterior e Interior: Nicaraguan Institute for Foreign and Domestic Trade
INEC	Instituto Nacional de Estadísticas y Censos: National Institute for Statistics and Consensus.
INIES	Instituto Nicaragüense de Investigaciones Económicas y Sociales: Nicaraguan Institute for Economic and Social Research
INSSBI	Instituto Nicaragüense de Seguridad Social y Bienestar: Nicaraguan Institute for Social Security and Welfare
JS19J	Juventud Sandinista 19 de Julio: 19th July Sandinista Youth Association
MED	Ministerio de Educación: Ministry of Education
MEDA	Marco Estratégico de Desarrollo Agropecuario: Strategic Framework for Agricultural Development
MICE	Ministerio de Comercio Exterior: Ministry of Foreign Trade
MICOIN	Ministerio de Comercio Interior: Ministry of Internal Trade
MIDINRA	Ministerio de Desarrollo Agropecuario y Reforma Agraria: Ministry of Agricultural Development and Agrarian Reform
MIPLAN	Ministerio de Planificación: Ministry of Planning
MINSA	Ministerio de Salud: Ministry of Health
OTPI	Organización Territorial de la Producción y el Intercambio: Territorial Organization of Production and Exchange
PAN	Programa Alimentario Nicaragüense: Nicaraguan Food Programme
RAAN	Región Autónoma Atlántico Norte: Northern Atlantic Autonomous Region
RAAS	Región Autónoma Atlántico Sur: Southern Autonomous Atlantic Region

SPP	Secretaría de Planificación y Presupuesto: Planning and Budget Office
UCA	Universidad Centroamericana: University of Central America
UNAG	Unión Nacional de Agricultores y Ganaderos: National Union of Farmers and Ranchers
ZE	Zona Especial: Special Zone

Introduction

THE RESEARCH PROBLEM AND FOCUS

During the 1980s, governments in several post-revolutionary Third-World societies introduced a series of economic and planning reforms which represented a major departure from orthodox socialist principles and practice. These reforms generally sought to deal with problems associated with shortages of consumer goods, public-sector and balance of trade deficits, inflation, parallel markets and popular discontent by:

(a) encouraging a partial shift away from centralized planning and direct state control of production and exchange, towards decentralization and the regulation of the economy through macroeconomic policy instruments;
(b) expanding the role of petty commodity production[1] in the economy;
(c) lowering the investment ratio[2] and shifting the accumulation/consumption balance in favour of the latter;
(d) altering the domestic terms of trade in favour of agricultural producers and increasing the provision of goods and services to rural areas;
(e) reducing government and balance-of-trade deficits through devaluation, stricter controls on social expenditures and reductions in subsidies.

The purpose of this study is to analyze why the shift from 'orthodoxy' to 'reform' occurred in these countries at this point in time. Obviously this subject covers an extremely broad area. In the 1980s, there were in the world approximately twenty-five countries which could be classified as Third-World socialist countries[3] and many experimented with economic policy reforms. Apart from the number of countries involved, the reforms affected diverse policy areas associated with economic and social development as well as the political system itself. Given the scope involved, I have chosen to delimit the subject area in certain respects.

Firstly, a small number of countries which may be categorized as dependent 'transitional' economies[4] have been selected for study.

They are Nicaragua, Mozambique, Vietnam[5] and Cuba. The case studies relating to the latter three countries are essentially based on secondary sources readily available in English and Spanish. Here my intention is to describe the shift in policy approach and identify the types of conditions that prompted the reforms.

The selection of Mozambique, Vietnam and Cuba was determined partly by the availability of literature but also because of their contrasting social and economic structures and levels of development. Nicaragua is the focus of a more detailed study which draws not only on secondary materials but also on primary sources, as well as my own research on economic and food policy issues carried out in that country since 1980.[6]

Secondly, while the review of the policy changes takes us up to 1990, the more detailed analysis of why the shift from orthodoxy to reform occurred focuses particularly on the initial stages of the reform process, notably during the early and mid-1980s.

Thirdly, rather than studying in detail all aspects of economic and social policy reform, the central focus is on changes in food policy, that is, on policies affecting the production, processing, marketing, distribution and consumption of food. This focus has been adopted for a number of reasons. It has been said that analyzing the food situation of a particular country provides a window for viewing the broader situation regarding development processes and socioeconomic and political relationships (Barraclough, 1991; Benjamin *et al.*, 1984). This is particularly so in the type of countries which concern us here, given that they are largely agrarian-based economies where much national and family income is derived from food production, processing and marketing. In addition, a large proportion of household expenditure tends to be allocated to food consumption.

Associated with these general characteristics are the dual features of poverty or low levels of living, and limited industrialization. Food production, marketed surpluses and savings (both voluntary and forced) associated with peasant/farm income and the domestic terms of trade[7] assume a crucial role in the development process from the point of view of basic needs provisioning and accumulation.[8] Focusing on food policy in the context of post-revolutionary societies, however, provides a window for viewing not only the situation as regards 'poverty' and 'development', but also 'transition'. The food question is intimately related to three issues that lie at the heart of the debate concerning transition in underdeveloped countries, namely the forms and extent of appropriation of surplus by the state; the reproduction of the proletariat both as a factor of development and a dominant historical subject (Fitzgerald and Wuyts, 1988a, p. 3); and the transformation of social relations which characterize agrarian petty commodity production.

Much of the discussion surrounding economic policy reform in socialist countries involves the so-called 'plan versus market' debate and the question of how to articulate different forms of production within the framework of a socialist development strategy. One of the key questions here relates precisely to relations between the state and agrarian petty-commodity producers who are primarily food producers. Such relations tend to be contradictory. The post-revolutionary state has traditionally sought to appropriate large quantities of surplus from the peasant/agricultural sector in order to finance industrialization and provide cheap food for the urban working class and other support groups such as the army and the bureaucracy. At the same time the state has attempted to develop agriculture through increases in productivity and the transformation of social relations. Such attempts have often been resisted by sectors of the peasantry which, in many instances, have responded by reducing levels of marketed surplus.

This scenario of conflicting or 'contradictory' interests involves also other major actors on the post-revolutionary stage. Crucial to the whole development issue is the question of the domestic terms of trade and the quantity of manufactured goods made available for peasant consumption. Increasing the supply of such goods to rural areas and/or increasing food-producer prices may run counter to the interests of an urban working class and a bureaucracy concerned with cheap food and access to manufactured products. The technocracy may well favour not only a high accumulation rate and restrictions on consumption but also investment in heavy industry as opposed to industries producing basic manufactures required in rural areas, or basic consumer goods. A key source of state finance may also be enterprise profits achieved to a large extent on the basis of an austere wages policy, which will have repercussions in terms of worker productivity and support. Another source may well be large-scale monetary emission which through inflationary effects can affect real incomes and popular support for the regime.

The way, then, in which major social groups relate to issues associated with surplus appropriation, reproduction and transformation is likely to be contradictory. A central theme running through this study is that these contradictions express themselves in forms of struggle or generate distorsions that play a decisive role in accounting for a set of crisis conditions which place the need for radical reform firmly on the policy agenda. Such reforms, however, should not be seen, as is often the case, merely in terms of a belated recognition of policy errors on the part of government leaders and planners, or a pragmatic response to economic crisis, social discontent and external pressures, or, indeed, as simply the result of an intra-party power struggle which sees the 'moderates' claiming victory over the 'ideologues'.

Rather, I argue that the introduction of radical economic and food policy reforms and their specific content should be analyzed in terms of a response on the part of the state to (a) a set of crisis conditions generated to a large extent by what may be referred to as contradictory class and state practices which undermine the capacity of the state to mobilize and appropriate surplus, plan the economy and maintain hegemony; and (b) changes in social structure, civil society and participatory processes which alter the balance of social forces and the capacity of different groups to influence the policy process.

Such contradictions are crucially linked to the fundamental structural changes which characterize post-revolutionary societies. The redistribution of income and wealth, rapid industrialization, agricultural modernization, the transformation of social relations, expanding the role of the state in the economy – all imply major changes in state–society relations and in social structure. Post-revolutionary transformation also implies new forms of representation and organization of the mass of the population. Revolutions of national liberation against colonial domination or dictatorship can provide a greater space for mass participation in the policy process. This study will look at the way in which such developments have enabled certain groups to influence more directly the policy process.

Post-revolutionary development generally implied, in addition, significant changes in the mode of insertion of the transitional society in the world economy. This process tends to express itself in a struggle between the revolutionary state and a world or regional power with economic and/or geopolitical interests in the transitional society. Domestic class forces and social groups, as well as foreign capital and governments, align themselves in different ways to what in effect constitute two alternative societal 'projects'.[9] In order to understand the shift from orthodoxy to reform it is crucial to look also at the nature and effects of this struggle.

This study is divided into four parts:

Part I   describes relevant aspects of the transition from orthodoxy to reform in mainstream socialist societies, notably the Soviet Union and China. I begin by discussing the historical origins (both theoretical and concrete) of orthodox socialist development policy and look briefly at the types of economic and food policy reforms which have been introduced during several decades of post-revolutionary development up to the mid-1980s. I then examine a number of different approaches which have been adopted for explaining the reform process and attempt to identify those aspects or variables which are of use for understanding the reform process in the type of countries that concern us here. Part I ends by examining what is specific about this group of 'dependent transitional economies' and raises the question of the limits to which one can generalize about the experience of socialist countries in general or, indeed, about post-revolutionary Third-World societies.

Part II   consisting of Chapters 2, 3 and 4, reviews on a country-by-country basis the types of reforms which were introduced in Mozambique, Vietnam and Cuba and attempts to identify the principal factors and conditions that prompted the policy changes. Each chapter commences with a brief introduction outlining the nature of the agrarian/food question at the time of the revolution or independence. These case studies go on to identify the central characteristics of food and development policy in the particular country concerned during the pre-reform era, continue with a review of the policy reforms, and end by attempting to identify, from the secondary sources available, those key elements and contradictions that are pertinent for understanding the shift from orthodoxy to reform.

Part III   provides a deeper analysis of the reform experience of one country – Nicaragua. This section consists of four chapters. Chapters 5 and 6 trace the evolution of Sandinista development policy from the initial emphasis on the expansion of the state and co-operative sectors, large-scale investment projects and urban basic-needs provisioning, to a more peasant-orientated strategy during the mid-1980s and finally on to economic stabilization and adjustment towards the end of the decade. Chapter 7 analyzes the nature of the crisis which prompted the mid-1980s shift in strategy. Chapter 8 looks more closely (than in the preceding case studies) at the relationship between these policy reforms and changes in social structure, the organization of groups at the level of civil society and in the extent and forms of participation of different social groups in the policy process.

Part IV summarizes the way in which governments in all four countries responded to what I refer to as a crisis of the post-revolutionary state, identifying both the similarities and differences in policy approach. It goes on to specify the component features of that crisis and examine the types of changes occuring in social structure, at the level of civil society and in 'participation' which affected the capacity of different social/interest groups to influence the policy process. A short concluding section characterizes the specificity of the reform process in dependent transitional economies, and attempts to conceptualize what may be called the economic and political 'logic' behind the reforms.

Notes

1. The term 'petty commodity production' refers to family-based units of production which possess means of production and rely principally on unpaid family labour to produce commodities (Bernstein, 1986, p. 9).
2. The investment ratio refers to the percentage of GDP or Global/Gross Social Product accounted for by investment.
3. Classifications of Third World 'socialist' countries vary, of course, but generally include Afghanistan, Albania, Algeria, Angola, Benin, Capo Verde, China, Cuba, Ethiopia, Ghana, Grenada (1979–83), Guinea-Bissau, Guyana, Kampuchea, Korea (PDR), Laos, Madagascar, Mongolia, Mozambique, Nicaragua, Vietnam, Yemen (PDR), Zimbabwe. Several others, notably Myanmar (Burma), Surinam, Iraq, Libya, Tanzania and Somalia are sometimes included as well (See Fitzgerald and Wuyts, 1988a; Jameson and Wilber, 1981; Szajowski, 1981; Wiles, 1982).
4. As indicated in the final section of Part I of this study, 'transition' implies, *inter alia*, a process of transformation of certain structures and social relations which characterize dependent capitalist formations, as well as profound changes in the mode of insertion of the post-revolutionary society in the world economy. Crucial here, and to the idea of socialism, is the notion that patterns of production, distribution and accumulation will be determined to a greater extent by what has been referred to as 'a socially determined rationality' or social control, and to a lesser extent by 'the logic of capital' centred on the profit motive (Fagen *et al.*, 1986, p. 10).
5. The case study of Vietnam deals with the experience of North Vietnam (Democratic Republic of Vietnam (DRV)) up to 1975 and goes on to consider policy changes affecting the Socialist Republic of Vietnam (SRV) which was formed following the reunification of the North and South.

6. Throughout most of the 1980s I worked as a researcher at the Centre for Research and Studies of the Agrarian Reform (CIERA) in Managua.

7. The term 'surplus' assumes different meanings in different contexts and schools of thought. At the level of the national economy, economic surplus may be defined as the difference between aggregate net output and aggregate essential consumption (Saith, 1985, p. 17), that is, that consumption necessary to reproduce the labour force (Fitzgerald, 1986, p. 42). Agricultural surplus generally refers to marketed surplus in the form of commodities – food as wage goods, raw materials for industry and agro-export products for foreign trade. It may also assume the form of a financial flow or transfer of net investible resources exacted through such mechanisms as voluntary savings, taxation or transfers effected though the relative prices of agricultural and industrial products, and what for agricultural producers are adverse terms of trade (Goodman and Redclift, 1981, pp. 73–7). In Marxist analysis, the appropriation of surplus from peasant producers also relates to what is referred to as 'devalorized labour time' which derives from the fact that peasant households produce for self provisioning, that is, 'use-values' – using unpaid family labour. As Goodman and Redclift point out, this represents a potential source of subsidy to non-farm capital since it has the effect of reducing the cost of the labour inputs involved in commodity production, which in turn 'exerts downward pressure on the relative prices of these commodities' (Ibid., p. 78).

8. The importance of food, both from the point of view of economic development and social well-being, has been stressed in much of the research and literature of recent years on 'food security' and 'basic needs' (Barraclough, 1991; Hopkins and Van Der Hoeven, 1983; Streeten, 1979; World Bank, 1986a).

9. This line of argument has been developed by O.Nuñez (O. Nuñez, 1987).

Part I

Orthodoxy and Reform in Socialist Countries

1 What Can Be Learnt from Theory and the Experience of the Soviet Union and China?

INTRODUCTION

A considerable body of literature now exists which documents and explains the shift from orthodoxy to reform in mainsteam socialist societies. In Part I of this study I refer to some of this literature and, in particular, the experience of the Soviet Union and China. In doing so I will identify those features of development strategy in socialist countries which may be labelled 'orthodox' and look briefly at the nature of the economic and food policy reforms which have been introduced.

I then examine a number of approaches which have been adopted for understanding the reform process. Attention is focused firstly on the writings of those who stress the question of systemic constraints associated with so-called state-centred accumulation models. I then consider an alternative approach which links policy reforms to changes which have occurred in the balance of social forces. Here, several crucial variables or areas of analysis are identified which will be examined more closely in the case studies contained in Parts II and III. With particular reference to Bettelheim's analysis of the reform experience of the Soviet Union in the 1920s and that of modern-day China, I highlight the importance of referring to the question of class struggle. Other areas of analysis associated with changes in social structure, developments at the level of civil society and changes in institutionalized forms of 'popular participation' are also identified. Part I ends by (a) assessing the relevance of the experience of the Soviet Union and China for understanding the reform process in dependent transitional societies; (b) examining the specificity of the latter; and (c) considering variations within this group which have some bearing on the nature of the reform process.

ORTHODOX SOCIALIST DEVELOPMENT STRATEGY

From much of the Marxist literature on transition and the historical post-revolutionary experience of the Soviet Union and China, socialist development has come to be associated with centralized planning, direct state control of the means of production and exchange or sweeping collectivization of petty commodity producers, as well as rapid industrialization centred on heavy industry.

Planning and the Market

According to Engels, production and distribution in socialist society would not be determined by the law of value;[1] rather, commodity production would cease once the means of production had been 'seized' by society: 'Direct social production and direct distribution preclude all exchange of commodities, therefore also the transformation of the products into commodities. . .' (Engels, 1975, p. 366). What society produced would be determined by a plan which prioritized the production of goods according to their socially useful effects. As Engels stated: 'The useful effects of the various articles of consumption, compared with one another and with the quantities of labour required for their production, will in the end determine the plan.' (Ibid., p. 367).

Planning, it was assumed, would be a relatively straightforward exercise since it was envisaged that socialist revolution would occur in countries with a high level of development of the productive forces, where production would be concentrated in relatively few enterprises, thereby facilitating expropriation and the co-ordination and administration of resource flows, and where conditions of abundance, characteristic of advanced capitalism, would minimize conflicts over resource allocation.

This scenario, however, bore little relation to the objective conditions that characterized 'actually existing socialism' (Bahro, 1978) in its infancy – conditions associated with low levels of industrialization and the dispersion of production among many small-scale enterprises and petty-commodity producers. Such conditions precluded the expropriation of much of the means of production and meant that commodity relations would continue to exist. The key development questions became, rather, how to combine planning and commodity forms, and how to transform not only social relations of production but also, as Saith points out, economic structures through industrialization and the modernization of agriculture (Saith, 1985, p. 2).

During the three-year period of civil war and foreign intervention which followed the Russian Revolution in 1917, economic strategy was characterized by a highly centralized system of economic administration and measures to eliminate commodity and money relations. Private trading was abolished, requisitioning and rationing of food introduced, and a system of wage payments in kind put into effect. The policies of 'War Communism', however, soon generated acute contradictions. In the debates that ensued, very different positions regarding the relationship between plan and market, agriculture and industry emerged.

These were expressed clearly in the writings of Bukharin and Preobrazhensky. For Bukharin, plan and market would necessarily have to coexist, and could do so in harmony. His association of the market with decentralization and democratization meant, moreover, that the market was essential not only for the health of the economy but also for socialist society. The operation of market forces need not constitute a threat to socialism if the 'commanding heights' of the economy (banking, foreign trade and large-scale industry) were under state control and if the power of certain groups, such as the 'kulaks', could be contained through measures including taxation and co-operativization. Outlining Bukharin's position, Littlejohn points out: 'planning should aim to minimize the inevitable temporary disruptions of the natural order which occur in the process of development of socialism'. As such, Bukharin placed considerable emphasis on such aspects as planning techniques, balanced growth, even tempos and agriculture as the basis of industrialization (Littlejohn, 1979, pp. 214–17).

For Preobrazhensky, there was an inherent conflict between plan and market. His concept of Primitive Socialist Accumulation (PSA) referred to the measures necessary to obtain the resources to support accumulation and the growth of the socialist sector of the economy (Millar, 1978, p. 392). PSA meant:

> accumulation in the hands of the state of material resources mainly or partly from sources lying outside the complex of the state economy. . .In conflict with the law of value (the law of PSA determines), both the distribution of means of production in the economy and the distribution of labour power, and also the amount of the country's surplus product which is alienated for expanded socialist reproduction. (Preobrazhensky, 1965, pp. 84–5)

In practice this meant that planning must subordinate the market mechanism and that agriculture would provide the surplus to finance accumulation and the growth of the socialist sector of the economy. The concept of PSA stressed the need to squeeze agriculture and the peasantry through 'unequal exchange' or the manipulation of the domestic terms of trade through fixed prices (the so-called 'price scissors') set for agricultural and industrial products. PSA, however, involved far more than just a net transfer of resources from agriculture to industry. It was, rather, the key mechanism on which the transition from one mode of production to another was based. As Saith explains:

> PSA encapsulates a wide-ranging structural process. . .It also includes not just flows of surpluses but also flows of labour and changes in the ownership of stock and assets. . .Since PSA is really a process, it starts and ends, the latter occuring when the old mode of production has been entirely transformed into the new one. (Saith, 1985, p. 23)

The Soviet Union and the 'Stalinist Model'

Preobrazhensky's ideas were influential in shaping development policy in the Soviet Union from the late 1920s. The programme of forced collectivization, implemented between 1929 and 1938 and involving some 26 million peasant holdings, facilitated applying in practice the concept of PSA, although the idea of radical institutional change as a basis for PSA had not actually figured in Preobrazhensky's ideas.

A particular interpretation of Marxist theory, which gained prominence during the Stalinist era, was instrumental in associating socialist development with the rapid development of the productive forces. Stalin's 'Dialectical and Historical Materialism' gave primacy to the development of the productive forces as opposed to class struggle as the motor of history (Hindess, 1976, p. 2). It was theoretical positions such as these, reinforced by pressures and constraints associated with backwardness and external aggression, that gave rise to policies in the Soviet Union favouring centralized planning, forced industrialization and high rates of accumulation. Rather than following a strategy promoting balanced growth, sectors and activities regarded as the 'engines of growth' were given clear priority in resource allocation. In relation to agricultural production, the aim was not so much to increase and diversify food production, as to collect tribute to increase the availability of essential wage goods such as grains, potatoes and cabbage (Ellman, 1979, p. 92–8).

In order to ensure, then, that sufficient surplus was generated and appropriated, the state directly controlled the 'commanding heights' of the economy and imposed rigid controls over the domestic terms of trade. As Brus explains:

> Thus it was not enough to control and to regulate economic behaviour of economic units. The State had to take over the functions of an economic actor both on the macro- and on the micro-scale so as to secure the generation of savings, to collect them, to invest, to produce, and to distribute them. . .Enforcement of the desired rate of accumulation required strict control over the 'terms of trade' between the State and the peasants' and workers' and employees' households. The solution applied in all socialist countries, at least until the mid-1950s, was administrative determination of prices and wages combined with direct physical controls in particularly sensitive areas, such as extraction of agricultural produce by way of compulsory deliveries at nominal prices. (Brus, 1987, pp. 149–50)

China and the 'Maoist Model'

Many of the features of the 'Stalinist model' also characterized the first five-year plan in post-revolutionary China. A key difference, though, lay in the role of the peasantry as a protagonist in the movement to transform social relations. The existence of a large, poor peasant sector, the active involvement of much of the peasantry in the revolutionary process, and the limited importance of the rich peasantry[2] in rural society during the post-revolutionary period, meant that the type of state/peasant and urban–rural relations which existed in the Soviet Union were not reproduced in China (Saith, 1985, p. 30).

In relation to economic policy, important differences between the Stalinist and Maoist development strategies arose from 1956 onwards, when Mao Tse-Tung criticized the initial post-revolutionary strategy based on high rates of accumulation, the prioritization of heavy industry and excessive centralized state control of the economy (Gray, 1982, pp. 293–4). As indicated in the following quote, Mao had been critical of the Soviet model of collectivist agriculture:

The root of the failure to increase agricultural production in some countries is that the state's policy towards the peasants is questionable. The peasant's burden of taxation is too high while the price of agricultural products is very low, and that of industrial goods very high. . .The collective needs accumulation, but we must be careful not to make too great demands on the peasants. . .Except when we meet with unavoidable natural disasters, we should enable the peasants' income to increase year by year on the basis of increased agricultural production. (Mao Tse-Tung, cited in Ellman, 1979, p. 91)

In contrast to the Soviet emphasis on modern capital intensive techniques, the Chinese stressed the importance of 'walking on two legs', that is, combining modern and simple or capital-saving techniques (Spoor, 1988). This led to the rapid development of small-scale industry in both urban and rural areas (Ellman, 1979, pp. 137–8). The development of small-scale rural industries reflected another difference in approach, namely the attempt to maximize the use of resources available in the countryside for the benefit of agriculture. This involved, in addition, eliminating situations of widespread unemployment or underemployment by mobilizing labour for rural infrastructural activities (Ibid., p. 100). Whereas the Stalinist model aimed to squeeze the peasantry to provide resources for accumulation in the 'centre', the Chinese peasantry was squeezed, to a large extent, to provide resources for development at the local level.

Despite these differences, many of characteristics of the Soviet model continued to constitute key features of Chinese socialism. While the Great Leap Forward (1958–61), in its original conception, was based on Mao's criticisms of the Stalinist model, in actual practice it became identified with increasing state regulation and control. Accumulation continued at very high rates of around 30 per cent of national income until the beginning of the 1980s; heavy industry received clear priority in the allocation of investment expenditures (over 50 per cent between 1958 and 1978), while agriculture and light industry received little more than 10 and 5 per cent respectively; and it would seem that for much of the Maoist period, agriculture continued to be squeezed by the price scissors. While the essential needs of the mass of the population were generally guaranteed, 'luxury' consumption was virtually eliminated and the growth of consumption in general was less than that of national income (Ghose, 1984).

In rural areas, increased state control and regulation were facilitated by the amalgamation, during the late 1950s, of virtually the entire rural population into People's Communes which combined the tasks and functions associated with large-scale production units, local state administrative agencies and traditional village community institutions. From 1953 until the 1980s, a state monopoly existed on the procurement and marketing of four principal agricultural products – grains, cotton, velvet and vegetable oil crops. Some seventy products formed part of a fixed state purchasing system whereby producers were obliged to sell all surplus to the state's commercial departments at official prices. Referring to the Maoist era. Croll points out:

> The chief characteristic of the national food system is the degree to which the state has intervened and substituted the market in producing, distributing and allocating the staple food grains. It is not too much of an exaggeration to say that the operation of the national grain circuit by the state. . .is the unique cornerstone on China's food policies and the key factor determining grain intake and the food security of the people. (Croll, 1982, p. 326)

ECONOMIC AND FOOD POLICY REFORMS: PAST AND PRESENT

The above features associated with orthodox socialist development strategy were, of course, not immutable. Before the contemporary wave of economic policy reforms, both the Soviet Union and China experienced several periods of reform wherein an attempt was made to introduce new policies to deal with various combinations of problems associated with inefficiency and waste, shortages, low labour productivity, balance of payments difficulties and social tensions.

Reform in the Soviet Union

The NEP

Particularly relevant to the issue of economic and food policy reform in Third-World socialist countries is the reform experience of the

Soviet Union during the first decade following the Russian Revolution. The New Economic Policy (NEP), introduced by the Bolshevik Party in 1921, represented an abrupt departure from the policies which had characterized the immediate post-revolution period of 'War Communism', (Bettelheim, 1977; Carr, 1952; Nove, 1969). The NEP centred to a large extent on issues associated with food policy and the peasantry, and represented not only a new economic strategy but also a new strategy of class alliance in order to tackle the combined problems of declining agricultural production in general and marketed production in particular, poor living conditions of the mass of the rural and urban populations, and increasing discontent among sectors of the peasantry and the working class.

With regard to state/peasantry relations, the NEP experienced two phases. The first, involving the abandonment of the 'surplus-grain appropriation system' (requisitioning) in favour of the 'tax-in-kind system', 'implied a more or less socialist exchange throughout the country of the products of industry for the products of agriculture, and by means of that commodity exchange the restoration of large-scale industry as the sole basis of socialist organization' (Lenin, CW. vol. 33, 1966, pp. 95–6). The system of state-regulated buying and selling, however, was impossible to implement. It therefore became necessary to encourage commodity and money relations, as well as to renounce attempts to subject the peasantry to state controls.

Other policies which characterized the NEP sought to expand light industrial production organized in small-scale private or co-operative enterprises, particularly in rural areas, as well as trade and financial relations with the international market and economic relations with foreign capitalists through the granting of concessions. While the state retained control and ownership of the 'commanding heights' of the economy, some state enterprises were leased to capitalist entrepreneurs.

It is important to note for the analysis which follows that the NEP was seen by Lenin not merely as a tactical move or 'retreat' to boost production and contain the disaffection of the masses, but as a necessary component of a longer-term strategy of socialist transformation. As Bettelheim explains:

> a socialist transformation of production relations is possible only under definite political and economic conditions. In a country like Russia this transformation required the existence of a firm alliance between the workers and the peasants. In 1921 this alliance was not

firm enough. The first task of the proletarian party was to strengthen this alliance, which was one of the aims of the NEP.

Carrying through the task of the socialist transformation of production relations requires, furthermore, that the living conditions of the masses be such as to enable them really to devote themselves to this as the priority task. This means that the working people must not be absorbed by the fight against hunger and cold, and not be crushed by day-to-day difficulties, physical exhaustion, and sickness. . .Reestablishing acceptable conditions of life, ensuring the supply of food to the towns and balanced exchanges between agriculture and industry, ending unemployment as soon as possible, were therefore also among the necessary aims of the NEP. (Bettelheim, 1977, p. 444)

Partial Reforms of the Post-War Era

During three decades prior to *perestroika*, several reform initiatives were introduced in the Soviet Union. A major purpose of these reforms was to deal with the problem of inefficiency in state enterprises. A period of reform which began in 1957 was largely restricted to attempts to move away from the highly centralized planning system and introduce regional decentralization. When, however, the problems of the centralized system were reproduced at the regional level, the system was eventually scrapped (Nuti, 1981, p. 397). Another period of reform began in 1965, when the administration of Kosygin attempted a series of reforms that introduced profit as an indicator of enterprise performance and as a basis of material incentives to labour. This model of reform, which in theory (drawing on the ideas of Lange and Lieberman) supported a high degree of decentralization and a reduction in the role of the central planning apparatus while encouraging broad macroeconomic guidance, was implemented far more comprehensively in Hungary in 1968 (Ibid., p. 398). In the Soviet Union, implementation of such reforms was largely blocked by the state and Party bureaucracy.

There were also several attempts to correct macroeconomic and sectoral imbalances related to the allocation of resources for accumulation/consumption and agriculture/industry. The early 1960s saw the beginnings of a more consumer-orientated economic policy, when the decision was taken to purchase large quantities of grain from abroad. In the late 1960s the level of investment in agriculture increased significantly (Ellman, 1979, p. 97). In 1965 and 1972–74

measures were introduced to improve the price and incentive structure in agriculture (Rutland, 1985, p. 154), thereby contributing to a
significant increase in the real incomes of agricultural producers
(Ellman, 1979, p. 97). Schemes were also introduced which permitted subcontracting to small groups of agricultural workers. The
1971–75 Five-Year Plan (FYP) was the first in which consumer-goods
industries were expected to grow faster than producer-goods industries (although in practice this was not achieved) (Rutland, 1985, pp.
107–8). The next FYP saw a large increase in the allocation of
investment resources to agriculture. As a result, the share of total
investment accounted for by agriculture increased from 19 per cent in
1961–65 to 27 per cent in 1976–80 (Ibid., p. 154).

A more integrated attempt to improve economic and social conditions in agriculture began in 1982, with the launching of the Food
Programme which sought to boost and diversify agricultural production, as well as to improve the living conditions of rural families,
notably through housing programmes; education, health-care and
cultural projects; and the provision of consumer durables (Chernenko, 1985). While some changes in property relations were introduced to promote an increase in private small holdings, the main
stimulus to agricultural production was expected to come from
'increas[ing] capital investment in agriculture and. . .flood[ing] it
with machinery and other material means', as well as the more
efficient use of such resources (Ibid., p. 6). In terms of production
results, it was largely the state farms that benefited from these
developments.

Perestroika

Since the mid-1980s there has occurred in the Soviet Union a more
concerted effort at reform involving decentralization, or what has
been referred to as 'the redefinition of planning in terms of the use of
value forms instead of material balances to control the economy'
(Fitzgerald and Wuyts, 1988, p. 3). Apart from greater respect for
enterprise autonomy, the profit motive, material incentives, and
factor productivity, *perestroika* also provides a greater space for
co-operative and small-scale private economic activity.

As regards agriculture, a 1987 decree paved the way for a larger
role for private subsidiary farms (Schroeder, 1988, p. 182). In addition, production tasks were increasingly contracted out to groups of
workers or families (Nove, 1988, p. 11). Co-operative managers in

many regions acquired greater independence from the state, enabling them to take decisions about what to produce and where to sell once planned procurement targets had been met (*Guardian Weekly*, 23 October 1988, p. 18).

Changes in the price structure for food and agricultural products were also introduced. According to a leading government economic adviser:

> A radical and total reform of price formation is envisaged as well as a revision of all types of prices: wholesale, purchase retail and supply tariffs, into a unified coordinated system of prices. . .Subsidies on the price of goods will be substantially cut. In agriculture, prices will be constructed so as to take into account the real cost of fertiliser inputs, of machinery and other equipment, formally sold to agriculture at depressed prices. . .With the implementation of the reforms intended for the 1989–90 period. . .the number of prices set centrally is to be reduced, that is, to comprehend only the more essential staple products. (Aganbegyan, 1988, p. 8)

If fully implemented, such a policy would represent a radical departure from that of the previous decade, which had both heavily subsidized agricultural production costs, and maintained relatively stable producer and retail prices (Cook, 1987, p. 12). Under the new policy, prices for many food products are to be established on the basis of competition among co-operatives and state enterprises (Nove, 1988, p. 11).

Unlike any of the previous reforms, significant political and institutional changes have also been added to the reform agenda. Democratization and curbing the role and power of the bureaucracy are seen as essential both to radicalize the content of the reforms and to ensure their implementation. The possibility of implementing a radical programme, of economic reform however, would seem to depend also on overcoming opposition from sectors within the working class. As indicated by Mandel, such opposition has arisen as prices rise with only slow improvements in the availability of consumer goods, as enterprise managers attempt to reduce labour costs and link wages to productivity, and as state authorities seek to reassert the principle of distribution according to work, thereby threatening the considerable social wage (provision of heavily-subsidized goods and services which bears little if any relationship to work effort) enjoyed by workers (Mandel D., 1988, pp. 141–3).

While the economic policy reforms occuring in the Soviet Union and other Eastern European countries involve questions regarding the extent and forms of state control over the economy, the articulation of different property forms, enterprise efficiency and the accumulation – consumption balance which are of relevance to Third-World countries, their ultimate economic objectives would seem to be more specific to countries enjoying a far higher level of industrial development and where 'basic needs' have largely been met. As Fitzgerald and Wuyts point out: 'In "Second World" socialism, *perestroika* appears to be directed towards achieving international industrial competitiveness on the basis of advanced technology and towards raising non-essential consumption standards.' (Fitzgerald and Wuyts, 1988a, p. 3).

In the words of another writer, it was necessary 'to move the respective economies beyond a stage of basic industrialization to cope with new conditions requiring new growth sectors, such as electronics, services and biotechnology, or to universalize and routinise the reliance upon increased efficiency and innovation as the bases for continued growth' (Riskin, 1987, p. 164). Even the new-found emphasis on food and consumer-goods production focuses less on quantitative increases in the production of essential products, as on improvements in the variety and quality of products (Aganbegyan, 1987, p. 102–3).

Reform in China

China too has experienced several reform periods. Skinner has identified eleven periods or 'policy cycles' between 1949 and 1977 when there was a shift from 'radical' to 'liberal' policies – when 'normative power [was] phased out in favour of remunerative power' (Skinner, 1985, p. 396).

Referring specifically to food policy, Croll points out:

In examining the operation of food policies over the past 25 years, it is possible to identify periods when market forces, as opposed to state controls, have played a greater role in determining which foodstuffs are produced and consumed. . . .

Following the gradual decline of market forces generally between 1949 and 1956 there has been something of a pendulum-like swing between greater and lesser emphasis on them in determining the contents of the family food bowl. The Great Leap Forward in the late 1950s and the decade following the Cultural Revolution between the mid-1960s and mid-1970s were both marked by greater state control and market restrictions. . . .

On the other hand, the years 1956–7, 1962–4 and again the present period dating from 1976 can be identified as years in which market forces were more pronounced. . . . (Croll, 1982, pp. 332–3)

What is clear is that until the 1980s, reform attempts were only partial and piecemeal, or relatively short-lived. No such claim can be made of the reforms initiated in the late 1970s, following the launch in December 1978 of the Four Modernizations Programme. The latter called for an accelerated drive to modernize agriculture, industry, defence and the scientific/technological apparatus, in order that China might attain the levels of economic and social development characteristic of the advanced capitalist countries by the middle of the twenty-first century (Deng Xiaoping, 1985, p. 16).

The initial phase of the reform process, which lasted until the mid-1980s, centred primarily on rural reforms and the implementation of the household contract responsibility system. The latter involved a radically new form of articulation of state, collective and private ownership or control. As explained by one Chinese economist:

Land is owned publicly by villages, which are responsible for assigning contracts for certain farm products and for supplying certain means of production. Villages must also provide guidance for production and product mix, and map out overall plans for farmland and water management. Within this framework, farmers make their own decisions for production and labour. . . . (Xue Muqiao, 1987, p. 19)

Under this system, households were obliged to sell a certain quantity of products at a relatively low official price, another portion at an above-quota price, while any additional surplus could be sold on the free market. In practice, the activities and power of the people's comunes were drastically curtailed as direct-production functions passed to private household units and government functions passed to the traditional village township.

Whereas the first stage of the rural reforms focused on changes at the level of production, the second stage, initiated in 1985, centred on the marketing system. Price controls were lifted on products such as vegetables, meat, eggs, poultry and fish. The number of agricultural products with official prices was reduced from 113 to 25 – these 25 products accounting for 30 per cent of the total value of farm sales (Gao Shangquan, 1987, p. 20). Local authorities, however, were still required to keep price rises within certain limits. The state procurement system was also transformed. As Bettelheim explains:

> those peasant families who were obliged to deliver a minimum quantity of cereals, meat, fish, fruit or vegetables at prices below those of the market, saw such contracts eliminated. Henceforth, the peasants were only subject to various local taxes and the payment of supplies purchased from the state. That part of production that they do not consume themselves is freely sold either at variable prices according to the market situation or to the state at fixed prices. (Bettelheim, 1988, p. 8)

Another feature of the rural reforms has been the encouragement to small-scale industry, run either collectively or privately, and free to employ wage labour. The rural reforms have been complemented by others affecting industrial planning and enterprise management, as well as the wage system and relations with foreign capital and the world market. Developments in these areas, however, have been far less dramatic than those affecting the rural economy.

EXPLAINING THE REFORMS

Systemic Constraints

Much of the literature on economic and food policy reform in the Soviet Union, Eastern Europe and China has attempted to understand the reforms as a response to situations of economic crisis or stagnation resulting primarily from imbalances and constraints associated with centralized or imperative planning systems and collective property forms. These are said to give rise to macroeconomic and intersectoral disequilibria, microeconomic inefficiency, and low labour productivity, from which emerge problems associated with shortages, quality control and waste.

Agriculture and the food system have been particularly affected by these types of problems. As Ellman points out, Soviet agriculture is 'a high-cost agriculture, requiring massive inputs of land, investment and labour' while 'the investment, labour and price policies pursued in the distribution sector were not favourable to the general availability of good quality food' (Ellman, 1979, p. 97). Shortages, notably of meat and dairy products, also constituted a serious problem. These resulted to a large extent from a retail price policy which enabled consumers to purchase many food products at well below production costs. According to one estimate, food subsidies increased from 3.5 billion roubles ($3.9 billion at the official exchange rate) in 1965 to 54.6 billion ($67.2 billion) in 1983, and accounted for 14 per cent of all state budgetary expenditures (Cook, 1987, p. 12–14).

In summary, it may be said that the system of collectivist agriculture which operated in the Soviet Union from the late 1920s and which, as we saw, changed only slowly from the 1950s onwards, suffered two major drawbacks from the point of view of its role as supplier of wage goods and surplus. Firstly, the emphasis on increasing marketed surpluses of *essential* food products led to low levels of production of meat and dairy products and to poor quality food in general. Secondly, to achieve satisfactory levels of production, massive quantities of modern inputs had to be pumped into agriculture. According to Ellman, the flow of capital goods to agriculture was such that the latter was, in fact, a net receiver, rather than a net supplier of resources to industry:

> collectivisation did not lead to an increased net transfer of commodities from agriculture. Hence Stalin's 1928 implicit argument for collectivisation, based on the idea that it would lead to an increased net transfer of commodities to industry, turns out to have been wrong, at any rate in the Soviet case. (Ellman, 1979, p. 96, 1978)

In the case of China, the direction of the transfer of resources is less clear (Idem., 1979, p. 108). What is clear is that the 'bureaucratism' and 'egalitarianism' which characterized the commune system acted as a disincentive to individual effort and initiative and resulted in low levels of labour productivity (Bettelheim, 1988, p. 8; Ghose, 1984, p. 254). Other features of the Maoist 'model' such as 'grain as the key link' in agriculture and local grain self-sufficiency, (Croll, 1982, p. 329) acted as a constraint on the diversification of agriculture and the production of raw materials needed for light industry.

Much of the discussion regarding the limitations of orthodox socialist models has centred on the technical limitations of the centralized planning system which restrict its capacity to substitute the price mechanism as a means of allocating scarce resources. Arguments along these lines were put forward early this century by writers such as Barone and Mises. While the former emphasized the impossibility of gathering and processing information from the millions of economic agents which take decisions about what to produce and buy (Barone, 1935), the latter (Mises, 1935) claimed that given the absence of monetary exchange and consumer sovereignty[3] planners could not take rational decisions governing production and distribution (Rutland, 1985, p. 30).

Once the so-called 'Lange–Lerner solution' to these problems had been put forward,[4] alternate lines of criticism emerged. Prominent amongst these were the arguments of Hayek who questioned the assumptions underlying the debate regarding allocative efficiency. The market, he believed, was not prone to equilibrium but was highly unstable given the constant appearance of new products, techniques and tastes (Hayek, 1949). Under such circumstances, it was argued, what was required was 'a high degree of responsiveness of economic organizations to their changing environment' (Rutland, 1985, p. 38). The bureaucratic centralization characteristic of socialist societies stifled such responsiveness. In contrast, private property, free exchange and competition, it was argued, encouraged it.

During the 1960s, criticism of centralized planning systems intensified increasingly from the perspective of writers on the left. While recognizing the potential of the socialist economic system to mobilize and use existing resources in accordance with the social interest, writers such as Brus emphasized the need for 'a planned economy with a "built-in market mechanism"' (Brus, 1972, p. 129). Responsibility for a whole range of decisions regarding production and distribution should, it was argued, be transferred from central planners to the enterprises directly involved. Decentralization and the use of the criterion of profitability as a basis for enterprise decisions were considered necessary to overcome some of the major problems which characterized the centralized model, notably the limited responsiveness of supply to demand; the stifling of innovation and individual creativity and motivation; high costs per unit of output; sectoral disproportions; the sheer complexity of planning; and the related problems of bureaucratic inertia (Ibid., pp. 147–56).

More recent discussions of the limitations of the centralized planning systems (Nove, 1983; Fitzgerald, 1988a; Fitzgerald and Wuyts, 1988a) have drawn on the ideas of Kalecki and/or Kornai and their respective concepts of 'accumulation bias' (Kalecki, 1986) and 'soft budget constraint' (Kornai, 1986). These features of the centrally-planned model are held to be primarily responsible for problems associated with shortages, inflation and balance of payments deficits, and can have an adverse effect on income distribution and production efficiency (Fitzgerald, 1988a, p. 6).

Both Kalecki and Kornai were concerned with the negative effects of the high rates of investment which characterized socialist economies. Kalecki, however, believed that accumulation bias resulted from the tendency of government planners and leaders to prioritize future, as opposed to present, consumption, while Kornai argued that high levels of investment stemmed from specific institutional characteristics of the socialist system which gave state enterprises easy access to state finance and subsidies (Fitzgerald, 1988a, pp. 7–8). Such a situation is said to derive from the 'paternalism' which characterizes relations between the socialist state and the state enterprise (Kornai, 1986, pp. 52–61) and is the effect of a credit policy where access to funds is not constrained by considerations of profitability or own saving (Fitzgerald, 1988a, p. 8). High levels of investment increase the demand for producer goods (the output of Department I) which, in turn, constrains the production of consumption goods (Department II). This creates not only intersectoral imbalances but also tensions regarding the allocation of consumption goods between enterprises and households. As Fitzgerald explains:

> Households, in contrast [to state enterprises], have a 'hard budget' based on salary income, but must suffer from the continuous 'suction' of consumer goods and services. . .from distribution channels by enterprises and government entities for 'on site' consumption by their own workforces, and in the last resort, for special commissariats etc. Thus there is a double conflict over resources: between Departments I and II inputs on the one hand, and between enterprises and households for Department II output, on the other. (Fitzgerald, 1988a, p. 9)

Thus Kornai establishes a direct relation between the institutional characteristics of the centrally-planned system and the problem shortages:

Paternalism is the direct explanation for the softening of the budget constraint. And, if softening occurs, it will entail several phenomena connected with shortage: the almost insatiable demand for materials and the tendency to hoard them, the almost insatiable demand for labour and the tendency to hoard it, the almost insatiable hunger for investment, and so on. (Kornai, 1986, pp. 56–60)

Such characteristics also generate serious problems of inefficiency and waste in the use of resources, which relate essentially to the fact that considerations of profitability and demand do not play a major role in determining the behaviour of state enterprises. Labour efficiency and discipline are also affected by a commitment to full employment which characterizes socialist strategy, as well as the lack of attention to the question of material incentives. These conditions result in low labour productivity and low productivity of investment.

Reform as a Phase of Socialist Development

The type of systemic constraints associated with state-centred accumulation models have been well documented. As we have seen, they derive to a large extent from certain institutional characteristics of the socialist system associated with accumulation bias and the soft budget constraint. Moreover, the state-centred system may make an important contribution to development during the initial post-revolutionary phase, given its capacity to mobilize productive resources in the short-term and bring about crucial structural changes affecting the distribution of income and wealth, the nature of social relations and the balance of social forces, as well as external relations. It is precisely this capacity which makes it possible to move some way towards quickly eliminating the worst features of underdevelopment, associated, for example, with extreme poverty, malnutrition and poor health; an extremely narrow industrial base; and subordination to foreign interests.

The capacity of this system, however, to administer and coordinate the resource flows which characterize a more complex and diversified economy, and to foster the types of technological innovation and new branches of industry associated with modern society, is increasingly called into question. Hence, the limitations of the centrally-planned system reveal themselves particularly in the more developed socialist economies.

According to White, reformism and market socialism represent the latest phase of a process of socialist development. What he refers to as the 'dynamic of socialist transition' consists of three phases. Firstly, during the phase of 'revolutionary voluntarism', involving the revolutionary seizure of state power and socialist reconstruction, 'state-building combines with mass mobilization: markets are seen as matrices of antagonistic class power and subjected to increasing controls. The policy agenda calls for rapid social and institutional transformation'. A second phase of 'bureaucratic voluntarism' follows, in which 'the strategic task of the era becomes rapid economic development and the state takes on the key role in steering the social economy . . .through a network of increasingly complex bureaucratic organizations'. During this stage considerable tensions emerge between the 'revolutionaries' or the politico-administrative elite and a new breed of bureaucrats and technocrats. Reformism and market socialism are said to constitute a third phase:

The population wearies of postponed consumption, and increased social differentiation leads to proliferating sectional interests and demands which beat on the doors of Party hegemony. The traditional methods of directive planning become more and more ineffective as the economic structure becomes more complex and social demands diversify. There are thus moves to change the institutional mix, with more scope for markets, greater political pluralism and cultural diversity. The policy agenda focuses on economic efficiency and productivity, intensive rather than extensive development. (White G., 1983, pp. 32–3)

In analyzing the rural reforms in China, Ghose also argues that the need for new policies arose in response to a very different set of economic and social conditions that had evolved over three decades of change:

Development efforts over the period 1949–78 . . .brought about fundamental changes in China's rural economy . . .The old policies had played their role, and their very achievements had generated new problems which in turn called for modifications of the old policies. On the other hand, new capabilities had developed which made different state policies feasible. The industrial sector generated a growing surplus and the need for extracting a surplus from agriculture declined proportionately. An economic surplus had emerged in the rural sector and capital-investment could increasingly replace labour-investment. The problem of ensuring a minimum level of living for the entire population had been largely solved and attention could shift to a rapid improvement in the levels of living. Production conditions in agriculture had been sufficiently improved to initiate a process of specialization and diversification. (Ghose, 1984, pp. 271–2)

Explanations such as these highlight correctly the link between reform and changes in objective conditions associated with economic development and social change. In doing so they reveal the limited value of analyses which explain policy changes merely in terms of a belated attempt to correct policy 'mistakes', or as a reflection of changes in the ideology of the party leadership. This latter element appears in many journalistic and academic accounts of policy changes in the Soviet Union and China where the leadership factor – read Mikhail Gorbachev and Deng Xiaoping – is seen as the crucial element in explaining the reform process. The following type of statement illustrates the explanatory weight sometimes given to the leadership question: 'new leaders commonly launch reform initiatives to shed the stigma of past associations . . .To prove themselves as bold and legitimate rulers, successors attempt to chart a new course more responsive to popular needs' (Perry and Wong (eds), 1985, p. 7). As the analysis of the reform process in Third-World socialist economies will show, the leadership question may have a limited explanatory value for understanding why reforms are introduced. In the four countries I have selected for study, important changes in economic policy took place without there having occurred previously any significant change in the leadership of the ruling party.

The type of explanation put forward by White seems to imply that at a certain level of development of the productive forces, market socialism will necessarily come into being. This raises, though, a number of questions, some of which are posed by White himself. How do we account for the experience of some socialist countries, with relatively high levels of industrialization, which have not engaged in deregulation or decollectivization to any significant degree? How, also, do we explain why a country like Cuba retreated from a policy line favouring material incentives and private markets? This type of analysis is also of little help in explaining why economic reforms with certain similar features to those in Eastern Europe and China were also introduced during the 1980s in newly-emerged socialist countries such as Mozambique or Nicaragua. The same might be said of the Soviet Union during the early 1920s when the NEP was introduced.

To answer these questions it is important firstly to move away from broad generalizations about the types of problems facing all socialist societies and establish the specificity of the crisis to which post-revolutionary states respond when introducing reforms. A point which has already been raised, and will be developed further below, is that the nature of the crisis in the Soviet Union and certain Eastern European countries is very different from that experienced in most dependent transitional economies. Secondly, it is wrong to see the reforms merely as pragmatic responses to economic crisis conditions, or simply in terms of instruments of 'crisis management'. The reform process must also be analyzed in the light of changes occurring in the balance of social forces, that is, in the capacity of different social groups to influence, through diverse means and practices, patterns of mobilization and distribution of resources, as well as decision-making processes associated with government policies. The nature of such changes may also vary considerably from one society to another. This is not meant to imply that generalizations are not possible but to recognize that important differences in the nature of the reform process exist not only between developed and underdeveloped transitional societies but also within each category.

As I mentioned earlier, the experience of the Soviet Union in the 1920s, provides a useful reference point for understanding the contemporary reform process in several underdeveloped transitional economies. As Bettelheim's analysis shows, the NEP and other major policy changes introduced by the Bolsheviks, emerged in the context of a crisis of the state[5] which had serious political as well as economic manifestations. Hegemony, as much as surplus mobilization and appropriation, was at stake. Popular discontent, strikes, uprisings, and support for counter-revolutionary forces indicated a serious weakening, if not breakdown, of the system of alliances that had enabled the Party to exercise leadership.

The measures which constituted the NEP attempted both to increase agricultural production and marketable surplus, as well as to bring about a realignment of class forces wherein a broad worker–peasant alliance would constitute the social basis of state power while forces opposed to the revolution would be correspondingly weakened (Bettelheim, 1977, pp. 485, 513). This new approach involved an attempt to regain the trust of the middle and rich peasantry, not only so that these social groups might contribute towards the fulfilment of more immediate economic and political objectives, but also so that, on the basis of this trust, the Bolshevik Party could recoup its capacity to transform social relations without alienating large sectors of the population. Particularly important here was Lenin's notion of voluntary co-operation (Ibid., pp, 477–592).

Bettelheim makes the point in his analysis of the NEP that the content of the policy changes was determined by three main factors: theoretical analysis, the lessons of experience and the demands of the masses (Bettelheim, 1978, p. 234). The lessons of experience would seem to refer here to a more realistic assessment of the capacity of the party/state to direct and transform the economy. In considering the question of the demands of the masses and the capacity of different social groups to influence the policy process, it is important to examine (a) the way in which conflicting class forces express themselves and how practices they engage in affect the state: (b) changes occurring in social structure and at the level of civil society: and (c) the extent and forms of participation of the masses in decision-making processes associated with policy design.

Class Struggle and Contradictory Class Practices

In the context of socialist societies it is necessary to focus on what one writer has called (referring to the peasantry in North Vietnam) 'avoidance and non-cooperation strategies' (Fforde, 1984) of different classes or social groups. The practices which characterize such 'strategies' play a crucial role in influencing decision-making processes. In relation to the working class, practices involving widespread absenteeism, 'foot-dragging', pilfering, and so on, are clearly manifestations of discontent which may amount to what one writer has called a 'perceptual plebiscite' in a system where the role of elections is restricted (Schultz, 1981, p. 5). Similarly, in relation to the peasantry, failure to pay taxes, deliver grain quotas to state marketing agencies, participate in communal infrastructural works, or follow directives regarding cropping patterns and techniques, can constitute a powerful expression of class interests which may prompt policy changes. Moreover, such strategies may imply various levels of support for counter-revolutionary forces through the provision of food and other supplies, as well as information regarding, for example, troop movements. Why practices as these can have such an impact relates to the central role of the post-revolutionary state in the process of surplus mobilization and appropriation. The types of practice to which I have referred may seriously undermine the capacity of the state to fulfil this role.

The way in which practices such as these can play an important role in bringing about policy changes is brought out clearly in the case of the NEP. In his writings and speeches justifying the NEP, Lenin stressed the fact that it was a response to social contradictions. Declining levels of agricultural production and marketing of food products derived not so much from problems associated with the material conditions of production but essentially from the fact that middle and rich peasants reverted to subsistence production when faced with shortages of goods to buy. As Bettelheim explains:

> what was decisive was the petty-bourgeois practice of 'giving nothing for nothing'. . .[which] . . .took precedence over solidarity with the soldiers. . .with the town workers. . .or even with the peasants in those regions where the harvest had failed.
>
> In noting this fact, we are not, of course, drawing up some sort of 'indictment' of the Russian peasants of that time, but noting a class practice, and the Bolshevik Party's inability to transform it (whereas the subsequent experience of the Chinese Revolution has shown that it can be done). (Bettelheim, 1977, p. 242)

Much of the Russian peasantry had supported the Bolshevik Party during the civil war in a common cause against forces which sought to recover the power of the landlords, but when these forces had been defeated peasant demands turned to issues associated with requisitioning and free trade. During the winter of 1920/21 expressions of peasant discontent manifested themselves in much of the country. Inflation, food shortages and the paralysation of factories due to lack of fuel also strained relations between the Bolshevik Party and the working class, and strikes broke out in some of the major industrial centres. These events contributed to the revolt at the Kronstadt naval base in March 1921, by which the participants had hoped to initiate a country-wide movement to dislodge the Bolsheviks from power. The Kronstadt rising explicitly supported peasant demands associated with free trade (Ibid., pp. 361–6).

These forms of discontent reflected the emergence of antagonistic contradictions which in turn reflected the inability of the Bolshevik Party to manage relations with the peasantry and the transformation of social relations in the context of the objective economic and

structural conditions existing in the Soviet Union at that time. This
was recognized clearly by Lenin:

> We know that so long as there is no revolution in other countries,
> only agreement with the peasantry can save the socialist revolution
> in Russia. . . .
> We must try to satisfy the demands of the peasants who are
> dissatisfied and disgruntled, and legitimately so . . .It will take
> essentially two things to satisfy the small farmer. The first is a
> certain freedom of exchange, freedom for the small private pro-
> prietor, and the second is the need to obtain commodities and
> products. . . .the vastness of our agricultural country with its poor
> transport system, boundless expanses, varying climate, diverse
> farming conditions, etc., makes a certain freedom of exchange
> between local agriculture and local industry . . .inevitable. In this
> respect, we are very much to blame for having gone too far; we
> overdid the nationalization of industry and trade, clamping down
> on local exchange of commodities. Was that a mistake? It certainly
> was. (Lenin, 1965, pp. 215–19).

While most of the literature relating to China tends to see the policy
changes as a pragmatic response to planning and institutional limitations inherent in the 'Maoist model' which impeded growth and
productivity, certain writers have stressed the role of social/class
conflict in the policy process. Several writers stress the role of peasant
discontent and unrest in 'detonating' the reforms (Bettelheim, 1988;
White G., 1985a; Petras and Selden, 1981).

According to Bettelheim, among the principal factors contributing
directly to the abandonment of the Maoist model was peasant discontent, along with certain negative effects of the system of popular
communes and the imperative of the planning system on production,
investment and local initiative. Discontent was fomented through
what White refers to as a 'triple subordination of the short-term
interests of peasant households' to the primacy of a) national industrialization, which meant excessive procurement quotas, low prices
for agricultural produce and restrictions on investment resources for
agriculture; b) accumulation over consumption; and c) collective accumulation over household accumulation' (White G., 1985a, p. 7).

Discontent gave rise to 'a strong peasant movement (especially in
the interior) . . .pressing for decollectivization. This base movement
was to be one of the first detonators of the transformation of the

relations of production in the countryside' (Bettelheim, 1988, p. 5). While overt conflict was minimized through effective local controls on political activity, resistance took numerous other forms, including reduced intensity of labour at work, refusal to obey party directives concerning production, diverting energies away from collective activities towards private activities, withholding labour from state projects, petty concealment and evasion, and so on (White G., 1985a, p. 6; Perry, 1985, p. 178).

As Bettelheim observes: 'the decisions taken by the plenum in 1978 "officialised" what the peasant movement had initiated; they opened the door and became part of a much larger "strategic turn" made up of the "four modernizations" in agriculture, industry, defence and science' (Bettelheim, 1988, p. 8).

Changes in Social Structure and the Expansion of Civil Society

In addition to considering the role of class struggle in shaping the reform process, it is also important to refer to changes occurring in social structure, and developments taking place at the level of civil society. The types of demand put forward by the Russian peasantry and the measures contained in the NEP were influenced by changes that had occurred in rural social structure. Important here was the process of internal differentiation among the peasantry, whereby: 'In a very large number of cases the peasant "poor" (proletarians and semi-proletarians) have become middle peasants. This has caused an increase in the small-proprietor, petty-bourgeois "element"' (Lenin, 1965, p. 341).

It is also necessary to refer to the influence of new social groups that emerge through the process of economic development. Particularly important in the case of China, the Soviet Union and the Eastern European countries is the role played by a 'middle class' or 'intelligentsia' of professionals, technicians, managers, scientists and educators, closely associated with or inserted into the state apparatus, and whose interests and world view differ from or clash with those of the traditional cadres (White G., 1983a, pp. 181–2).

The nature of the interests of this emergent group and its relationship to the mass of the population has been the subject of considerable debate. Bettelheim, for example, refers to the existence within the state of a ruling class or a 'party bourgeoisie' (Bettelheim, 1988, p. 6), and in one text goes so far as to argue that the post-1976 policy changes in China reflect 'the resurgent influence the bourgeoisie, and above all the bourgeoisie present in the machinery of the state and of the party, who were tending to strengthen their authority, to "free themselves" from the authority of the masses, and so to be able to dispose of the means of production which, in a formal sense, belong to the state' (Idem., 1979, p. 43). Others place more emphasis on the relationship between policy reform and the emergence of a technocracy adhering to an ideology of modernization and frustrated with the declining capacity of orthodox planning systems to 'deliver the goods' (White G., 1983b; Petras and Selden, 1981).

Here the question of relations with the advanced capitalist countries is also important, notably the planner/technocrat's concern about an apparent widening of the economic/technological gap between East and West; the increasing economic and trade links with the West as the socialist economies become more complex and diversified; and the growth of a middle-class consumer culture stimulated by the increasing penetration of Western cultural influences through communications and travel. As Petras and Selden point out, influences and relations such as these 'find resonance within the political structure, converging with the interests of managerial and technological personnel and petty commodity producers . . .affect[ing] . . .domestic class relations . . . (Petras and Selden, 1981, p. 197)

The important point when dealing with the question of changes in social structure and the emergence of new social groups is not merely the quantitative growth of such groups, but also developments taking place in the area of civil society. It is necessary to look at the way in which the individuals that compose such groups associate and organize in 'private' institutions (universities, trade unions, producer/consumer groups, professional associations, and so on). This type of analysis is important in three respects. Firstly, it tells us something about the capacity of such groups to articulate interests and constitute themselves as 'pressure groups'. Secondly, the expansion of these institutions opens up the possibility of qualitative changes in the mode of leadership of the dominant group, away from what Gramsci called 'domination' or exercising power by means of coercion, towards 'hegemony', which relates to the system of relations between classes and social groups; whereby power is secured on the basis of a broad popular consensus, achieved through political, intellectual and moral leadership (Gramsci, 1971). Hegemony implies that the ruling group must build a system of alliances and concern itself not only with its economic–corporate interests but with the interests of other social groups (Mouffe (ed.), 1979, p. 181). Thirdly, it is the restricted development of the institutions associated with civil society which partially explains why the 'state-centred' model is quickly put in place during the post-revolutionary phase. The relative absence of such institutions means that, in the context of a defeated or severely weakened bourgeoisie, the autonomy and intervention of the politico-administrative apparatuses of the state is likely to be that much greater. This situation recalls that analyzed by Marx in *The Civil War in France*, when referring to Napoleon's regime 'it was the only form of government possible at a time when the bourgeoisie had already lost and the working class had not yet acquired the faculty of ruling the nation' (Marx and Engels, 1940, p. 56, cited in Bengelsdorf, 1986, p. 206).

Popular Participation and the Policy Process

Considerations regarding the role of the masses in shaping the reform process through more direct means associated with institutionalized forms of participation have not figured prominently in the literature of economic policy reform in socialist countries. This reflects to a large extent the theoretical legacy of both non-Marxist and Marxist political and social scientists regarding the nature of politics and the policy process in 'communist' systems, particularly in the Soviet Union. The 'totalitarian' (Friedrich and Brzezinski, 1956), 'bureaucratic' (Meyer, 1967) and 'institutional pluralism' (Hough, 1972) approaches which have dominated non-Marxist thinking on Soviet politics since the 1950s, have all emphasized the hierarchical nature of decision-making processes. In the first, politics, reflected in conflict between groups, is non-existent; in the second, it is largely restricted to the upper echelons of the party–state complex; while in the third, it involves state institutions and certain other 'elite' groups such as professionals, managers, and so on (Holmes, 1986, pp. 383–96).

Marxist approaches to politics in the Soviet Union and Eastern European countries (apart from official government positions) have also stressed the concentration of power in the hands of the party/bureaucracy which forms either a new class (Bettelheim, 1976 and 1988; Djilas, 1966; Šik, 1981) or a ruling stratum (Deutscher, 1966; Trotsky, 1967). Common to all these approaches is the idea that the masses play a highly limited role in the political and policy process and that communist regimes are largely unresponsive to citizens' demands.[6]

While the vast majority of the population may belong to mass organizations, it is often argued that the latter exist primarily 'to explain communist party policies to their members, to encourage members both to support these policies and to participate actively in their implementation . . .' (Holmes, 1986, p. 217). Such organizations are generally considered, therefore, to have little input into the policy process. Western political scientists frequently describe communist governments as 'mobilization regimes' which control and direct the political involvement of the masses.

Restricted institutionalized participation has also been a feature of socialist development in several Third-World countries during specific periods in their post-revolutionary histories (Lowy, 1986, p. 267). As Fagen *et al.* explain:

> The common legacy of underdevelopment – lack of resources, trained personnel, and democratic and participatory traditions – coupled with the heritage of authoritarian models in actually existing socialisms – militate against such participation. So too do imperialist intervention and the centralizing and bureaucratic tendencies evident when attempts at comprehensive planning are made in fragile and impoverished economies. (Fagen *et al.*, 1986, pp. 21–22).

Since the 1970s, however, there has emerged a considerable body of literature indicating that the level of institutionalized participation in socialist societies was far greater than was generally assumed; was on the increase; and enabled certain groups to influence the process of policy design. (Schulz and Adams, 1981). As we shall see, important initiatives took place in Mozambique, Cuba and Nicaragua which strengthened participatory structures and practices and gave some meaning to the slogan 'People's Power'.

These aspects, associated with changing forms of representation and the extent and efficacy of institutionalized forms of participation, constitute another area of analysis which must be taken into account when explaining the shift from orthodoxy to reform.

THE SPECIFICITY OF THE DEPENDENT TRANSITIONAL SOCIETY

The current wave of economic and food policy reform in the Soviet Union, Eastern Europe and China has been the subject of much discussion and analysis. Far less has been written about the process of policy reform which occurred during the 1980s in a group of Third-World countries, which may be categorized as 'dependent transitional societies'.[7] It is to this subject that we now turn our attention, by studying the experience of economic and food policy reform in Mozambique, Vietnam, Cuba, and, in somewhat more detail, Nicaragua.

The category of 'dependent transitional societies' comprises economies on the 'periphery' of the world system, and engaged in a process of 'transition'. The latter may be defined in terms of an attempt to transform social relations and structures characteristic of 'dependent capitalism' and to subordinate patterns of production, distribution and accumulation to social and economic priorities determined by a more or less centralized planning process (Fagen *et al.*, 1986, p. 10–20). The fact that they are 'peripheral' implies a specific form of insertion in the international division of labour. Historically, these economies supplied raw materials to the world market, failed to develop a significant industrial base and were highly dependent on external markets. During the post-revolutionary period they remained dependent on large-scale inflows of external aid. These types of relationship rendered such economies extremely vulnerable, not only to international market conditions but also to external pressures and attacks – both economic and military – as post-revolutionary governments attempted to redefine relations with foreign powers with which they were previously linked (Fitzgerald, 1986 and 1988a).

Many of the issues discussed above relating to the accumulation/consumption balance, the efficiency of the state sector, and the articulation of different property forms, are also central to the question of reform in dependent transitional economies. Yet, precisely because they are dependent, because the level of development of the productive forces is much lower, and because throughout most of their post-revolutionary history they have had to endure serious external aggression of one form or another, many of the major problems facing governments in such countries are qualitatively different. Here we are dealing with a set of countries where the post-revolutionary environment for launching and sustaining a development effort is particularly harsh.

Within the context of these constraints, the crucial problems facing the post-revolutionary state in these societies relate to the provision of *essential* goods and services (basic needs), the creation of basic infrastructure and incipient industrialization, as well as building a broad-based popular alliance (national unity) to facilitate the mobilization of resources, policy implementation and defence. As such, the priority concerns of leaders and planners in these countries have related less to the typical issues, referred to earlier, which dominate the policy agenda in the Soviet Union and China, namely those associated with the adjustment of the planning system to a more complex and diversified economy; the need to achieve international industrial competitiveness; or the satisfaction of consumer demands for non-essential or quality goods (Fitzgerald and Wuyts, 1988a, p. 3).

The four countries I have selected for study have all been influenced by the type of state-centred planning and accumulation models described above, and have experienced many of the problems associated with centralized planning systems. Moreover, as Littlejohn points out, the limitations of the planning system may be even more apparent in the context of the underdeveloped socialist economy given that 'the state sector is frequently run on lines influenced by the "model" of Soviet central planning . . .while the organizational conditions for this (especially the administrative resources and management skills) are not present.' This will also affect the capacity of the state to regulate the private economy (Littlejohn, 1988 p. 10).

While the types of problem inherent in the centralized planning model have affected these economies, two other central issues lie behind the policy changes. Firstly, there is the double-barrelled problem of how to meet the subsistence requirements of the working class, the army and the bureaucracy, and how keep the peasantry producing a marketable surplus. Secondly, there is the question of how the group exercising state power can maintain its ruling position. Crucial here is the concept of hegemony. As Simon points out, hegemony involves 'making such compromises as are needed to adapt the existing system of alliances to changing conditions and the activities of opposing forces' (Simon, 1982 p. 37). As far as the process of post-revolutionary development is concerned, consensus is crucial, both from the politico-military point of view of preventing 'counter-revolutionary' forces gaining a social base, and from the socioeconomic perspective of facilitating the role of the state in resource mobilization, specifically, enabling it to mobilize the productive energies of the people in tasks associated with economic and social development and social change.

In the case of the dependent transitional economy, problems associated with basic-needs provisioning and social tensions can be mitigated to some extent by large inflows of 'solidarity' aid or during periods when there is a positive response on the part of the masses to mobilization campaigns. Acute crises of basic-needs provisioning and of hegemony are, however, likely to manifest themselves. In the case studies that follow we will see that the crisis of the state which prompted the reforms was related to a large extent to the declining capacity of the state both to appropriate surplus for basic needs provisioning and to secure hegemony.

There are, of course, important socioeconomic differences among the countries selected which had an important bearing on the nature of the process of economic and food policy reform. Particularly relevant were those which related to the level of development of the productive base, social structure, political system and institutionalized forms of participation, as well as relations with the world economy.

Regarding the first of these variables, we see, in Tables 1.1 and 1.2, that the levels of technical advancement in agriculture and industrialization achieved in Cuba and Vietnam were higher than those in Mozambique and Nicaragua. Also, Cuba, while having experienced severe economic pressures associated with trade and financial embargoes imposed by Western countries, did not have to endure the effects of a prolonged war on national territory. There was, then, a considerable difference in the level of development of the Cuban economy and the extent to which the basic needs of the mass of the population had been met (See Table 1.3). As we will see, these conditions can have an important bearing on the types of constraints and contradictions that affect the development process, the nature of demands expressed by different social groups, and the response of the state.

The relative strengths and weaknesses of different interest groups may also reflect differences in social structure. While in Vietnam and Mozambique the vast majority of the population was rural-based, in Nicaragua and Cuba the majority was concentrated in urban areas (see Table 1.4). In Vietnam, virtually the entire rural population was integrated in a co-operative of one sort or another, whereas in Mozambique the majority consisted of individual producers. In Cuba the vast majority of the rural and urban labour force was made up of salaried workers. In Nicaragua the majority of the urban population belonged to the so-called 'informal sector', while the class composition of the rural population was highly heterogeneous.

During the 1980s, Nicaragua stood out from the other countries as having a more pluralistic political system, not only in relation to the

TABLE 1.1   *Levels of technological development in agriculture, 1984*

	Tractors in use (units)	Tractors per 000 ha. of arable land	Irrigated agric. area (ha)	Irrig. land as % arable area	Fertiliser consumption (00 gm/ha.)*
Mozambique	5 750	2.0	78	2.7	48
Vietnam-SRV	39 000	6.4	1 750	28.5	627
Cuba	66 000	25.8	1 030	40.2	1 642
Nicaragua	2 400	2.2	83	7.6	557

SOURCES   FAO, *FAO Production Yearbook*, 1985; World Bank, *World Development Report*, 1987.
* Hundreds of gm of plant nutrients per hectare of arable land.

TABLE 1.2   *Structure of production** (percentages of GDP or Gross Social Product)

	Year	Agriculture*	Industry*	Services*
Mozambique[1]**	1985	35	11	53
North Vietnam[2]	1975	29	55	16
Cuba[3]**	1983	14	51	34
Nicaragua[1]	1985	23	33	44

SOURCES   [1] World Bank, *World Development Report*, 1987.
[2] Fforde and Paine, 1987, p. 151.
[3] Díaz Vázquez.[8]
* Since the categories and definitions used by these countries vary, this table is intended to provide only a very crude indication of variations in economic structure.
** Due to rounding, figures do not total 100.

TABLE 1.3   *Basic needs: nutrition and infant mortality, 1985*

	Nutrition Kcal.[1]	Protein gm.[2]	Infant mortality rate[3]
Mozambique	1 678	30.1	123
Vietnam-SRV	2 240	n.a.	49
Cuba	3 122	75.7	16
Nicaragua	2 425	n.a.	69

SOURCE   World Bank, *World Development Report* 1987.
[1] Daily per capita calorie supply.
[2] Per capita per day; 1981–83 average; Source: FAO.
[3] Deaths per 1000 under 1 year of age.

TABLE 1.4   *National, agricultural, urban and economically-active population (EAP), 1980 (in 000s and percentages)*

	National	Agricultural	Urban as % of total[1]	EAP Total	EAP in agric.	% in agric.
Mozambique	12 123	10 242	19	6 904	5 832	84.5
Vietnam:						
SRV	54 175	36 555	20	24 930	16 822	67.5
DRV*	24 550	21 900**	11	10 952+	9 276++	84.7
Cuba	9 732	2 315	71	3 567	848	23.8
Nicaragua	2 771	1 260	56	825	384	46.6

SOURCE   FAO, *FAO Production Yearbook*, 1985.
[1] World Bank, *World Development Report*, 1987.
* Corresponds to 1975 data for North Vietnam (Fforde and Paine, 1987, Tables 8, 10).
** Refers to population in rural areas.
+ Refers to population of working age.
++ Refers to population of working age in rural areas.

existence of a multi-party system, but also in relation to the active mobilization of major social groups through mass organizations. In all four countries large mass organizations existed but their capacity to operate as effective pressure groups varied considerably. Their primary purpose was very often to facilitate the implementation of policies and mobilize support for the regime rather than to participate actively in the process of policy design. In Nicaragua, however, this latter role was more pronounced. Nevertheless, alternative participatory structures in the other three countries did exist and through these, social groups were able to exert some influence over the process of policy design.

Finally, pressures for change in economic policy also came from outside. The extent to which these economies were affected by the world economic recession, the debt problem, and related 'adjustment' pressures exerted by leading international finance agencies and certain Western governments varied considerably. The degree of dependence on Western trade, loans and aid on the one hand, or the Eastern bloc on the other, was a crucial variable in this respect. Major differences in external relations characterized the selected countries during the early and mid-1980s. Both Cuba and Vietnam were extremely dependent on Eastern bloc assistance, notably the Soviet Union. Mozambique became increasingly dependent on Western aid. Nicaragua continued to receive important quantities of aid from Western sources but depended to an ever greater extent on the Eastern bloc countries.

On analyzing the shift from orthodoxy to reform in each of the four countries, we will see how these differences conditioned both the content and trajectory of the reform process. On balance, though, it will be argued that the orthodox, state-centred accumulation model, and the response on the part of different social groups and imperialist powers to the process of post-revolutionary structural change, generated a set of conditions which bore similar characteristics in all cases. Moreover, certain developments associated with the changing balance of social forces, notably the strengthening of rich peasant interests and of certain urban 'middle-class' groups, were generally shared by all four countries.

In this chapter I have pointed to the need to incorporate in the analysis of the reform process in socialist countries the question of changes which have occurred in the balance of social forces. In particular, I have stressed the importance of considering the nature of class struggle, changes in social structure, developments occurring at the level of civil society, and forms of institutionalized participation. Such issues lie at the heart of the examination which follows in Part II of the cases of Mozambique, Vietnam and Cuba. Since I have had to rely on what amounts to a fairly small body of secondary literature, certain gaps inevitably appear in the analysis. For this reason a deeper study of Nicaragua is presented in Part III.

Notes

1. According to Marxist economic theory, production and distribution in a market economy are said to be regulated by the law of value whereby commodities are exchanged according to the amount of 'socially necessary labour power' used in their production. The law determines not only exchange ratios but also the quantities of goods produced and the allocation of labour to different branches of production (Brus, 1972, pp. 91–92).

2. Throughout this study I use the tripartite classification of 'poor', 'middle' and 'rich' peasants. The term 'poor peasants' refers to those producers or rural families which, because of limited access to land and other means of production, must sell their labour power for a significant part of the year. The category 'middle peasants' refers to those that are able to meet the subsistence requirements of the household – inputs, implements, food, clothing, etc. – largely on the basis of what they produce on the land. Such produce may be either used for self-provisioning or sold in order to

purchase certain essential items. The term 'rich peasants' refers to those who produce a surplus over and above that which is required for the simple reproduction of the household. This surplus permits the acquisition of additional means of production and labour power and enables the producer to expand production and increase the consumption levels of the household. As Bernstein points out: 'insofar as they initiate and maintain a cycle of extended reproduction based on accumulation they come to form a category of capitalist farmers' (Bernstein, 1977, p. 67).

3. Consumer sovereignty has been defined by Brus as 'the adaptation of the composition of production to consumer preferences expressed as effective demand' (Brus, 1972, p. 32).

4. Lange and Lerner had argued that central planners could, in fact, manage the factors of production and obtain an equilibrium price structure not by processing millions of bits of information but by observing the movement of demand and supply and, through successive approximations, adjust prices accordingly (Rutland, 1985, p. 30–1; Brus, 1972, p. 27–31).

5. As used in this study, the term 'crisis' implies not only some sort of fundamental breakdown in functioning or reproduction, but also the likelihood of a qualitative restructuring or change of form. By using the term 'crisis' of the state', then, I wish to convey two specific meanings. The first relates to the inability of the state to perform its role as the institutional complex that (a) mobilizes resources for basic needs provisioning, accumulation and defence, and (b) directs the process of post-revolutionary transformation of economic and social structures. The second refers to a fundamental change in the characteristics of the state. If, following Jessop, we characterize the latter in terms of 'an institutional ensemble of forms of representation, internal organization, and intervention' (Jessop, 1982, p. 228), then a crisis of the state may be said to involve also the likelihood of an abrupt qualitative transformation in one, a combination or all of these aspects. In the context of this study what is particularly relevant are the changes, expressed in the policy reforms, which occurred in the forms of state intervention in the economy.

6. Some writers, such as Lane, have adopted an alternative position, arguing that real possibilities did exist for groups or organizations such as trade unions and others 'to communicate their interests . . .to the law makers', maintaining, however, that this possibility was more restricted for 'amorphous social groups' such as peasants, white-collar and manual workers, and consumers (D. Lane, *The End of Inequality? Stratification under State Socialism*, Lada, Penguin, p. 235).

7. Numerous labels can and have been used to describe these societies. See, for example, White G., 1983b.

8. Díaz Vázquez J. (1986) *Cuba: Integración Económica Socialista y Especialización de la Producción*, Havana, Editorial Pueblo y Educación, p. 13.

Part II

Economic and Food Policy Reform in Mozambique, Vietnam and Cuba

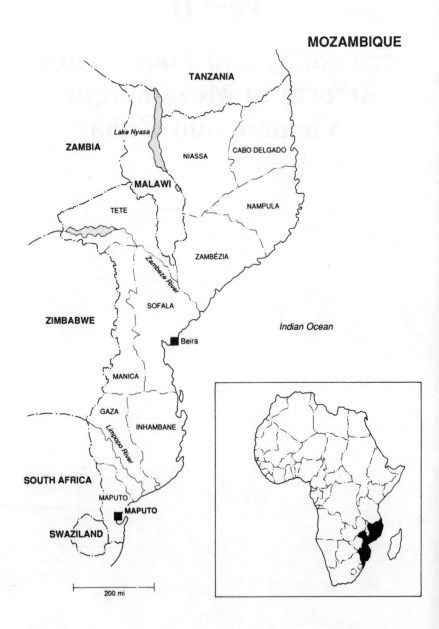

2 Mozambique

INTRODUCTION

Following Mozambique's independence from Portugal in 1975, development strategy emphasized the need for rapid and profound structural change. The FRELIMO-led government inherited an economy with a highly rural-based and impoverished population. Over 80 per cent of the country's ten million people lived in rural areas. FAO data indicate that 85.5 per cent of the economically-active population depended for their livelihood on agriculture (FAO, 1986, p. 65). A large proportion of the economically-active male population was made up of 'semi-proletarians' who, under colonial rule, had been obliged through a system of forced recruitment to work several months of the year as seasonal plantation workers. An estimated 100 000 men from the south of the country were also employed in the gold mines of South Africa. The local population that remained on the land was forced to grow certain crops, such as cotton, rice and cassava.

A system of family plots and communal tenure arrangements was preserved under Portuguese rule to facilitate the simple reproduction of the rural household (Hanlon, 1984, p. 18). Through forced labour and forced cropping, the colonial system ensured cheap supplies of labour and raw materials, food for the mass of the rural population, and foreign exchange. Most food for the cities and towns, however, was produced by Portuguese settler farmers. The settler population, which numbered approximately a quarter of a million, also controlled urban and rural trade. The colonial agricultural sector, producing both food and export crops, comprised some 4600 farms totalling 2.5 million hectares (Moore Lappe and Beccar-Varela, 1980, p. 44) – an area roughly equivalent to that cultivated by approximately 1.6 million peasant families.

The colonial system had restricted social differentiation among the peasantry. It had effectively eliminated the middle peasantry engaged in non-commoditized subsistence production. The extent to which commodity relations had penetrated peasant production is indicated by the fact that the latter accounted for an estimated 31 per cent of total marketed production in 1970 (Hanlon, 1984 p. 100). The colonial system had, however, constrained the growth of an indigenous agrarian petty bourgeoisie and sector of landless labourers (O'Laughlin, 1981). By 1970, an estimated 97 per cent of peasant families with 86.6 per cent of the land cultivated by Mozambicans, could be classified as poor or 'lower-middle' peasants with less than 15 acres (6 ha.) (Hanlon, 1984 p. 180).

Lack of Portuguese capital investment and Mozambique's insertion in the international division of labour as a supplier of raw materials (such as sugar, tea, cotton and sisal) resulted in extremely limited industrial development and a very small urban proletariat. Colonial pass and labour laws restricted rural-to-urban migration and the growth of an indigenous urban 'informal' sector. As Hanlon points out: 'The ban on trade by Africans has left Mozambique as one of the few countries where bus and train stops are not thronged with vendors' (Ibid., 22). World Bank data indicate that in 1965, Mozambique had the eighth lowest urban population ratio in the world, with city and town dwellers accounting for just five per cent of the total population (World Bank, 1987, p. 266).

The independence period (1974–76) saw the abrupt exodus of most of the settler population. The departure of the Portuguese had an immediate and dramatic impact on food production and marketing, leading to serious problems of urban provisioning and shortages of inputs and consumer goods in rural areas. Actions taken by the South African government exacerbated the post-independence crisis. The country's main source of foreign exchange and key source of income and investment capital for peasant families in southern Mozambique was seriously threatened when the South African government announced major cuts of approximately 70 per cent in the quota of mine labourers (Pinsky, 1985, p. 285). Rural-to-urban migration accelerated sharply as a consequence of both the relaxation of the colonial pass laws in 1974 and the disarticulation of the rural economy which resulted from the rupture of trade networks, reduced employment opportunities, and attacks from Rhodesia.

The nature of the food problem facing the revolutionary government had both an immediate and a strategic dimension. The former concerned the question of how to fill the vacuum left by the Portuguese and reactivate the production and marketing circuits they had controlled. A particularly pressing problem was that associated with urban food shortages which had worsened with the rapid growth of the urban population. The strategic question centred on how to transform the highly exploitative social relations which characterized Portuguese colonial rule and continue to mobilize and appropriate the surplus needed for urban provisioning and accumulation.

POST-REVOLUTIONARY FOOD AND DEVELOPMENT POLICY

Orthodox Principles

The development strategy which unfolded during the early years of the post-Independence period emphasized the need to develop the agricultural sector, 'socialize' the rural population, establish a heavy industrial base, centrally plan the economy and prioritize the state sector. As stated in the Central Committee Report to the Third Congress of FRELIMO:

> Our strategy for development rests on agricultural production. The Communal villages are the fundamental level for liberating the people in rural areas.
>
> Industry is the dynamising factor for economic development. The construction of heavy industry constitutes the decisive factor for our total independence, enabling us to break from our integration into the imperialist system.
>
> The building of Socialism demands that the economy be centrally planned and directed by the State . . .The state-owned sector of production must become dominant and determinant; so the establishment of state-owned firms is a priority objective . . .All the strategic sectors of the economy must be under state control. (FRELIMO, 1977, pp. 43–4)

The most accessible of the abandoned plantations and settler farms were quickly organized as state farms (Hanlon, 1984, p. 100) which, in conjunction with the co-operativized peasantry, were expected to constitute the primary source of domestic surplus (Littlejohn, 1988, p. 14). By 1980, the state farms accounted for an estimated 52 per cent of total marketed agricultural production (Hanlon, 1984, p. 100).

In order to improve the access of the poor peasantry to social services and to facilitate political mobilization and planning, the government encouraged a process of social concentration whereby the dispersed rural population would come together to live in 'communal villages'. By the end of 1982 an estimated 1350 communal villages existed, inhabited by approximately 1.8 million people, some 18 per cent of the rural population (Munslow, 1984, p. 213). Rural development strategy at the village level stressed the importance of self-reliance, the use of low-level technologies and the mobilization of collective labour to expand social services (Mackintosh and Wuyts,

1988, p. 6) While the government urged producers to form co-operatives, few did so in practice. By 1983, only 230 of the communal villages had formed co-operatives (Ottaway, 1988, p. 216).

Government policy towards the private sector sought to relegate private enterprise to the 'non-strategic' sectors of the economy, where 'private activity will be allowed in so far as it scrupulously fulfils its social objectives and participates in national production, within the framework of the aims laid down by the State and in accordance with the interests of the popular masses' (FRELIMO, 1977, p. 45). The exodus of the Portuguese and the formation of state farms and co-operatives had the effect of drastically reducing the importance of this sector in agriculture. Between 1970 and 1980 the percentage share of marketed production accounted for by private farmers fell from an estimated 69 per cent to 10 per cent (Hanlon, 1984, p. 100).

State-Centred Accumulation

During the late 1970s, greater stress was laid on capital intensive development and the expansion of the state farm and agro-industrial sector. For the first time, large numbers of combines were imported, and while the number of imported tractors was roughly equivalent to that entering the country during the last years of Portuguese rule, the machines tended to be larger (Ibid.). Between 1978 and 1982 the area under state farms increased by 40 per cent. In 1981 a long-term development plan was drawn up which envisaged a massive increase in the size of the state farm sector from 350 000 acres (141 700 ha.) to 2.5 million acres (1 million ha.) (Ibid.).

The rationale behind the prioritization of the state farm sector is generally explained with reference to a combination of ideological and conjunctural factors associated with an impending urban food crisis and the need to rapidly mobilize existing resources. The latter, it was thought, could best be achieved in those areas where the state directly controlled the means of production. This prioritization was explained by FRELIMO in the following terms: 'The state-owned enterprises are the quickest means of responding to the country's food requirements because of the size of the areas they cover, their rational organization of human and material resources, and the immediate availability of machinery' (FRELIMO, 1977, p. 46).

When, during the early 1980s, the war with the South African-backed Mozambican National Resistance forces (RENAMO) escalated, the concentration of resources on the state farms was also justified for security reasons. As Mackintosh explains:

> The industrial and large-scale state farming activities . . .take on a strategic importance. State food farms provide a production nucleus which provides food for the army and the rest of the state sector, and contributes to feeding the towns. They provide a production nucleus which may be militarily defensible, and which can therefore provide a focus for the organization of other activities including agricultural extension and marketing. (Mackintosh, 1986, p. 576)

The 'state-centredness' of the development model should also be explained with reference to certain structural conditions associated with the level of development of peasant economy and the institutions of civil society in rural areas. Rural society, where the vast majority of the national population resided was, at the time of independence, not only starved of essential resources but also characterized by dispersed settlement patterns and (apart from certain religious organizations) a dearth of autonomous local institutions. Even the traditional leadership structure, based on chiefs or *regulos*, had been manipulated or destroyed by the Portuguese (Ottaway, 1988, pp. 224–5). Given, then, the total absence of any countervailing sites of economic, administrative and political power it was hardly surprising that the state attempted to assume the dominant role it did.

The priority accorded to the state farm sector was clearly reflected in the allocation of investment capital. Official figures indicate that between 1977 and 1983 state farms received an estimated 90 per cent of agricultural investments (Mackintosh and Wuyts, 1988, p. 13), an estimated four-fifths of which consisted of machinery and other imports (Littlejohn, 1988, p. 14). In contrast, only 2 per cent of agricultural investment was in co-operatives. Many producer co-operatives were disbanded during this period for lack of support from the government, although a number of co-operatives around the capital, Maputo, did receive more support from 1980 onwards, when the government created the Green Zones Office in order to provide them with technical assistance. Within two years there was, in fact, a five-fold increase in the number of co-operatives operating in this area (Benjamin and Danaher, 1988, p. 3). The policy of encouraging agricultural production around the major cities also involved measures to encourage private farmers.

The state attempted to control the use and allocation of resources through centralized planning, the main site of which was the National Planning Commission. As Mackintosh and Wuyts point out: 'Material investment planning . . .became a major method by which the state intended to plan the economy as a whole, and to develop the balance between the different sectors' (Mackintosh and Wuyts, 1988, p. 10). Investment tended to be concentrated on large-scale agricultural and industrial projects, and the mechanization of state farms.

During the early 1980s, there was a substantial shift in the accumulation/consumption balance in favour of the former. Investment as a percentage of GDP increased considerably from around 6 per cent in 1978/79 to 20 per cent in 1981 and 1982 (Ibid., p. 11). The government explicitly stated the need to restrict consumption in order to liberate more resources for rapid import-substituting industrialization (Ibid., p. 14). As was explained in a 1982 report of the Ideological Department of the Party:

> If we buy these [essential food] products . . .then the money we spend is used up and will not be productive. If on the contrary we make a sacrifice in this phase, so that instead of buying rice, flour, meat, fish we use the money for the construction of factories, then in four or five years the sacrifice we are making today will produce all these goods. (Ibid.)

This prioritization was reflected in changes in the composition of imports. Whereas between 1976 and 1982 the percentage share of total imports accounted for by machinery increased from 13.6 to 21.7 per cent, that of consumer goods declined from 26.8 to 20.2 per cent (see Table 2.1).

Trade and Urban Provisioning

The state also intervened heavily in the marketing system, setting producer and retail prices for the principal agricultural and manufactured products. State wholesaling companies were established to procure agricultural produce or distribute inputs as well as certain consumer goods. Within this framework, private traders were to play an important role at the level of rural retail trade, although this role expanded well beyond the bounds envisaged by the government (Mackintosh, 1986, pp. 562–3).

The period 1979–80 saw a revival of private commercial enterprise

TABLE 2.1   *Changes in the composition of imports, 1976, 1978, 1981–84*
(current prices in millions of meticais and percentages)

Year	Consumer goods Value	%	Intermediate goods* Value	%	Machinery Value	%	Total Value	%
1976	2427.0	26.8	5398.0	59.6	1233.0	13.6	9058.0	100
1978	4907.4	28.5	9032.1	52.5	3259.0	19.0	17198.5	100
1981	6303.5	22.3	16665.5	58.8	5348.6	18.9	28317.6	100
1982	6362.1	20.2	18353.1	58.1	6858.5	21.7	31573.7	100
1983	7134.0	27.9	13547.1	53.0	4890.3	19.1	25571.4	100
1984	7723.1	33.7	11210.4	49.0	3969.8	17.3	22903.3	100

SOURCE   Based on National Planning Commission (see Mackintosh, 1986, p. 560).
* Includes raw materials and spare parts.

in the cities. Following independence, the government took over numerous small-scale retail and service enterprises abandoned by the Portuguese. Towards the end of the decade, however, the state transferred control of many of these enterprises back to the private sector. When this wave of privatization had been completed, the state controlled 40 per cent of wholesale trade, while 20 per cent of retail trade was in the hands of consumer co-operatives (Hanlon, 1984, p. 195).

Whereas only approximately 70 000 people were organized in producer co-operatives in 1981 (Dolny, 1985, p. 230), a network of consumer co-operatives expanded rapidly from 1977. By mid-1982, some 13 000 co-operatives claimed a membership of nearly half a million and benefited an estimated 2.3 million consumers (Binkert, 1983, p. 41). A non-discriminatory subsidy policy ensured that consumers also benefited from subsidies on several food and manufactured products. In the early 1980s, direct consumer subsidies accounted for approximately 20 per cent of total recurrent government expenditures (Ibid., p. 53). A rationing system for basic food products also operated in the principal urban centres.

The urban areas, in particular, were highly dependent on imported cereals, which were heavily subsidized. Grain imports, which had risen from approximately 100 000 to 200 000 tons between 1970 and 1976, were maintained at a level of 300 000 between 1978 and 1982. This quantity far exceeded the registered levels of domestically-produced marketed grain. Roughly half (46.7 per cent) of all grain imported over the 1978–82 period consisted of food aid (Hanlon, 1984, p. 287).

ECONOMIC AND FOOD POLICY REFORMS

Changes in the Sectoral Allocation of Resources

In the build up to FRELIMO's Fourth Congress in 1983, government and party leaders began to criticize certain aspects of development strategy and called for a new policy approach. While many of the goals and features of Mozambican socialism outlined above remained intact, a number of important changes in priorities were considered. In stark contrast to the tone of the Third Congress report cited above, which had emphasized the need to develop heavy industry and prioritize state sector enterprises, a Party document entitled *Draft Theses for the Fourth Congress* stated that the short- and medium-term role of industry would be 'to produce essential goods such as clothing, blankets, pots, plates, cutlery, soap, lamps, matches, batteries, hoes, machetes, ploughs, bicycles etc.'. The document also stressed the need to 'give priority to the communal villages and the cooperatives' and also to support 'family' and private agriculture. It also redefined the role of state farms and their relations with other sectors or forms of production: 'As production units of the people's state, the state owned agricultural and agro-industrial complexes are to produce food and raw materials, and generate profit, for the benefit of the whole community. The state farms are to take on specific responsibilities in supporting communal villages and cooperatives in terms of technical assistance, inputs, and the marketing of produce.' (FRELIMO, 1983, pp. 11–12).

The reforms eventually approved at the Fourth Congress focused on the need to direct more resources toward the 'family' and private sectors of the rural economy, to rearticulate marketing circuits and control the activities of internal class forces, which were seen to be undermining socialist development strategy. A more gradual approach towards collectivization was adopted as measures were taken to encourage poor peasants to form associations as an initial stage in the co-operativization process (Munslow, 1984, p. 219). In practice, however, the government tended to reduce its level of support for co-operatives (Mackintosh, 1986, p. 577). An important exception, though, concerned the ongoing support provided to the co-operative movement in the Green Zones around Maputo. Between 1982 and 1987 the number of co-operatives in this area increased from 32 to 210, while membership rose from 2100 to 11 500 (Benjamin and Danaher, 1988, p. 5).

The attempt to stimulate peasant and private forms of production involved measures to improve access to credit, land and consumer goods, as well as increased producer prices. Small commercial farmers were encouraged to form associations, primarily as a means of obtaining credit. This process had, in fact, begun earlier. In one province alone (Gaza), more than 300 associations were formed by the end of 1982 (Munslow, 1984, p. 219). The access of agricultural producers to land was also improved as a number of state farms were broken up and redistributed to both individual peasants and private farmers (Littlejohn, 1988, p. 16). The expanded flow of resources to private farmers was linked to increased state procurement through a system of contracts. Mackintosh refers to the example of rice producers in Gaza Province which, in return for the use of irrigated state lands and access to inputs and technical assistance, were obliged to sell 60 per cent of their produce to the state at official prices (Mackintosh, 1986, p. 565).

The Report of the Economic and Social Directives Commission in 1983 stated that the stock of goods for sale in rural areas would increase by 20–23 per cent by 1985. To increase the supply of agricultural inputs, implements and basic consumer goods, more emphasis was placed on developing small-scale local industries. Changes also occurred in the composition of foreign aid and imports, as consumer goods increased their share of total imports from a fifth in 1982 to a third in 1984. The value of other categories of imports (intermediate goods and machinery) fell sharply, reflecting an overall decline in imports (see Table 2.1 on page 55). Sweden, which at one time provided over 80 per cent of all foreign exchange investment in the state farms, began to provide more production inputs and consumer goods. The establishment of trade relations with China in August 1982 gave Mozambique access to a relatively cheap source of agricultural implements and basic consumer goods (Munslow, 1984, p. 217).

These changes in the composition of imports were reflected in the accumulation/consumption balance. In 1983, the investment ratio[1] declined from the level of 20 per cent recorded during the previous two years, to 15 per cent (Mackintosh and Wuyts, 1988, p. 10). However, the availability of goods for private consumption continued to be restricted by the ongoing priority established for 'social' or 'institutional' consumption. Mackintosh cites a top official of the Ministry of Internal Commerce who claimed that the army and health and education centres absorbed up to half the supply of some products (Mackintosh, 1986, p. 573).

The Rearticulation of Marketing Circuits

In order to increase both the access of rural producers to agricultural inputs and consumer goods, and the sale of agricultural produce, the reforms sought to rearticulate marketing circuits which had collapsed during the post-independence period. This was to be achieved not only by expanding the supply of consumer goods in rural areas but also through increased producer prices, a degree of deregulation and restoring the value of the local currency.

Significant changes in the price system were introduced in order to boost marketed production and reduce the gap between official and open market prices. This process had, in fact, begun in January 1982, when producer price increases of 50 per cent or more were announced for maize, millet and cassava (Binkert, 1983, p. 57). In May 1985, prices of certain goods were deregulated (Mackintosh, 1986, p. 571). By 1987, the prices of all fruit and some vegetables and meat products had been freed. The government continued to set basic grains prices but both producer and consumer prices experienced major increases (Ottaway, 1988, p. 219; Mackintosh and Wuyts, 1988, p. 28).

The state attempted, however, to use its economic power to restrict price increases, particularly in the major cities. Large quantities of fruits and vegetables, for example, produced fairly near the capital, were transported in convoys to Maputo and sold in the market-place. To undercut the prices charged by private vendors, some of this produce was sold directly to the consumer through a network of state stalls (Mackintosh, 1986, p. 571).

The attempt to rearticulate marketing circuits involved removing a number of controls on private wholesale trade, notably restrictions on the inter-provincial transport of goods. The number of outlets for marketing agricultural inputs and products, as well as consumer goods, was also expanded. The state provided increased support to the network of retail co-operatives. According to the Report of the Fourth Congress, these outlets were to become the 'the basic structure of retail trade'. At the same time the number of procurement centres for agricultural products, including both fixed posts and mobile brigades, was expanded (Barker, 1985, p. 70). By raising agricultural producer prices, expanding the supply of inputs and consumer goods in rural areas, increasing the number of procurement posts, and developing contractual relations with farmers, the government aimed to increase state procurement levels by 40–45 per cent between 1982–85.

While private trading was encouraged, the state attempted to curb black market activities and regulate domestic trade. This involved keeping a watchful eye on speculation, hoarding, and corruption; attempting to develop the organization of wholesale marketing by the state and retailing by co-operatives; and defining priority areas governing the pattern of allocation of essential goods.

Decentralization

The economic policy reforms introduced during 1983/84 also sought to curtail the activities and practices of certain institutions and social groups that were seen to be undermining socialist development, notably the centralized bureaucracy and dealers in the black market. Decentralization of the planning and administration of agricultural production was to play a crucial role in this respect.

Decentralization manifested itself at different levels. At the level of the state farm, a number of the larger complexes were broken up into smaller units (Roesch, 1984, p. 312). Enterprise managers were granted increased administrative powers, with the combined purpose of not only increasing efficiency but also 'making them responsible for success or failure' (Mackintosh, 1986, p. 572). Enterprise managers were also responsible for organizing extension work in the areas where the state farms were located.

The decentralization of planning involved increasing the powers of provincial and district authorities. Provincial governments were to play a more prominent role in economic decision-making, with increased power over economic policy and the planning of production in state enterprises. The Fourth Congress recognized that if serious problems of transport, marketing and distribution were to be alleviated, it was necessary to reinforce planning at the district level to provide for a more rational utilization and integration of resources locally (Munslow, 1984, p. 218). State wholesaling activities were decentralized to the provincial level (Mackintosh, 1986, p. 572). At the central level, the importance of the National Planning Commission decreased as decision-making powers were transferred to the ministries directly involved with production and trade.

Diminishing the power of the central bureaucracy also involved attempts to transfer desk-bound technocrats to work in state enterprises. Shortly after the Fourth Congress, for example, the government announced that twenty-seven highly-qualified people working in the central state apparatus would be transferred to jobs running state farms and factories (Hanlon, 1984, p. 206).

The transfer of labour from 'non-productive' to 'productive' activities affected not only professionals and technicians but also the unemployed. To resolve problems associated with urban overcrowding which had resulted from increased rural-to-urban migration, 'Operation Production' was launched soon after the Fourth Congress. This involved the forced migration of large numbers of the urban unemployed to underpopulated rural areas, primarily in the north of the country (Saul, 1985, p. 98). This particular measure, however, was shortlived, being abandoned a year later because of its unpopular character (Pinsky, 1985, p. 280).

In an attempt to ensure that planning remained in tune with both peasant interests and the reality of resource availability, Regional Centres for Participatory Development were established in the main agricultural regions of the country. These centres had the fourfold purpose of finding ways of increasing productivity by relying primarily on local skills and resources, developing co-operative work methods, co-ordinating the activities of regional officials responsible for different aspects of agricultural production and marketing, and providing a channel through which the ideas and demands of agricultural producers could be heard (Barker, 1985, p. 71).

From 'Reform' to 'Adjustment'

Agreements with the World Bank and the IMF prompted a new wave of reform measures in 1987. In January of that year, the government announced an Economic Recovery Programme (ERP) which devalued the metical from 40 to 200 to the US dollar and reduced or eliminated consumer subsidies on food and other products. The government attempted to increase fiscal revenues by expanding the tax base and raising taxes on such goods as cigarettes, beer and fuel, as well as the cost of public services (*AED*, 7 February 1987, p. 14). Wage rises of 50 per cent took effect and plans were announced to introduce a new system of productivity bonuses. Further policy changes, conforming to the adjustment prescriptions of the leading international lending agencies, were announced in mid-1987. These involved another major devaluation, more price deregulation and further privatization (Ottaway, 1988, p. 220).

In an attempt to boost domestic food production, farmers were allowed to charge higher prices. A system of fixed prices for certain goods was replaced by a minimum pricing system. Price and marketing controls were gradually lifted on all but a 'hard core' of goods which were granted exemption until the security and emergency situation improved (*AED*, 29 May 1989, p. 11). Commercial farmers, many located in urban green belt areas, profited from these measures.

Stricter regulations were introduced governing the disbursement of credit, which was more closely linked to profitability. A number of state enterprises in both urban and rural areas were privatized. Several of the large agro-industrial complexes were dismembered and operated as smaller units (Ottaway, 1988). The ERP also accelerated the decentralization and privatization of foreign trade which had begun during the early 1980s. By early 1988, nearly half of the country's export enterprises were privately-owned, while 230 enterprises, including 65 private companies, were importing on a regular basis (*AED*, 18 November 1989, p. 15).

Smaller but more frequent devaluations continued throughout 1988 and 1989 which reduced considerably the gap between official and black market rates, which had stood at 40 and 1000 meticais, respectively, on the eve of the ERP. By December 1989 the exchange rate had reached 830 to the US dollar, approximately half the black market rate. The state bureaucracy was also reduced in size and many workers in non-profitable enterprises were dismissed. As in previous years, the unemployed were encouraged to move to rural areas and engage in agricultural activities (*YICA*, 1989).

Despite the trend towards liberalization and privatization, FRELIMO continued to stress, throughout the late 1980s, the need to adhere to basic socialist principles and the 'vanguard role' of the party in national development. It was not until the fifth party congress, held in 1989, that major political reforms were contemplated, involving the separation of the role of party and state and the possibility of a multi-party system.

While the ERP stimulated economic growth and exports, the social cost was extremely high. Real wages plummeted, creating considerable hardship for workers. In December 1989 the first of a series of strikes was organized. During early 1990 thousands of people joined in a national wave of strikes that involved workers in numerous sectors and regions of the country. In response, the government eased up somewhat on wages policy (*Africa South*, March/April 1990, p. 20).

Meanwhile, famine conditions continued to threaten central and northern regions of the country. It was estimated that in 1989 some 2.9 million rural dwellers could not produce enough to feed themselves (*AED*, 17 April 1989, p. 13) while over seven million people, half the national population, still depended on food aid (*The Economist*, 31 March–6 April, 1990).

In 1989, the government announced a food security and rural development programme which was to concentrate resources in forty food producing districts. These areas were to receive farm implements and seeds, as well as benefit from small-scale irrigation projects and improvements to economic and social infrastructure. To alleviate the impact of the adjustment process on vulnerable groups, it was announced that poor families would receive government support to buy medicines, food and school books. Plans were also drawn up which would enable a hundred thousand people to receive a cash food allowance the following year. (*AED*, 27 November 1989, p. 15)

Such programmes, of course, were contingent upon foreign aid. By the end of the decade, however, the government and people of Mozambique faced a new threat – that of 'donor fatigue'. In December 1989, it was reported that pledges of food aid for the following year were approximately half the level requested by the government (*New African*, April 1990, p. 18). As the attention of many Western governments and aid agencies shifted to Eastern Europe and (during 1990) the Middle East, and donors became frustrated with the seeming permanency of the Mozambican crisis, there was a danger that levels of external assistance would be significantly reduced.

EXPLAINING THE REFORMS

The main purpose of the reforms introduced following the Fourth Congress has been summed up aptly by Mackintosh in the following terms:

> The government aims to retain and strengthen its capacity to plan the state sector, while at the same time decentralizing economic decision making and economic management, in order to improve its effectiveness. At the same time, the authorities are seeking to increase private investment and private economic activity, with an emphasis on indigenous small and medium-sized enterprises in

both agriculture and industry, and to stimulate local markets by deregulation. (Mackintosh, 1986, p. 572)

Why, then, were such significant changes in economic and food policy introduced by the government?

Economic Crisis Conditions

During the early 1980s the Mozambican economy experienced severe difficulties as levels of production declined and domestic trade circuits disintegrated. This situation resulted from a number of conditions associated primarily with the elimination of the type of coercive mechanisms referred to earlier, on which the reproduction of the economy had previously depended; the limited capacity of the state to fill the gap left by foreign enterprises, Portuguese farmers and technical personnel; planning imbalances which tended to marginalize certain sectors and social groups; and the effects of external aggression and war. The situation was also aggravated by chronic drought conditions in several parts of the country.

By 1980, serious food shortages were appearing in the cities. During the early 1980s, famine conditions began to threaten certain provinces and eventually became reality in late 1983 and early 1984 following a lethargic response from Western donors to appeals for food aid (Hanlon, 1984, p. 252). The country's GNP, which had recovered slightly from 71 100 million to 83 700 million meticais between 1975 and 1981, fell sharply to 55 600 million in 1984 (Ottaway, 1988, p. 216).

Serious problems associated with basic food production had emerged in the late 1970s. In Table 2.2 we see a marked decline in cereals production following 1977. Between 1976 and 1983, per capita cereals production fell by 42 per cent, while per capita food production declined by 23 per cent.

Both state agricultural enterprises and peasant producers experienced serious difficulties. Despite the priority accorded to the state farm sector, the production performance of the latter was extremely poor. The limited capacity to repair and maintain machinery, lack of skilled personnel, and labour shortages seriously undermined a development strategy centred on large-scale capital intensive production. While marketed production of the 'modern' (that is, state) farm sector of cereals (maize and rice) was, during the late 1970s, roughly equivalent to pre-independence levels, production of livestock and

TABLE 2.2   *Indices of cereals and food production, 1976–83*

	1976	1977	1978	1979	1980	1981	1982	1983
Cereals								
National	116	115	104	96	103	101	96	90
per capita	138	131	100	102	98	90	82	80
Food[1]								
National	97	97	96	98	101	102	102	97
per capita	115	110	104	102	100	98	96	89

SOURCE   FAO (FAO, 1986, Tables 4, 8, 9, 13).
* 1979–81=100.
[1] Refers to commodities that are considered edible and contain nutrients.

vegetable products fell considerably (Raikes, 1984, p. 101). Low levels of productivity meant that, rather than generating surplus, the state farm sector incurred substantial losses, which in turn exacerbated foreign exchange difficulties (Littlejohn, 1988, p. 14).

An even more serious situation affected peasant production which, it has been estimated, accounted for approximately 70 per cent of gross agricultural production (Raikes, 1984, p. 105). This production included not only the major staples of cassava and maize but also important agro-exports such as cotton and cashew. Production in this sector was seriously affected by a combination of low prices, the disruption of marketing channels, and the extremely limited supply of basic inputs, tools and consumer goods. While the national economy was highly dependent on the import of capital, intermediate and consumer goods only a tiny proportion of these ended up in the hands of the peasantry. As Raikes explains: 'Given a very serious foreign exchange shortage and its rationing according to plan, the enormous preponderance of machinery, equipment, and spare parts and fuel for the industrial and state farm sectors in total imports, this leaves very little for consumer goods for the peasantry, especially since over 60 per cent of imports of consumer goods are of basic foodstuffs for the cities' (Ibid). The marginalization of the peasantry in the structure of resource allocation had major implications both for food and agro-export production in general, as well as the profitability and performance of the state sector, which was highly dependent on labour, food and raw materials derived from the peasant sector (O'Laughlin, 1981). Marketed production, in particular, was affected, as many peasant households reverted to a subsistence economy.

War conditions and attempts by the South African government to destabilize the Mozambican regime and economy played an important part in this scenario. During the early 1980s, the RENAMO forces, supported by the South African government, rapidly extended their military actions, destroying in the process transportation and marketing networks. These actions contributed to the disarticulation of trade circuits in rural areas, as well as those connecting town and countryside. In early 1984, Samora Machel reported that some 900 shops had been destroyed by RENAMO and that this had affected supplies and marketing for 4.5 million people (Saul, 1985, p. 100). Agricultural production and the levels of living of the rural population were further affected by the systematic destruction of infrastructure related to energy, communications and social services, as well as attacks on co-operatives. The war also served to reinforce certain biases which characterized the planning process, notably those favouring development in and around the cities and in the state farm sector, that is, in sites that were more easily defensible.

The post-1981/82 period witnessed a serious procurement crisis, which was compounded in subsequent years as inflationary pressures widened the gap between official and parallel market prices. As indicated in Table 2.3, registered procurement fell sharply during the first half of the 1980s for most major crops, with the exception of maize, which fluctuated sharply.

In Table 2.4 we see that by 1982, officially-marketed domestically-produced grain only accounted for 30 per cent of all marketed grain.

Although total export revenues continued to increase during the late 1970s and beginning of the 1980s, the visible trade deficit rose sharply from $145 million in 1976 to around $600 million in 1982 (see Table 2.5). The value of imports had soared following 1978, from an annual average of approximately $340 million during 1975–77, to $550 million in 1978–79, reaching around $800 million in 1981–82. Over the same period, the overall balance of trade deficit (visible plus invisible trade) increased from zero to just over $500 million.[2] During the early 1980s, the balance of trade deficit emerged as a major constraint on economic development. By 1983, foreign trade revenues accounted for little more than a third of imports (Mackintosh and Wuyts, 1988, p. 10) and the country had become heavily dependent on foreign loans and grants.

Particulary alarming was the collapse of agro-export earnings following 1982: FAO data indicate that revenues from agriculture,

TABLE 2.3   *Registered marketing of selected crops, 1975–85 (in 000s of tons)*

	Rice	Maize	Beans	Cashew	Cotton	Copra	Sunflower
1975	98	95	14.8	160	52	50.4	8
1978	70	44	10.1	90	74.2	60	7
1980	43.6	65	9.6	87.6	64.9	37.1	11.8
1981	28.7	78.3	14.9	90.1	73.7	54.4	12.1
1982	41.5	89.2	6.9	57	60.7	36.6	10.8
1983	17.3	55.8	4.7	18.1	24.7	30.7	7.3
1984	19.1	82.6	3.5	25.3	19.7	24.8	5
1985	17.9	58.6	n.d.	n.d.	5.7	24.0	n.d.

SOURCE   National Planning Commission, (see Mackintosh, 1986, p. 559; Egero, 1987, p. 91).

TABLE 2.4   *Sources of marketed grain, 1982 (in 000s of tons)*

	Wheat	Maize	Rice	Total
Commercial imports	46	20	42	108
Donations arrived	82	71	45	198
Local marketed prod.[1]	1	89	42	132
Total	129	180	129	438

SOURCE   Hanlon, 1984, p. 287.
[1] Does not include black-market sales.

TABLE 2.5   *Visible trade deficit and import coverage, 1976–82 (in millions of dollars and percentages)*

	1976	1978	1980	1982
Visible trade deficit	145	361	519	603
Import coverage (%)[1]	103	48	48	38

SOURCE   Based on Mackintosh and Wuyts, 1988, p. 10; Hanlon, 1984, p. 280.

[1] $\dfrac{\text{Export earnings} + \text{Balance on invisibles}}{\text{Imports}}$

TABLE 2.6   *Agriculture, fish and forestry exports (in millions of dollars)*

1980	1981	1982	1983	1984	1985
133.2	146.0	153.7	98.5	77.4	68.6

SOURCE   *FAO Trade Yearbook*, 1985.

TABLE 2.7   *Index of agro-industrial and light industrial production, 1973, 1980, 1982*

Product	1973	1980	1982
Rice	100	36	35
Sugar	100	58	41
Cashew Nuts	100	59	44
Edible Oil	100	82	78
Textiles	100	95	60
Soap	100	86	112
Beer	100	70	58
Hoes	100	24	90
Bicycles	100	15	38

SOURCE   Hanlon, 1984, p. 284, based on National Planning Commission. Base year   1973=100.

fishing and forestry fell from $153.7 million in 1982 to just $68.6 million three years later (see Table 2.6).

Production of many processed food and manufactured products also fell sharply during the post-revolutionary period. This is illustrated in Table 2.7 which presents data for nine product sectors between 1973 and 1982. The (constant) value of production in the light industrial and processed food branches fell by 38 per cent between 1981 and 1984, whereas that of the heavy industry and energy branches declined by 67 per cent over the same period. Total industrial production fell by half (see Mackintosh, 1986, p. 560).

Shortages of basic products, price control and inflation led to the development of a parallel economy where prices bore little relation to those set by the state. The implications of this situation for economic development are explained by Mackintosh:

the gap between the tiers of the market in Mozambique has now reached the stage where it is a positive block on the development

of the economy. The effect has been to both devalue and devalor-
ize the local currency. . . Reversing this situation is a precondition
for the re-establishment of intrarural trading and of exchange
relations between the state and the rest of the economy. This in
turn is an essential basis for re-establishing state procurement.
Only by making local money again acceptable for general exchange
can the state recover the capacity to procure food. The present
market situation reduces production, and it distorts the pattern of
investment and economic activity towards profits to be made by
trading and speculation. The overall effect is that the government
has largely lost the capacity to direct the evolution of the economy.
(Mackintosh, 1986, p. 574)

Planning Limitations and the Loss of Hegemony

This situation was also a product of the type of planning approach
adopted by the revolutionary government during the late 1970s and
early 1980s, which emphasized rapid industrialization, modernization
and large-scale projects. Highly ambitious goals were set which
aimed at eliminating underdevelopment within a decade – the 1980s
being proclaimed the decade of the 'big jump'. According to Egero:

ideology came to dominate the content of state plans. Rather than
being the sum total of locally based production and development
plans, their point of departure were the centrally defined goals for
1990. This increased the internal contradiction in the planning
process between central demands and local means. (Egero, 1987,
p. 100)

A chronic shortage of reliable data and technical/professional staff
further weakened the planning process. Littlejohn argues that the
low levels of productivity which resulted in losses in the state farm
sector stemmed from the types of planning methods adopted:

Given the huge difficulties of obtaining and transmitting information on the production processes of these farms, an appropriate
form of central planning should have included a considerable
amount of delegation of decisions to the levels where the information was available. . .Not only were the connections between state,
cooperative and family agriculture ignored, with consequent ef-

fects on labour supply, but the very form of planning made it difficult to correct plans in the light of the information available to the more experienced workers on these farms. (Littlejohn, 1988, pp. 14–15)

The upshot of this situation was what one writer has referred to as a problem of confidence in planning (Egero, 1987, p. 101). As a government report put it: 'this situation brings many cadres to doubt, not this type of planning but any type of planning or planning as a method.'[3] Recognizing the ineffectiveness of official planning and management methods, many state farm managers reverted to alternative methods which were frequently based on the types of colonial management techniques which characterized settler farms and plantations. As Littlejohn explains:

the failure of the central planning agencies to establish pertinent forms of information flow, and appropriate forms of decision making at the various organisational levels, led not only to negative economic growth, but also to the blocking of any socialist transformation of the state farms themselves. (Littlejohn, 1988, p. 15)

Problems associated with organization, methods and resources seriously affected the implementation of plans, programmes and policies. In this respect the Mozambican state has been characterized as an exceptionally 'weak' state. According to Ottaway: 'The Government has a very limited capacity to affect what actually happens. It can draw up plans, make laws, and issue decrees, but it cannot implement them: and it can set up institutions of all sorts, but it cannot make them operational.' (Ottaway, 1988, p. 222).

However, the limited capacity of the state to direct the evolution of the economy should not be analyzed solely in terms of economic problems associated with the low level of development of the productive forces and macro-economic disequilibria, but also in terms of political conditions associated with the loss of hegemony of FRELIMO and the declining capacity of the vanguard to mobilize the energies of the mass of the population in accordance with national development objectives. This situation contrasted with that which had existed some years earlier. As Pinsky explains, referring to the period immediately following independence when the country was desperately short of technical, administrative and productive capacity:

the one resource FRELIMO could bring to bear on its post-independence reconstruction projects was the ability, developed during the arduous years of the liberation struggle, to mobilize and organize popular participation and popular forces in order to generate self-reliant solutions to problems. (Pinsky, 1985, p. 281)

The economic reforms, it seems, were part of an attempt to recover this capacity.

The Marginalization of the Peasantry

The post-1977 development model had clearly failed to address the needs of the mass of the agricultural population. As indicated earlier, the overwhelming majority of the agricultural population were poor peasants. The post-independence government did not introduce a major land redistribution programme and, despite the early emphasis on collectivization and the establishment of communal villages, only a tiny percentage of the rural population was actually organized in some form of producer co-operative.

The alienation of the rural population was not only a product of decisions taken at the central level, regarding the allocation of resources among different economic sectors and forms of production, but also a consequence of the type of relations which existed between the state farm and the local population. As Littlejohn points out:

the failure to meet their own targets meant that state farms gave little help to cooperatives, and the attempts at extensive growth of surface area cultivated alienated the neighbouring peasantry, many of whom also formed part of the work force of the state farms themselves, where poor working conditions and disregard of their views further alienated them. (Littlejohn, 1988, pp. 15–16)

The inability of the government to address the material needs of the peasantry was clearly recognized in the Party's *Report on the Preparation of the (Fourth) Congress*:

We are not bothering about manufacturing the hoe because we are waiting the arrival of the tractor we must import. We are distributing tinned beans, that cost foreign exchange, in a communal village that produces beans and from where no one has bothered to collect surplus production. We overload the peasant with items he does not use but do not provide him with a lamp, cloth, a file or a hammer. Nonetheless we expect him to exchange his production for goods he does not need.

Likewise. . .the failure to support small-scale projects and local initiative has the effect of demobilizing the people. They make great sacrifices to make large-scale projects possible, but they do not feel the support of state structures in improved living standards and in the fight against hunger.

The result of all this was that peasant-producers were increasingly drawn into the web of the parallel economy in order to obtain essential inputs and consumption goods. Once locked into these circuits, tensions with the state necessarily intensified for this was a world the state was attempting to suppress.

By 1982, peasant support for the revolution was waning. Referring to the situation in one of the major agricultural regions (Baixo Limpopo), Roesch describes a set of conditions that point to a potential crisis of hegemony:

Attendances at local political meetings dropped. Enthusiasm and goodwill began to be replaced by apathy and cynicism. The increasingly difficult economic situation initiated a gradual but growing process of peasant demobilization, which came effectively to block the processes of social, political and ideological transformation that the creation of the communal villages had set in motion. Though Frelimo continued to enjoy – and still enjoys – widespread popular support in this rural area, the crisis of reproduction made it increasingly difficult for the party to sustain the level of popular support needed for the social and economic transformations it was seeking to bring about in the countryside. (Roesch, 1984, p. 309)

Popular Participation

To what extent and how, then, did peasant discontent influence the policy process? Here it is important to refer to the principle of participatory democracy which had been a central feature of the development process in post-revolutionary Mozambique. At the outset, the revolution attached considerable importance to the idea that the people would play a major role in shaping the decisions that affected their lives. Initially, small committees known as *grupos*

dinamizadores, serving a multiplicity of functions (popular mobilization, the 'eyes and ears' of the revolution, as well as administrative,
social and judicial functions), were set up throughout the country,
operating at the level of the workplace, the neighbourhood or the
village. These, together with frequently-held mass meetings, constituted one of the main sites of popular participation.

Decisions taken at the Third Congress in 1977 stressed the need
not only for socialist transformation of the economy but also for
popular democracy. As Pinsky points out, the primary achievement
of the Congress was:

> To constitute FRELIMO as a political party with a very explicit
> commitment to popular democracy and the transition to a socialist
> society. Party members were to work in constant contact with the
> population, and rural, town, provincial, and national assemblies
> were to be democratically elected to ensure popular control over
> the state apparatus at each level. Particular emphasis was to be
> given to the rural assemblies as a political counterweight to the
> relatively privileged cities. (Pinsky, 1985, p. 292)

In late 1976 and throughout 1977 new democratic institutions and
forms of participation emerged. Firstly, mass organizations representing youth, women and workers were established. Secondly, the
People's Assembly – an institution with certain consultative and
legislative functions – was established at different levels with candi-
dates being chosen on the basis of universal adult suffrage (Saul
(ed.), 1985, p. 80). National planning meetings at local, district and
regional levels were held to discuss issues and policies associated with
urban planning and collective rural development. In addition, the
practice of holding public meetings in workplaces or residential areas
whenever leaders were visiting in order to discuss problems openly
was institutionalized (Hanlon, 1984, p. 146).

Following the Third Congress, the Party itself was transformed
from a small, largely urban-based organization into one with ten-
tacles that spread throughout the society. Over a period of several
years FRELIMO created an infrastructure that increased the potential for greater contact with the mass of the population. This process
of party-building is described by Scott:

> After the third congress in 1977. . .a 'party structuring' campaign
> was undertaken in order to recruit members and set up committees

at provincial, city, and district levels. By early 1979, party cells had been established in factories and collective farms, as well as in government ministries. . .By 1980. . .'Frelimo had become firmly implanted throughout the country'[4] and by the time of the fourth congress in 1983, some 4200 cells had been created in Mozambique. (Scott, 1988, pp. 30–1)

While the structures of participatory democracy were developed during the late 1970s, effective participation (in terms of the capacity of different social groups to have a direct bearing on decision-making processes associated with policy design) remained fairly weak. The principle of democratic centralization adopted by the party, as well as the ongoing influence of colonial attitudes and social relations, often meant in practice that 'commandism' gained the upper hand. Also, the distinction between the role of the vanguard party and the state became increasingly blurred, with the effect that popular organizations and party cells ended up primarily as channels for communicating state directives to the people, rather than fulfilling the function of conveying demands associated with popular interests upwards.

The party began to reassert a more independent position in 1980 when problems associated with corruption, bureaucratic inefficiency, worker apathy and rural demobilization became more apparent (Saul, 1985, p. 82) In response, FRELIMO launched the 'Political and Organizational Offensive' which, as Saul points out, attempted to strengthen the party, revitalize party cells, repoliticize the development process, repopularize economic strategy and ensure that 'the drive toward Mozambique's long-term socialist development goals was not preempted by a bureaucratic petty-bourgeoisie' (Saul, 1985, pp. 87, 91). This process culminated in the launching in 1982 of a national dialogue in preparation for the Fourth Congress to be held the following year. As stated by Hanlon: 'More than anything else, it was by holding thousands of meetings throughout the country in the build-up to the Fourth Congress that the leaders realized the anger and resentment that had been growing up because of the economic problems in rural areas' (Hanlon, 1984, p. 146).

Through this participatory process, workers and peasants were able to influence the policy process and shape the proposals discussed at the Fourth Congress. At the Congress itself, workers and peasants were well-represented, with the majority of the delegates being drawn from their ranks. In the run-up to the Congress the membership of the party was expanded to 110 323 members, 54 per cent of whom were peasants and 19 per cent workers. (Ibid., p. 140) At the Congress itself the Central Committee of the party more than doubled in size and was weighted less in favour of technocrats and more in favour of workers, peasants and the pre-independence FRELIMO fighters (Saul (ed.), 1985, p. 95).

Rich Peasant Interests

Given that the central thrust of the reforms was geared towards stimulating private agricultural production, it would seem important, when analyzing the intervention of different social groups in the policy process, to differentiate peasant interests. Unfortunately, in the literature on the reform process in Mozambique, there has been little attempt to do this. There is some evidence to suggest that rich peasants were influential in many areas of the country, in part due to the fact that, unlike much of the rural male population, they enjoyed stable residence and did not have to migrate in search of employment (O'Laughlin, 1981). In certain areas of the south, social differentiation among the rural population had intensified. The expansion of agriculture in the Green Zones around Maputo, for example, saw certain 'mining' families with some capital take up commercial farming on abandoned settler farms in order to supply to urban market, (Ibid.).

Government support for rich peasants/private farmers seems in part to have been founded on a problematic twofold assumption which has been pointed out by Littlejohn. It was assumed, firstly, that private farmers were capable of producing the type of rapid results needed in a shortage economy, and secondly, that poor and middle peasants were not involved in marketing. As such: 'rich peasants and private farmers were seen as the source of marketed agricultural surplus, while poor peasants were probably seen as potentially or actually involved in wage labour, whereas middle peasants were considered to be self-supporting (and hence less involved in market relations)' (Littlejohn, 1988, p. 17).

External Pressures

Perceptions such as these were clearly reinforced by pressure from Western donors which built up during the early 1980s (Ibid; Saul (ed.), 1985, p. 410; Ottaway, 1988) As the accumulation drive continued and foreign exchange earnings declined, the government had to rely increasingly on Western sources of aid to complement Eastern bloc development assistance, which appeared to have reached definite limits following the rejection in 1981 of Mozambique's request to join the Council for Mutual Economic Assistance (CMEA).[5]

By 1983, the OECD countries provided the majority of Mozambique's imports – their share of imports having increased from 41.2 per cent in 1979 to 57.8 per cent in 1983 (See Egero, 1987, p. 90). As Egero points out:

> Whatever had been the prospects of recovery in 1980, three years later Mozambique's foreign debt was over 1.3 billion dollars, three fourths of which referred to development projects still in progress. The state had no means to pay its debt service, and was forced to ask for a renegotiation of the whole debt burden. (Ibid., p. 92)

In September 1984, Mozambique joined the International Monetary Fund (IMF) and the World Bank, following *rapprochement* with the Reagan administration and the waiving of the US ban on non-emergency bilateral aid to Mozambique. Following the signing of the Nkomati Accord with South Africa in March of that year,[6] USAID began to provide development assistance amounting to approximately $10 million a year (Ottaway, 1988, p. 219). By 1987, United States aid to Mozambique totalled $85 million.

Considerable pressure was applied by these and other development agencies, which prompted a change in government strategy. Citing Cliff *et al.*, Mackintosh and Wuyts state that:

> one of USAID's principal stated objectives for aid in Mozambique [is] that of entering into a policy dialogue so as to induce the earlier arrival of a market based economy and a thriving private sector. Furthermore, [the authors] point out that in doing so, USAID relies on and aims to support the leading role of the IMF and the World Bank in setting the tone and the pace of this dialogue. (Mackintosh and Wuyts, 1988, p. 29, citing Cliff *et al.*, 1986, p. 19)

The United States government placed particular emphasis on the need to develop private agriculture (Littlejohn, 1988, p. 17). Conditions attached to the USAID agreement required that goods obtained be channelled to the private sector (Saul (ed.), 1985, p. 410; Ottaway, 1988, p. 219). As we saw earlier, World Bank and IMF insistence on the need for a major devaluation and cuts in subsidies bore fruit in 1987. The mid-1987 reform package had been negotiated with the IMF, which had agreed to a $36 million loan (Ibid., p. 220).

FRELIMO versus the 'Aspirants to the Bourgeoisie'

In analyzing the political economy of the Mozambican reform process it is important to consider other changes that had occurred in the balance of social forces. During 1982, FRELIMO launched an 'offensive' against the 'internal class enemy' which was seen as undermining the possibility of socialist development. During the late 1970s, two social groups rapidly increased their control over the means of production and exchange, considerably improved their material position and increasingly marginalized workers and peasants in the structure of resource allocation. These groups, referred to by FRELIMO as 'aspirants to the bourgeoisie', consisted of what Hanlon refers to as the commercial group, based on private commercial capital and accumulating through the black market, and the state group, consisting of a technocratic elite within the bureaucracy (Hanlon, 1984, p. 187).

The position of both these groups was significantly reinforced during the 1979/80 period when technocrats came to control decisions regarding the sectoral allocation of scarce resources and the party itself came to justify hierarchy and privilege. It was a period when, as Hanlon points out, decisions were taken to import tractors for large-scale state projects, or to grow white potatoes consumed by the urban middle classes, rather than to import the hoes the peasantry needed or to increase the production of peasant crops such as sweet potato or cassava (Ibid., p. 194). It was also a period in which the private sector expanded as the state privatized small businesses it had inherited from the Portuguese, and implemented its green zones policy, encouraging both private and co-operative farming around the main cities. The problems of shortages and inflation associated with a war economy created a propitious environment for speculative trading and black market activities. Government control on prices and the geographical movement of goods meant that private commercial capital operated largely illegally. Sources of produce destined for the black market expanded not only through 'leaks' in the official channels but also as 'traders themselves began to invest their speculative profits in farming and fishing, both to provide a cover, and as a route to further illegal trading' (Ibid., p. 196)

As Hanlon points out, the two groups had a 'community of interest' and developed a symbiotic relationship that was often semi-legal. Whereas the commercial group needed the tacit approval of the bureaucracy, the state group required access to the types of goods which characterized middle-class lifestyles. These were available on the black market or through legal enterprises (for example, restaurants) that obtained part of their supplies from the black market. Gradually, illegal practices and corruption increased within the bureaucracy (Ibid., p. 196).

In the early 1980s, it became obvious that the activities of the black market operators were seriously undermining not only basic development programmes but also the possibility of effective state control over the economy (Ibid., p. 208). Moreover, much of the bureaucracy eventually came to see the black market as impeding, rather than assisting, the reproduction of urban middle-class households. These changing conditions and perceptions led to a rift between the two factions of the 'aspiring bourgeoisie'. The position or legitimacy of the technocratic elite was also weakened during this period when it became apparent that many of the plans, programmes and policies it proposed were clearly failing. As popular discontent rose, the party itself initiated actions to curb the power of the commercial and state groups.

Problems associated with the black market, shortages and centralization were interpreted by FRELIMO as resulting not so much from errors in development strategy but from the class struggle and the fact that the 'aspirants to the bourgeioise' were gaining the upper hand. As one FRELIMO report put it:

> The internal bourgeoisie now has more economic power than it held immediately after independence. It has infiltrated the trade circuits and the state apparatus. Hence the blackmarket is not essentially an effect of economic difficulties and low production. . .it is above all the action of the class enemy.

While statements such as these clearly served an ideological purpose to divert attention away from the types of problem discussed in Part I, inherent in orthodox socialist development strategies, they are important in so far as they highlight the role of contradictory class practices in contributing to the crisis which prompted the reforms.

Referring to the technocratic elite, a document prepared by the Central Committee of FRELIMO noted:

they try to distort the class character of our revolution by transforming it into a technocratic process through which they can control power.

This social stratum actively opposes any measures that aim at simplifying organization and methods, democratizing leadership or increasing the worker's share in planning and controlling production. . .They are unable to learn from the people. . .So they reject the small-scale projects that require the intelligence, sensitivity and understanding of the people and prefer the projects that come ready made from abroad. (FRELIMO, 1983, pp. 71–72)

CONCLUSION

Varying interpretations exist as to which interests and social groups stood to gain from the process of economic reform. Some writers stress the pro-farmer character of the reforms. According to Mackintosh and Wuyts, for example:

The government is seeking ways to assist the small scale sector effectively, and there are many variations being tried between a 'building on the best' strategy of channelling resources to the more successful, and strategies, including the discussion of peasant associations, as ways of channelling resources to a wider number of poorer farmers. (Mackintosh and Wuyts, 1988, p. 30)

Others have interpreted the reforms in terms of an attempt by the technocratic elite within the state apparatus to consolidate its position. According to Hanlon, this would be achieved by 'join[ing] with the workers and peasants against speculative capital. . .[and trying] to move commercial capital into production while it supported and tried to create rich peasants as new potential allies, then working with both these groups to block support for poor peasants' (Hanlon, 1984, p. 209).

Some writers interpret the reforms as a tactical concession. Littlejohn, for example, argues that the failure to channel more resources towards rural co-operatives and the poor and middle peasants indicates the extent to which planners and government/party leaders still adhere to 'a statist conception of socialism whose corollary is that market relations are a temporary concession in adverse circumstances' (Littlejohn, 1988, p. 16)

Others argue that the reform process in Mozambique is, in essence, similar to the adjustment process affecting many Third-World 'capitalist' economies which aims to reduce, both in the short and long term, the role of the state in the economy and develop private enterprise (Ottaway, 1988).

These interpretations reflect not only the different analytical positions of the writers concerned but also the vagueness and uncertainty of several reform initiatives and the diverse interests and social forces influencing the reform process. The gravity of the economic crisis (declining levels of production, productivity, procurement and foreign exchange earnings) stemmed both from the impact of the war and the inadequacy of orthodox approaches to socialist development, which concentrated resources in state enterprises and large scale projects, thereby marginalizing important forms of production and creating conditions conducive to the development of a parallel economy. During the early 1980s, FRELIMO clearly recognized the limited capacity of the state to implement a state-centred accumulation model, and the distorted effects which derived from such a model.

Peasants were not passive bystanders in this process, but responded through class practices or 'survival strategies', which compounded problems associated with the mobilization and appropriation of surplus, and a process of 'demobilization', which threatened the hegemony of FRELIMO. This latter process was particularly worrying for FRELIMO, taking place as it did in the context of a war in which counter-revolutionary forces operated in many rural areas. Participatory structures developed by FRELIMO provided the mass of the rural population with some possibility of influencing in a more direct manner the process of policy design. It is quite possible that rich peasant interests assumed a prominent role in this process and that technocratic fractions within the central state apparatus attempted to shift the sectoral allocation of resources in favour of the rich peasant/private farmer sector, believing that therein lay the best possibility for rapidly increasing production.

FRELIMO did not intend, however, to abandon the central principle of socialist development strategy relating to the concept of social control over patterns of accumulation and resource allocation. This, it was believed, would be achieved partly through ongoing administrative interventions and direct control of limited but key areas of marketing and production. More importantly, however, it would be achieved by (a) creating conditions for a functioning economy; and (b) curbing 'uncontrolled patterns of private accumulation' by relying on policy instruments that would enable the state to manage, at least to some extent, the market (Mackintosh and Wuyts, 1988, pp. 3, 29).

Having failed to ally itself more closely with the Eastern bloc countries, the FRELIMO government turned increasingly towards Western donors and lending agencies. As relations with the West intensified towards the middle of the 1980s, so too did pressures from such agencies. During the latter half of the decade, USAID, the World Bank and the IMF were able to exert a decisive influence on the direction of the reform process.

Notes

1. This refers to government investment as a percentage of GDP.
2. Figures relating to the trade deficit are calculated on the basis of (a) government trade data in meticais presented in Mackintosh, 1986, p. 560 and Mackintosh and Wuyts, 1988, p. 10; and (b) exchange rate data presented in Hanlon, 1984, p. 280.
3. Instituto Nacional de Planeamento Fisico, 1984, p. 31, cited in Egero, 1987, p. 101.
4. Isaacman and Isaacman, 1983, p. 124.
5. The OECD estimates that gross disbursements of aid from the CMEA averaged $37.8 million between 1982 and 1985. This amounted to 13.3 per cent of Mozambique's total gross aid (see Lawson, 1988).
6. The Nkomati Accord was the 'Agreement on Non-Aggression and Good Neighbourliness' signed in March 1984, according to which each party agreed not to support armed opposition groups.

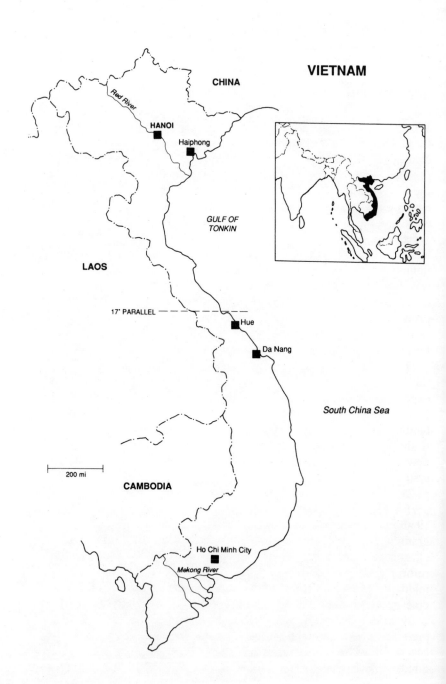

3 Vietnam

INTRODUCTION

When Vietnam was partitioned in 1954, the North could be described as an extremely poor, agrarian-based economy, where production centred on subsistence wet-rice cultivation (Fforde and Paine, 1987, p. 24). Data for 1960 indicate that 43 per cent of national output in the Democratic Republic of Vietnam (DRV) was accounted for by agriculture, while 77 per cent of the national labour force was engaged in agriculture.

Extremely low levels of industrialization, urbanization and proletarianization existed. Of a total population in the mid-1950s of 14 million, over 90 per cent lived in rural areas. Much of this population was located in the densely populated Red River Delta and relatively concentrated in villages. Throughout several centuries, agricultural producers had formed part of communal structures which were responsible, *inter alia*, for allocating land (on what was seemingly a fairly equitable basis) and collecting taxes.

The period of French colonial rule which dated in the North from the 1880s to the 1950s saw profound changes in rural society. Agro-export production, centred on tea, coffee and rubber, expanded and, as Fforde and Paine observe: 'individualized' mechanisms such as landlordism, usury and manipulation of trade started to replace the traditional 'corporate' sources of social and economic power. The new and rising social groups did not fit easily into the communal system, which began to fall into decline (Fforde and Paine, 1987, p. 25).

Having gained control of large areas of the North since the late 1940s, the Vietminh introduced in 1953 an agrarian reform programme which sought to eliminate landlordism and the old rural elite, and redistribute 'land to those who work it'. The agrarian reform took a more radical turn in 1955, when rich and 'upper-middle' peasants also came under attack in an attempt to prevent the emergence of a new villlage elite (Gordon, 1978, pp. 28–9).

By 1958, the revolutionary government had defined a more comprehensive development strategy, which followed fairly orthodox Marxist–Leninist lines, emphasizing large-scale collective agriculture, direct state control of the 'commanding heights' of the economy (banking, trade and industry), the need for centralized planning, and rapid industrialization centred on heavy industry. Capital formation associated with the latter process was financed primarily through foreign aid from the Soviet Union and China. Industrialization, however, required large quantities of 'complementary inputs' (Fforde and Paine, 1987, p. 38), the primary source of which was the domestic economy. Particularly important among these was food.

The 'food problem' facing the revolutionary government, then, centred on two pivotal aspects. Firstly, there was the question of how to meet the subsistence requirements of a rapidly-expanding peasantry. This problem was particularly acute now that the possibility no longer existed of increasing production via the traditional 'extensive' growth model based on the incorporation of virgin land beyond the Southern border (Ibid., pp. 26–7, 30). Secondly, there was the question of how to increase the extremely low levels of mobilizable surplus which characterized the agrarian economy in order to meet the subsistence requirements of the urban population and the growing demands of industry. Related questions concerned the need for the state to establish alternative mechanisms of surplus appropriation now that the landlord–usurer group had been eliminated. Surplus acquired by this group (which had often demanded payment for land and loans in kind) had served to supply the towns and cities with food. The post-revolutionary state was also confronted with the problem of how to appropriate surplus from a peasantry organized in communal structures which, throughout several centuries, had developed the capacity to resist the impositions of the central authorities, defend local interests and engage in 'avoidance strategies' which, amongst other things, restricted tax payments (Ibid., pp. 17–22).

POST-REVOLUTIONARY FOOD AND DEVELOPMENT POLICY

Agriculture and the Collectivization of Rural Producers

How, then, did the post-revolutionary state deal with these questions? Particularly important was the post-1958 emphasis on the rapid collectivization of rural producers (Bhaduri and Rahman, 1982, p. 53). During 1959 and 1960 an estimated 86 per cent of all peasant households joined mainly 'low-level co-operatives' where land was collectively worked but where the families retained ownership rights

TABLE 3.1 *Population and number of co-operator families in North Vietnam (in millions)*

	1960	1965	1975
Total population	16.10	18.63	24.55
Urban	1.40	1.84	2.65
Rural	14.70	16.79	21.90
Cooperator families	2.40	2.81	3.38
Lower level	2.06	0.78	0.09
Higher level	0.34	2.03	3.29

SOURCE   Fforde and Paine, 1987, Tables 8 & 70.

TABLE 3.2 *Legal ownership,* area and use of land** in North Vietnam*

	%		000 ha.
State farms	2	Total land area	15 840
Co-operatives	92	Agricultural land***	2 301
Private	4	Rice land	1 163
Municipalities and		Other crop land	946
religious ground	2	Natural pasture	192
		Forest and forest land	10 620

SOURCE   * Gordon, 1982, p. 9.
** Fforde and Paine, 1987; Tables 1 & 67 (official preliminary figures for 1974).
*** Refers to land used for agriculture and not land that could be used for agriculture. Excludes ponds, lakes, bog, streams, etc.

and were paid rent by the co-operative. By 1968, however, approximately 80 per cent of all co-operatives were of the 'higher level' type where both land and labour were collectivized (Fforde, 1984, p. 6). By the mid-1970s nearly 3.4 million families, or 95 per cent of all peasant families, were organized in co-operatives (see Table 3.1) which, according to official figures, controlled 92 per cent of farm land in North Vietnam (see Table 3.2).

From the late 1960s, official policy towards the petty commodity sector, or so-called 'family economy', in the North sought to restrict private agricultural activities to farming on what was known as '5 per cent land', that is, land allocated to co-operative members and their families for private use, the amount of which was officially expected to correspond to about 5 per cent of the land held by the co-operative. On this land households could engage in intensive small-scale production of pigs, chickens, fruit and vegetables, as well as intensive rice cropping. It has been estimated that income from this source accounted for between 40 and 65 per cent of total family income (Werner, 1984, p. 50; Nguyen Huu Dong, 1982, p. 23).

In the mid-1970s, the government's development policy stressed the need to accelerate the trend 'towards large-scale socialist agricultural production', reduce the role of the family economy and reassert social control over production as dictated by the plan (White C., 1982b, p. 48). Economic control of agricultural production was to be concentrated in the co-operative management committee which was expected to adhere closely to party directives. This approach was the basis of the New Management System introduced more extensively from 1974 onwards following an experimental period dating from 1971. As we will see below, the implementation of this policy, as well as efforts to contain private production, were relatively ineffective.

Industrialization and the Development of the Productive Forces

Following the drive during the 1950s to redistribute and collectivize the land, official policy in North Vietnam emphasized the need to combine the transformation of social relations with the development of the productive forces. This was expressed in the concept, given official expression in 1960, of the 'three necessary revolutions' in social relations; ideology and culture; and science and technology, with the latter regarded as key (Fforde, 1985, p. 4; Post, 1982, pp. 24–5).

Ever since the latter half of the 1950s, the public investment programme was weighted in favour of large-scale modern industry, with government leaders adhering to the Soviet doctrine of the 'law of priority development of producing means of production' as opposed to consumption goods (Spoor, 1985, p. 76). The priority attached to forced industrialization related in part to a belief in what Fforde and Paine refer to as 'neo-Stalinist assumptions': that the fundamental constraint upon economic development was the availability of industrial fixed capital (Fforde and Paine, 1987, p. 38). The upshot of this approach was that much of the investment programme centred on large-scale, slow-yielding projects associated, for example, with the production of steel, chemicals and hydroelectric power.

Government industrial policy also stressed the need to produce the means of production required to modernize agriculture.[1] This choice of policy related not only to ideology or socialist economic growth theory, but also to the objective reality of Vietnamese agriculture, where cultivable land was tremendously scarce and the agricultural land/rural population ratio of 0.1 hectare/person was amongst the lowest in the world. This dictated the need to intensify agriculture and to develop industries producing agricultural machinery and inputs – a need which became more pressing with the partition of the country in 1955. Previously, as Fforde and Paine point out:

> rapid population growth was only offset by expansion at the extensive margin permitted of the open Southern border. This meant that closure of the frontier would precipitate, sooner or later, a subsistence crisis in the North unless economic resources could be found to finance economic development and the investment needed to raise agricultural output. (Ibid., pp. 26–7)

As such, the intensification of agriculture during the post-partition period was imperative. It was this need that determined to some extent the types of industry developed. Hence the term 'heavy industry' as understood in official policy documents, referred also to industries producing insecticides, fertilizer, pumps and tractors, as well as threshers and other agricultural implements (Ibid., p. 44).

The pressures to intensify agriculture were reinforced during the 1965–73 period when US bombing reduced the cultivable area. While the increased supply of inputs boosted rice yields from approximately 1.82 tonnes per ha. during 1960–65 to 2.23 tonnes per ha. in 1973–75, production was affected by a fall in the sown area from 2.38 to 2.2 million ha. over the same period. Overall, staples production grew just 8.8 per cent (Ibid., p. 105).

From the late 1950s, then, the government encouraged a process of rapid industrialization which diversified to a considerable extent the productive base of the economy. By 1965, a relatively modern industrial sector consisting of approximately 200 state enterprises was in operation, producing a fairly diverse range of products which, in addition to those already mentioned, included machine-tools, electrical motors, bicycles, batteries, light bulbs and other consumer goods (Ibid., pp. 58–9).

During the war years, however, it was impossible to sustain the levels of industrial expansion and diversification achieved during the first half of the 1960s. With the notable exception of agrochemicals, production levels of many goods essential to peasant agriculture and

TABLE 3.3   *Production levels of selected agricultural inputs and consumer goods in North Vietnam, 1960, 1965, 1975*

Product	1960	1965	1975
Agrochemicals			
Fertiliser (000s tonnes)	51.4	144.4	423.0
Insecticides (tonnes)	45	3676	4683
Implements and machinery			
Irrigation pumps (units)	71	1915	500
Ploughs (000s)	281.0	135.5	169.4
Spades, hoes and shovels (000s)	778	1250	1267
Consumer Goods			
Laundry soap (tonnes)	1834	6378	8656
Matches (mill. boxes)	182.7	154.0	168.8
Cloth and silk (mill. metres)	96.6	108	108
Leather shoes, sandles (000s pr.)	67	887	182
Bicycles (000s)	23.1	70.6	60.4

SOURCE   Fforde and Paine, 1987, pp. 168–71 – Tables 46 and 47, based on data published by the Statistical Office in Hanoi.

households did not increase significantly, or actually declined, over the 1965–75 period (see Table 3.3).

Data available for four years between 1960 and 1975 indicate accumulation levels of between 22 and 25 per cent of national income (Ibid., p. 152). While this was based largely on investment goods imports, it nevertheless required the extraction of considerable resources from agriculture to provide raw materials for industrial production, as well as food for the growing working class and technical/professional sector associated with state enterprises and the ministries which controlled them.

Procurement and the Appropriation of Surplus

To obtain raw materials for industry and food for the non-agricultural population, a tax-in-kind and quota system were imposed on the co-operatives. Through taxes, the state acquired, during the early 1960s, approximately 7 per cent of national grain production, while in 1965 an estimated 17 per cent of national production was obtained through the quota system (White C., 1985, p. 100).

Citing official figures, Fforde and Paine show that state procurement of staples averaged around 20 per cent on national output

TABLE 3.4   *Staples production and state procurement levels in North Vietnam*

	1960	1965	1974	1975
Staples output*				
(000s tonnes of paddy equiv.)	4698	5562	6277	5491
Staples supplied to state				
(000s tonnes)**	878	1125	1017	796

SOURCE   Fforde and Paine, 1987, Tables 68, 78, 93.
* Between 80 and 90% of output is accounted for by rice.
** Approximately 95% is rice.

during the first half of the 1960s but subsequently declined, accounting for just 15 per cent in the mid-1970s (see Table 3.4). Procurement levels of industrial and export crops were generally far higher and did not show such a negative trend (Fforde and Paine, 1987, p. 109).

The state also purchased a certain quantity of produce at 'incentive prices', which were raised repeatedly from around 10–20 per cent above the quota price in 1960 to a price which exceeded the latter by some 50 per cent in later years. By the mid-1970s, marketing co-operatives were purchasing above-quota grain at prices which were approximately 15 to 20 per cent lower than those on the open market. It has been estimated that between 10 and 15 per cent of the marketed output of most co-operatives was disposed of in this way in 1975 (White C., 1985, pp. 100, 110).

The decline in direct national procurement levels was partly accounted for by the increasing gap between official and free market prices, which encouraged the peasantry to restrict deliveries to the state. A shift also occurred during the 1970s towards local procurement by state agencies, which would either sign contracts with co-operatives involving the barter of rice for manufactured commodities such as agricultural inputs or, contrary to government policy, simply purchase agricultural products directly at free market prices (Ibid., pp. 101, 110).

Direct control by the state over the distribution of basic food products was greater than that indicated by the figures on procurement, given its control of food imports, upon which the economy had become increasingly dependent. It has been estimated that the country moved from a position of relative food self-sufficiency in the early 1960s to a level of dependency on food imports which was of the order of 10–15 per cent of staples supply in the mid-1970s (Fforde and Paine, 1987, p. 69). Apart from food, there were considerable imports of other important consumer goods such as cloth, laundry soap, bicycles and sugar. Between 1960 and 1975 the economy registered a ninefold increase in the value of imports of 'means of consumption', compared with a threefold increase for 'means of production'. The percentage share of total imports accounted for by consumption goods increased from approximately 13 to 30 per cent over this period (Ibid., pp. 214–15).

The domestic terms of trade and the imposition of taxes and quotas on agricultural producers ensured the transfer of surplus from agriculture to finance not only industrialization but also the state budget. Cheap agricultural products and relatively expensive industrial products had contributed towards high profits in the state industrial sector, which provided a significant proportion of the domestic revenues that financed the state budget.[2] It has been argued, however, that while the Vietnamese development model bore many similar characteristics to the Soviet model it differed considerably in the extent to which the peasantry was squeezed by the state (Post, 1982). Data for the 1964–75 period indicate that whereas official retail prices of staples and other food products rose 30 per cent, the average prices paid for agricultural means of production increased just 13 per cent. This positive movement in the terms of official trade, however, was counteracted by relative price movements on the open market, which moved against producers. On balance, though, Fforde and Paine maintain that farmers' real incomes probably rose over the 1960–75 period (Fforde and Paine, 1987, p.108). Several commentators note the apparent contrast in the living conditions of peasant and working-class families which are generally more favourable in the case of the former.[3] On the basis of this evidence, it would seem that high industrial profits were also a function of a low-wages policy.

To ensure that workers and cadres had access to essential food products and to facilitate a low-wages policy, a coupon system operated, whereby a portion of income was paid in coupons which could be exchanged for food, which was heavily subsidized by the state. In the mid-1980s, workers with cash incomes in the region of 300 to 400 dong a month could buy 13 kilos of rice at 0.4 dong a kilo, compared to market prices of between 40 and 60 dong (*FT*, 17 April 1985, p. 38). Food subsidies increased following reunification as did social expenditure in general, as programmes in health, education, housing and social security were expanded.

Socialist Transformation in the South

Following the reunification of the North and South and the creation of the Socialist Republic of Vietnam (SRV) in 1975/76, state policy towards the southern private economy varied considerably by economic sector and socioeconomic group. A relatively equitable land tenure system (resulting from land reform measures introduced in 1956 and 1970) meant that it was not necessary to introduce a comprehensive redistributive land reform programme. The stages typically associated with the socialist transformation of agriculture could, therefore, be reduced (Nguyen Tien Hung, 1977, pp. 160–1). The government sought to incorporate rural producers in the tax system and announced plans to co-operativize the peasantry quickly. Targets were set to achieve this by 1980. In practice, however, co-operativization proceeded slowly during the latter half of the 1970s.

While many of the large enterprises abandoned by foreign capital or their Vietnamese owners were quickly nationalized, the small-scale manufacturing and trading sectors remained relatively unaffected. When during the late seventies, however, the country moved once again to a war situation, the government sought to clamp down on the urban private sector, which was seen as complementing, if not collaborating with, Chinese efforts to destabilize the economy. As Schnytzer explains:

Hanoi's response to its perceptions [of an external and internal Chinese threat] was dramatic. On 23 March 1978, a government decree to 'transform capitalist commerce' was published. This led to the immediate closure of all private business enterprises in Vietnam and the confiscation of accumulated commodities. Further, the 'capitalist traders' were offered the choice between jobs on government-operated enterprises or opportunities to make new lives for themselves in the 'New Economic Zones'. (Schnytzer, 1982, p. 347)

Government policy towards certain elements of the so-called urban informal sector, notably in Ho Chi Minh City, involved an attempt to transfer millions of under-employed to the New Economic Zones (Le Hong Tam, 1984, p. 528) located in underpopulated and undeveloped rural areas where the government aimed to increase agricultural production. Rural-to-urban migration had left important farming areas underpopulated. As explained by White:

In the Mekong Delta in the late 1970s. . .the major priority was. . . getting tillers back to the land (population redistribution). The wartime bombing in the Mekong Delta had driven millions of peasants to the relative safety of the towns and cities. Unemployed urban dwellers were urged to leave the cities for New Economic Zones on which the priority was to get production going by any means possible, whether the form was private, co-operative or state farming. Many of these settlers returned to the cities as they were unaccustomed after years of living off US aid to the rigours of making a living from the land, especially in such harsh economic conditions. (White C., 1983, p. 254)

ECONOMIC AND FOOD POLICY REFORMS

Agricultural Incentives and the Contract Farming System

Policy changes affecting food and agricultural production and marketing were at the heart of the economic reform process initiated in 1979, when a new policy line emerged at the Sixth Plenum of the Central Committee of the Vietnamese Communist Party (VNCP) that recognized the importance of small-scale peasant or family farming in economic development, as well as the need to increase the allocation of resources to that sector. The contract farming system was formally introduced in 1981, whereby co-operatives, which previously organized the labour process and controlled the surplus, now sub-contracted land to teams of members or, peasant households for the final stages of the production process. Under the new system, the teams delivered a fixed quota to the co-operative but were then free to trade any surplus product on the open market (White, 1935, p. 97). A system of dual contracts operated whereby the co-operative received from the state a guaranteed supply of basic inputs and equipment at fixed prices, while delivering to the state a set amount of grain. In relation to agricultural production it was estimated that over 90 per cent of the collective organizations in the country had adopted the contract system by the beginning of 1984 (Duiker, 1985, p. 99).

The precise operation of this system and the types of social relationship involved, however, varied considerably. Writing at the beginning of the reform period, White explains:

it is possible to hypothesize that two major and very different patterns would emerge depending on the pre-existing mix of state and family sector inputs. In the first type, a high level of state-supplied inputs would enable the cooperative to continue to organise a number of steps of the production process effectively. This is the pattern which the government would prefer to see generalised since it maximises control by the socialist sector. . . However, in the more typical situation of low state inputs and heavy cooperative dependence on family sector contributions, it is likely that the new system entails a return to household organisation of production for all steps of the labour process. (White C., 1982b, p. 49)

Under the first type of contracting, the co-operative would continue to organize specialized teams to perform more technical operations while other, more manual, operations would be contracted out. The contract system meant that approximately half the work previously organized by the co-operative management committees passed to the control of households, individual workers or groups of workers.

Given the gender division of labour that operates in Vietnamese agriculture, the new system meant that most of the technical work (ploughing, water control and crop protection) which remained collectivized, was carried out by men, while operations that were subcontracted – transplanting of rice, weeding and some harvesting – were performed by women (Werner, 1984, p. 52; White C., 1982b, p. 49). During the war with the United States there had been a marked acceleration in the feminization of agricultural work. It has been estimated that at least 60 per cent of agricultural work and some 90 per cent of subcontracted tasks were performed by women in 1982 (Werner, 1984, pp. 52–4).

The contract farming system implied a significant transfer of control over the labour process from the collective to the family. As explained by White:

it is left up to the existing social relations between individuals within households and families which have received land on subcontract to determine what the distribution of work and product will be. Government policy is only concerned with the contractual relationship between the cooperative and the contractee (obligation to deliver a certain quota of production). . .Individual subcon-

tractees are expected to mobilise labour within the household. . .
as well as family members not resident within the household.
(White C., 1982b, p. 50)

Crucial to the reform process was an attempt to alter the rural–urban terms of trade in favour of the countryside. Agricultural producer prices, which had remained low for many years, were increased
in 1979 and were raised again two years later, when increases of
between 400 and 600 per cent were announced on forty agricultural
products (Spoor, 1988, p. 14). As White points out, however: 'Post-
war changes in the rural–urban terms of trade, and improvements in
peasants' standards of living, have probably been primarily outside
the realm of official price policy. That is they are the result of the
material incentives for increased productivity introduced by the
contract system in 1981 and the increasing trend away from official
trade towards barter or free market exchange.' (White C., 1985,
p. 105).

Ongoing Socialization

Despite the introduction of measures that involved a degree of
decollectivization and the relaxation of certain centralized planning
controls, the government did not intend to abandon the concept of
social control over the economy. The linchpin in the system of social
control was the co-operatives. During the first half of the 1980s there
was a major drive to accelerate the socialization of agriculture in the
South. In 1982 only about 15 per cent of the farming population of
the South was organized in some form of co-operative organization,
but by April 1984 this figure had risen to 45 per cent and reached 75
per cent a year later. By early 1985, an estimated 30 000 production
solidarity teams and 540 co-operatives had been formed in the South
(Duiker, 1985, p. 98; 1986, pp. 109–10).

The socialization of agriculture was seen as a prerequisite for
effective state control of strategic product markets. With the organization of producers in co-operatives, state procurement levels stood
to increase from 10 per cent of the harvest (tax on individual landholdings) to between 30 and 40 per cent (White C., 1983, p. 255). As
mentioned earlier, however, while the pace of co-operativization was
stepped up, the content of the socialization programme was relaxed
somewhat. 'Appropriate' forms of socialist organization were no

longer just the traditional large-scale co-operatives, but smaller 'semi-socialist' 'solidarity' or production teams. This shift in policy had been largely inspired by the failure to promote production collectives in the major grain-producing areas of the South, such as the Mekong Delta, where rich peasant producers were concentrated (Ibid.).

Procurement and Marketing

Changes also occurred in the three-tier procurement system for food. Obligatory grain sales (principally rice) from the co-operative to state marketing agencies decreased by nearly half, as of March 1983, to 10 per cent of planned rice production. The delivery quotas of families or teams to co-operatives were fixed for a five-year period. Agricultural taxes increased slightly to around 10 per cent of total grain production. Sales of above-quota paddy and pork at 'incentive prices' continued but state agencies were encouraged to exchange grain for manufactured goods (White, 1982a, pp. 100, 101).

During the early 1980s it was estimated that procurement levels were only half of planned levels. In response to this situation, a 1982 decree called for local self-provisioning and stated that the central government would only guarantee the needs of the regular armed forces (Ibid., p. 101). The geographical movement of grain and other essential products continued to be controlled via a system of roadside checkpoints. In 1987, however, restrictions on long-distance trade and the flow of food and raw materials to urban areas through private channels were lifted (*FT*, 18 April 1987, p. 2).

As production levels in agriculture and industry increased during the early 1980s, the major problems which concerned policy-makers shifted to those associated with the growing inability of the state to control marketing and the related problems of increasing black market activities and inflation. Of particular concern was the role of the bureaucracy and party cadres in contributing to these problems, through administrative inefficiency and corruption. A commentary on Hanoi radio described the problem in the following terms:

Distribution and circulation (of goods) have become the thorniest, most burning issue. On this front, serious manifestations of erroneous ideas and viewpoints and shortcomings in cadre organisation have occurred. . .depriving the state of its ability to control goods, money markets and prices; creating many difficulties in production and livelihood, and making quite a few cadres, party members and state personnel depraved. (see Chanda, 1984, p. 30)

Both the Third and Fourth Plenums of the Party Central Committee, held in December 1982 and June 1983 respectively, called for the expulsion of cadres engaging in corrupt malpractices (Ibid., p. 32).

Employment and the Urban Population

Attempts to relocate urban labour in agro-industrial districts in order to expand production on new or fallow lands, as well as to reduce population pressure and alleviate social and economic problems in urban areas, continued during the 1980s. The 1985 annual economic plan called for the creation of 400 agro-industrial districts by the year 1990, each of which would accommodate approximately 100 000 people and cover an area of 20 000 ha. (Duiker, 1986, p. 108). Such measures were seen as an effective way of dealing with the urban problem in Vietnamese society. While the total urban population was only 20 per cent of the national population in 1985, (World Bank, 1987, p. 266) rural-to-urban migration had rapidly expanded the number of city dwellers, particularly in the South. In Ho Chi Minh City, some 300 000 families were estimated to be living in extremely adverse conditions, while approximately 195 000 houses were without water (Esterline, 1987, p. 93). As Esterline points out: 'The migration helped to derail monetary reform because it sharply deepened the imbalance between demand and supply – thus fuelling inflation – and further reduced the quality of urban life' (Ibid). As the cities grew, more and more people engaged in petty-trading activities over which the state had little control. In Ho Chi Minh City, the already large number of small traders operating at the end of the war was estimated to have grown by a third a decade later (*The Economist*, 29 March 1986, p. 41).

The restructuring of the labour force looked set to affect other social groups when, for example, plans were drawn up in 1987 to remove up to one million jobs from the state payroll over a two-year period (*FT*, 7 May 1987, p. 26).

In 1985, the lack of control of the state over procurement and the need to reduce the budget deficit forced the government to adopt measures to reduce coupon subsidies. In August, the system was abandoned whereby a portion of the income of both workers and cadres had been paid in coupons which could be exchanged for cheap food. Instead, the cash component of workers' wages increased (Esterline, 1987, p. 93). As inflation increased, the government was obliged, less than five months later, to reintroduce rationing on eight basic products. (*The Economist*, 29 March 1986, p. 41). Additional measures to defend the real wages of workers were taken in May 1987, when a plan was introduced to increase basic wages, taking into account the so-called 'social price increment' since September 1985 (Esterline, 1988, p. 87).

Macroeconomic Policy and Economic Efficiency

Throughout the 1980s, reforms were also introduced affecting monetary policy and the system of state finance, as well as the operation and management of industrial and commercial enterprises. New tax regulations were announced, notably in 1980 and 1983, partly to contain or reduce the budget deficit, but also as a means of controlling the rapid growth of the private commercial sector. The 1983 fiscal reforms stabilized agricultural tax rates by fixing them for a three-year period based on criteria associated with yield per hectare and geographical location. Tax exemptions were also created to encourage co-operative forms of production and distribution (Spoor, 1988, p. 18).

Measures were introduced in 1981 to increase the financial autonomy of state enterprises and to expand the system of material incentives whereby groups of workers or individuals would obtain a set amount for a given quantity of products (turnover of goods or quantities of freight in the case of commercial enterprises) and bonuses for extra production (Ibid., p. 13; Post, 1982, p. 36).

The reform of the economic management system was carried further in 1984, when measures were taken to expand the use of economic accounting methods. Measures were also implemented to improve the managerial skills of government and party officials (Duiker, 1985, p. 99). While still under the centralized regulation of the state, industrial enterprises were given more independence in decisions affecting production and marketing. An increased percentage of profits could also be retained for reinvestment and social programmes. As Spoor explains: 'One of the main goals of this reform was to lessen the burden on the budget by making state enterprises more responsible for their expenditures (and losses) while on the other hand material incentives are given to them which will increase production and profitability, ultimately leading to higher budget revenue in the long-run.' (Spoor, 1988, p. 21). More radical measures were taken in this direction the following year.

In September 1985, a new currency was introduced in an attempt to restore a degree of confidence in the national currency and stabilize the dong/dollar exchange rate. The measure, however, failed dismally. Black market operators had apparently known about the measure well in advance, sold old dong and hoarded dollars. Within ten days the black market rate was nearly four times the official rate. Towards the end of the year, the inflation rate, according to one estimate, had reached approximately 500 per cent and in November a further devaluation of the dong of 80 per cent was announced.

Following the legalization of private enterprise in November 1986, further measures were introduced in 1987 to encourage private enterprise in Hanoi. This followed what were considered by the authorities successful market-orientated measures in Ho Chi Minh City which provided greater freedom of operation for enterprises with up to ten employees. Greater factory autonomy was also encouraged in decisions affecting production and marketing of products. To contain the expansion of the money supply, banks were allowed to attract and lend money at market rates, as opposed to heavily subsidized rates (*FT*, 1987: 24 February, p. 4; 18 April, p. 2; 7 May, p. 26).

From Piecemeal Reform to Shock Treatment

The reform dynamic slipped into a higher gear during 1988 and in March 1989 shock treatment was applied to an economy which had experienced a post-1985 fall in food production, runaway inflation and, during 1988, famine in several northern provinces. In just two years Vietnam moved further and faster than any other Third-World socialist country in adopting market-orientated reforms. The measures introduced followed closely the policy recommendations proposed by several IMF missions which had had meetings with the government to prepare the ground for a resumption of financial assistance.

The 1988 reforms implied major changes for agriculture, particularly in the south of the country. Policy changes introduced in April effectively withdrew from co-operatives their official status as superior forms of production and their role as the linchpin in socialist development strategy. The contract system was revised, enabling producers in co-operatives to retain approximately half of their production and perform individually most of the tasks associated with the production cycle for rice (*FEER*, 28 July 1988, p. 20). While the state still formally owned the land, leases were extended for periods of up to fifteen years to encourage investment (*FEER*, 17 November 1988, p. 110). A party Directive issued in August 1988, which admitted that 'party and state policies of the past had not actually encouraged peasants and agricultural production, thus causing many collectives and co-operatives to operate with poor results', called on local officials and state farms to return to peasants land that had been illegally or arbitrarily expropriated during the late 1970s (Ibid.).

Another important development in 1988 was the expansion of foreign investment which followed in the wake of a new liberal foreign investment code approved in December 1987 (*FEER*, 14 September 1989, p. 76). Initial foreign investment was concentrated to a large extent in oil drilling and exploration, but was also attracted to fishing, light industry and processing, as well as tourism (*FEER*, 27 April 1989, p. 70).

The March 1989 policy measures saw a major devaluation of the dong which succeeded in reducing considerably the gap between official and black market exchange rates. The system of differential exchange rates was abolished (Cima, 1990, p. 92). A strict credit squeeze was introduced along with positive interest rates. Dual pricing was largely eliminated, as prices of rice and many other essential goods and services were deregulated. Controls remained on just a few items such as fuel, electricity, state transport and postal charges (*FEER*, 28 September 1989, p. 22). Cuts in defence spending and most subsidies to state enterprises and workers enabled the government to eliminate the budget deficit (*The Economist*, 24 February 1990).

As a result of these measures, inflation dropped rapidly to just 3.5 per cent a month towards mid-year (Ngo Vinh Long, 1989, p. 33). Rice production also increased in both 1988 and 1989, enabling Vietnam to become a major exporter of rice. While the prices of certain food products declined somewhat, economic hardship intensified for hundreds of thousands of state enterprise workers and soldiers returning from Cambodia, many of whom were made redundant. By the end of the decade an estimated 20 per cent of the work-force was unemployed.

The possibility of alleviating the social impact of economic stabilization was extremely limited, given the lack of financial support from major international agencies. While following closely IMF recommendations, Vietnam remained ineligible for both IMF and World Bank financial assistance during the late 1980s. Even though the Vietnamese government had apparently been given a glowing report card by the IMF in September 1989, the US and Japan still opposed any new programme. (*FEER*, 28 September 1989).

EXPLAINING THE REFORMS

A Response to Crisis

The economic reforms of the early 1980s are generally explained in terms of a response on the part of the state to a series of crisis conditions which emerged during the latter half of the 1970s. For some, the reforms constituted an attempt to resolve what was essentially a productivity and procurement crisis. According to White, for example: 'The increasing problems faced during this period by the state in generating and controlling an agricultural surplus made necessary the recent economic reforms.' (White C., 1985, p. 97). Elsewhere, the same author observes:

> Whereas the intent of most previous structural reorganisations in agriculture had been to increase the formal organisation of the work force, to specify universal norms for production and distribution and to transform the social structure, the new policy is an attempt to mobilise existing informal social ties in order to increase productivity. (White C., 1982b, p. 50)

Werner also writes: 'The state was as a result [of peasants curtailing their transfers to the state] obliged to devise stronger incentives to motivate peasants to raise productivity and release their surplus to state collection agencies.' (Werner, 1984, p. 49). The contract system, she argues, was intended both to increase the motivation of workers and the number of hours or days worked. While co-op workers were officially obliged to work 200 days in collective production, in practice they often worked only 150 to 180 days (Ibid., p. 51). The gravity of the economic and food situation is indicated by the following data. According to official Vietnamese statistics, aggregate national income fell slightly more than 1 per cent between 1976 and 1980, while population increased nearly 9.5 per cent (Fforde, 1985, p. 9). The IMF estimates that per capita income fell from $241 in

TABLE 3.5 *National and per capita cereals production indices (SRV), 1974–83*

	1974	1975	1976	1977	1978	1979	1980	1981	1982	1983
National	93	88	102	93	87	93	100	107	121	126
Per capita	107	100	113	100	91	95	100	105	116	119

SOURCE Based on *FAO Production Yearbook*, 1985, Tables 8 and 13.

TABLE 3.6 *Staples output and per capita availability from domestic production in North Vietnam (Annual averages 1960–65 and 1973–75)*

	1960–65	1973–75
Total staples output (mill. tonnes of paddy equivalent)	5.19	5.65
Staples availability from domestic production (kilos per capita per month crude milled rice equiv.)	16	13

SOURCE Fforde, 1984, p. 8, based on official statistics.

1976 to $153 in 1980 (Luxmoore, 1983, p. 8). In Table 8.3, FAO data indicate that per capita cereals production fell by 15 per cent between 1974 and 1978 (FAO, 1986, p. 96).

Per capita food production was estimated to have fallen to 243 kg. in 1978, well below war-time levels. Some reports put average per capita caloric intake as low as 1800 Kcal. in 1979, considerably below recommended minimum levels (Werner, 1984, p. 48). Data on food production in North Vietnam indicate that total staples output only increased by 9 per cent between 1960–65 and 1973–75, while per capita consumption derived from domestic production fell from 16 to 13 kilos per month (see Table 3.6 and Fforde, 1984, p. 8).

Some writers have also stressed the political dimensions of the crisis. Writing at the beginning of the 1980s, Post observes:

the internal political situation cannot look too satisfactory from the point of view of the Communist Party leaders. Integration of the South continues to be difficult, with much cynicism and passive resistance and even sporadic guerrilla activities by supporters of FULRO (United Front for the Liberation of the Oppressed Race) in the Central Highlands. Potentially even more menacing, at the end of 1980 there were public manifestations of discontent with low standards of living in the port of Haiphong and Nghe Tinh province in the north, the first since the vesting of the Democratic Republic there in July 1954 and a very ominous warning to the Party. (Post, 1982, pp. 2–3)

The capacity of the party to exercise hegemony and to mobilize the energies of the people declined as the credibility of the party was undermined, not only through economic difficulties but also through corruption and inefficiency (White C., 1983, p. 262). The economic reforms coincided with measures to clean up the party. Between May 1979 and the end of 1980 the number of members expelled from the party has been put at as high as 13 per cent (Post, 1982, p. 29).

Conjunctural Circumstances

In explaining the crisis, it is important to stress the negative impact of a series of conjunctural circumstances which intensified the economic and social problems left by the war. During the latter half of the 1970s, the country experienced a series of poor harvests, due in part to adverse climatic conditions, but also to the declining effectivity of ideological and psychological factors (patriotism and responsibility for the survival of the family and friends) that had motivated producers in general, and women in particular, to increase the intensity of labour during the war years. While the South was theoretically in a position to meet the historic food deficit of the North (estimated by the FAO to be in the region of 2 million tonnes a year) it was in no position to do so given the impact of the war on key links in the food system such as transport (Post, 1982, p. 1).

The access of the peasantry and the working class to food and other essential goods and services was undermined by the reduction in external aid following 1975. Immediately after the war, China and the USSR reduced their levels of aid. This was partially compensated for, however, by an increasing reliance on Western and Arab loans and credits. By 1978, foreign debt to the convertible currency area had reached nearly 1.1 billion dollars. Following the intervention of Vietnam in Kampuchea in 1978 and the inability of the government to repay its external debt, several important donors suspended loans and grants to Vietnam, including the World Bank, the IMF and China. The decline in aid not only affected the general availability of goods and services for basic needs provisioning and material incentives, but also forced the state to be more concerned with procurement of domestic food production. As Fforde explains:

> a major consequence of the 1965–73 period was the shift to a chronic dependency upon imports of food from the Soviet bloc and China. This appears on balance to have eased the pressure of procurement upon the collectivised agricultural sector. . .It also reinforced the already strong tendency for the balance of incentives to encourage production for the 'outside' or free market, or at least for own-consumption when (as was usually the case) collective distribution was below subsistence. (Fforde, 1984, p. 8)

The decline in aid also generated inflationary pressures as the government resorted to bank credits and increased the volume of money in circulation to cover the budget deficit. In 1982, inflation was reported to have reached 80 per cent (Spoor, 1988, pp. 15, 19). Aid from the Eastern bloc countries stabilized somewhat once the country joined the CMEA in mid-1978 but it was not really until 1987 that the aid situation was alleviated, when the USSR reportedly agreed to double its annual contribution from approximately 1 to 2 billion dollars.

Meanwhile, the ongoing primacy assigned to defence expenditures meant that considerable resources continued to be diverted away from the peasantry and the working class towards maintaining the world's fourth largest army, of approximately one million troops, deployed along the northern frontier with China, active in Cambodia and stationed also in Laos. Military expenditures were estimated to account for 47 per cent of state expenditure and 28 per cent of national income in 1980 (Luxmoore, 1983, p. 16).

Government Policies and Systemic Constraints

Another set of factors contributing to the crisis relate to the negative or contradictory impact of certain government policies. Particularly relevant here was the impact of collectivization and taxation on agricultural production in the South, notably on production levels of the rich peasantry in areas such as the Mekong Delta. Also important was the planning imbalance favouring heavy industry and large infrastructural projects. Considerable resources continued to be channelled towards large-scale, slow-yielding development projects, which meant fewer investment resources to increase production in the short term. Moreover, a series of problems, not least the reduction of foreign aid, meant long delays in project implementation.

Shortages of inputs and consumer goods acted as a disincentive to peasant production and the marketing of produce through official channels. As explained by Werner: 'With the end of the war, the peasantry's willingness to produce for the state weakened. Since the supply of consumer goods was very sparse and access to agricultural inputs such as fertilizer, equipment and seeds was limited, peasants simply curtailed their transfers to the state in like manner.' (Werner, 1984, p. 49). Problems associated with the availability of inputs and consumer goods were compounded by others relating to the existence of a parallel market or the so-called 'outside economy'. As Fforde explains: 'Wartime inflationary finance had helped feed a steady erosion of the effectiveness of the State's pricing structure compared with that of the free market. By the late 1970s "outside" prices were ca. ten times State prices' (Fforde, 1984, pp. 9–10).

Conditions such as these, combined with the limited capacity of industry and other 'formal' sectors of the economy to absorb labour, contributed to the rapid expansion of the 'outside' economy in North Vietnam. Fforde and Paine estimate that only about half the additional 3.45 million people that reached working age between 1960 and 1975 were absorbed into the 'regulated' sectors of the economy. The remainder were available for 'outside' employment (Fforde and Paine, 1987, p. 78). It should be remembered that these figures do not reveal anything about the phenomenon whereby co-operative members, industrial workers, bureaucrats, and so on, sought additional sources of income by engaging in trading and other activities associated with the 'outside' economy.

The reforms were, in effect, an overt admission that the previous model of agrarian development was no longer viable. Under this model, land reform and co-operativization had transformed peasant society, substituting insecurity of access to land and increasing exploitation of labour, with security of tenure and the possibility of access to minimum subsistence requirements. While this model provided the peasantry with security of livelihood, it also provided the state with cheap agricultural commodities, obtained through centrally set prices and direct control over the procurement system, in order to supply industry, the army and the bureaucracy. Cheap food facilitated a low-wages policy which, combined with the low cost of domestic and imported raw materials and inputs, meant high profits for industry. As mentioned earlier, the latter provided a significant proportion of the government's domestic revenues.

This model could function when, during the later 1950s and early 1960s, much of the peasant population experienced a direct improvement in their levels of living, or when, as in war-time, the peasantry responded positively to moral incentives and nationalistic appeals, as well as the increased, albeit limited, availability of certain inputs and consumer goods provided by foreign aid. However, these conditions were to change dramatically during the latter half of the 1970s.

Fforde and Paine stress the serious problem of population density and the corresponding imperatives of efficient use of limited resources, the need for technological innovation, and product diversification. To achieve this:

> the likely optimal path. . .would involve a blending of family-based control of much – but not all – of the production process with extensive use of market relations in order to provide an efficient incentive structure. This would likely be under-written by a preservation of communal institutions to finance local social welfare and valued infrastructural investment. (Fforde and Paine, 1987, p. 124)

Unlike most other writers, however, Fforde and Paine maintain that the underlying causes of the crisis had less to do with the conjunctural circumstances that emerged during the late 1970s than with the essential nature of what they call the 'neo-Stalinist model'. They argue that many of the basic tensions and constraints which characterized the crisis were, in fact, present in the early and mid-1960s. The cracks in the model, however, were subsequently pasted over when the Soviet Union and China provided massive quantities of aid following the commencement of bombing by the United States in 1965. According to these authors: 'The state's economic and social policies. . .created the macro and microeconomic conditions for an "aggravated shortage economy"', in which administrative methods for acquiring surplus from agriculture and allocating resources, as well as the extensive use of subsidies, necessarily depressed agricultural output, restricted the availability of complementary inputs vital to rapid industrialization, caused inefficiency and chronic wastage in industry and led to existence of an 'outside economy' which undermined the plan and caused people and the state sector itself to rely increasingly on illegal activities (Fforde and Paine, 1987, pp. 39, 40,

50 and 60).' Several similar points are raised by Spoor (Spoor, 1988, pp. 4, 22).

Much of the journalistic and academic literature on economic policy reform in Vietnam analyses the change in economic policy in terms of the pragmatic response of leaders to a crisis situation. Where the emphasis lies in explaining the crisis inevitably varies -- some stressing more the 'errors' of socialist policies or a specific development model, others the aftermath of war and external pressures, or the 'counter-revolutionary' attitudes and actions of internal class forces. Other accounts, notably of the more journalistic variety, tend to see the reform process in terms of (as one *Financial Times* reporter put it): 'a power struggle between the ideologues and the reformers who are spearheaded by the pragmatists from the south', in which the latter gained the upper hand (*FT*, 11 July 1986, p. 3).

These types of approach, however, fail to take account of, or at least relegate to a minor plane, the role of different social forces and interest groups in shaping policy through various forms of struggle, pressure and participation in decision-making processes, and of the dialectical relation between policy and changes in the balance of social forces. It is difficult to find in the literature on Vietnam any systematic treatment of these aspects. From the literature available, however, it is possible to identify a number of elements which are relevant to this discussion.

Popular Participation

As regards the question of participation of social groups in decision-making processes, we learn from White that:

> there is a continuing interaction between government and agricultural producers over pricing policy, with co-operatives playing an important and complex intermediary role. . .Co-operatives. . . have. . .strengthened the collective bargaining position of agricultural producers. In part this is because co-operatives have provided peasants with a degree of self-government, equality and food security.' (White C., 1985, p. 99)

While co-operative management committees had considerable leverage in their negotiations with state agencies, there appears to have been little direct participation by peasant producers in the formal decision-making process associated with planning and policy design. As Deere explains:

> The. . .cooperatives are important not just as a productive unit, but also as a political unit. In the absence of a mass peasant association they serve as the primary vehicle for peasant political participation for nonparty members. There have been recurrent drives to assure democratic decisionmaking in the co-operatives. . . The managing committee is the key administrative link to the relevant organs of the state, entering into contracts regarding production targets, the provision of inputs, and state procurement levels. However, the genuine participation of the membership at the co-operative level has not necessarily resulted in influence in agricultural planning within the apparatus or party. (Deere, 1986, p. 121)

This is not to say that the party and the state were somehow divorced from, or out of tune with, peasant interests. Gordon makes the point that 'unlike some other ruling communist parties, the VNCP has remained closely in touch with the masses' (Gordon, 1978, p. 25). The party, with 1 553 500 members in 1976 (Post, 1982, p. 29), had numerous peasant cadres (Deere, 1986, p. 136), while the Women's Union, which was one of the country's most important mass associations, was linked closely to the party structure and was composed primarily of agricultural producers.

What is in doubt is the extent to which these links permitted effective participation in the decision-making processes associated with the process of policy design. Werner's description of the Women's Union emphasizes its role as an agency which facilitates the implementation of state directives and policies rather than as an agency for channelling demands upwards (Werner, 1984, pp. 52–3). Two writers who have studied the question of 'popular participation' in North Vietnam conclude:

> There definitely exists today a new kind of 'work democracy' at the grassroots level of agricultural co-operatives. But it is not clear how much contact this 'work democracy' has with what may be called 'political democracy' in terms of running the 'affairs of state', reorganisation of the Party, etc. In brief, there are extremely democratic institutions at the grassroots level with genuine

participation by the people. . .But from information that could be collected, their influence on the 'higher' State apparatuses and the Party organs is not apparent. (Bhaduri and Rahman, 1982, p. 54)

Relevant to this discussion is the point made by Gordon that, in contrast to the Maoist conception – where the motor force of change is seen as deriving from the dialectic between the masses and the party, the VNCP tended to see the former as deriving from a dialectic located within the party. According to this conception: 'action by the masses takes place only in response to the lead of the Party and, save in minor matters, the masses are not seen as as taking political initiative' (Gordon, 1978, p. 25).

Class Struggle and State/Society Relations

On the basis of these observations, it would seem that any attempt to understand the reform process in Vietnam in terms of the capacity of different social groups to influence the process of policy design through institutionalized forms of participation in decision-making processes encounters serious difficulties. A more appropriate starting point relates to alternative forms of pressure brought to bear by sectors of the peasantry. What Fforde refers to as ' "avoidance" and "non-cooperation" strategies to cope with unwanted demands from the State', served to undermine policy instruments and basic development goals associated with the growth of agricultural production and/or the extraction of surplus by the state. Such 'strategies' included the weakening of collective practices by channelling more energies towards private activities; restricting participation of co-operative members and their families in tasks associated with 'direct accumulation'; ignoring recommendations or directives associated with cropping patterns or the introduction of new technologies and production methods; retaining payments in cash or in kind due to state agencies either to increase sales on the open market or family consumption (Fforde, 1984; Luxmoore, 1983, pp. 22–3).

As indicated in the Introduction to this chapter, 'avoidance and non-cooperation strategies' were in no way a post-revolutionary phenomenon, but had been practised over several centuries by the Vietnamese peasantry. In contrast to the stereotypical image of the peasantry in many Third World countries as dispersed and unorganized, much of the peasant population of North Vietnam had been concentrated in villages and organized in communal structures.

Fforde and Paine explain that while a settlement pattern of this type facilitated to some extent surplus appropriation by the state, 'such corporate organisations could, by facilitating cooperation amongst their members, help defend local interests, for example, by organising tax-avoidance' (Fforde and Paine, 1987, p. 17). Thus the post-1954 government confronted a peasantry familiar 'with methods of coping with the extractive strategies of centralised nation-states. This meant that any attempt, however desirable to extract resources forcibly from the impoverished rural areas, would be met by the tactical response of people well-experienced in avoiding such strategies' (Ibid., p. 30).

Developments such as these at the level of civil society, then, restricted the capacity of the state to control resource flows. Other conditions which emerged during the 1950s also weakened the authority of the central state. Important in this respect was the exodus of Vietnamese state officials associated with the French colonial administration (Ibid., p. 35). Also important were the social tensions and divisions which emerged following the radicalization of the agrarian reform programme in 1955 – a process which had seen the category of 'class enemy' expanded to include not only the old rural elite of landlords, usurers and traders but also rich and 'upper middle' peasants (Gordon, 1978, pp. 28–9).

While the party sought to heal these divisions through the 'rectification of errors campaign' of 1956/57, it was unable, as Fforde and Paine explain, to create the type of grassroots structure that would facilitate surplus appropriation and ensure a broad base of support for the revolutionary government: 'The basic structural dichotomy of state and commune persisted, and the centre, as ever, could not fully control the periphery' (Fforde and Paine, 1987, p. 36).

While developments during the late 1950s and the first half of the 1960s associated with collectivization, the creation of state trading monopolies and the rapid expansion of the bureaucracy[4] facilitated control by the central state apparatus, the state/commune, centre/ periphery dichotomy was subsequently reinforced during the war years as the co-operatives became more autonomous. As White explains: 'They provided the institutional network for maximum local level economic self-sufficiency along with decentralisation of political decision making and initiative which are crucial ingredients for the success of a people's war' (White C., 1982a, p. 16).

These developments, then, associated with state–society relations and the institutions of civil society in rural areas, imposed limits on the practicability of the orthodox state-centred accumulation model. The state/commune dichotomy and class practices involving 'avoidance and non-cooperation strategies' undermined socialist development strategy in two important respects. Firstly, the accumulation model, based partially on the transfer of resources from the co-operatives to the state, was weakened. As White explains:

> The socialist government now finds it not only difficult to obtain low-priced agricultural commodities, but often co-operatives and peasants refuse to pay taxes, to repay loans, to pay their debts, to pay for agricultural inputs, etc.. . .In the conflict between government and peasant preferences in accumulation/consumption ratios, it is peasant pressure for greater consumption now which is increasingly carrying the day. (White C., 1985, p. 112)

Secondly, the state's capacity to direct the process of social change and development through planning and policy implementation, was undermined. In this respect Fforde goes so far as to argue that 'perhaps 75% of cooperatives in North Vietnam rarely if ever followed Party prescriptions during the mid 1970s' (Fforde, 1985, p. 12).

Changes in the Balance of Social Forces

Interpretations such as these paint a picture of considerable tension between the development and accumulation strategy defined by the state and the actions and interests of the peasantry in general. There is, however, another interpretation which differentiates peasant interests and raises the question of class struggle among different groups of rural producers. Gordon argues that from the mid-1960s onwards the rich peasantry came to dominate many co-operative managerial committees. This happened as an increasing number of rich peasant families joined co-operatives while at the same time village cadres and activists, concerned with the consolidation of the co-operative movement and acting in support of poor peasant interests, diverted their attentions to the war effort.

These developments served to undermine collective relations. Referring to a VNCP report assessing the state of co-operative organization following the cessation of US bombing in 1968, Gordon writes: 'An outspoken report showed that lack of democracy in cooperative management had distorted distribution of income, that collective management had been widely abandoned, and that the

Party's neglect had favoured the spontaneous development of capitalism. In particular, large areas of cooperative land had been given over to private hands' (Gordon, 1982, p. 7). According to Gordon, privately-used lands came to represent between a quarter to a third of all the lands held by the co-operatives.

Despite being declared illegal in 1969, this practice continued with a degree of support from the local level cadres and functionaries:

> Rich peasants would draw their strength from their control of the management committees in order to gain and use privately even more lands. And they would require collaboration from and alliances with various levels of Party and State bureaucracy. Private use of cooperative land depends on control of the cooperative bureaucracy, alliance with extra cooperative bureaucracy and state toleration of private trading. (Gordon, 1982, p. 11)

The conflict of interests among co-operative members is also indicated by Fforde. Moreover, it would appear that these conflicts intensified following 1974 and 1979, when the government attempted to implement a system for centralizing economic control in the management committees. The so-called New Management System curtailed the autonomy exercised by production brigades in many co-operatives and generated conflicts between brigade leaders and members of the management committees (Fforde, 1984, pp. 12–13). According to Fforde, some three-quarters of the co-operatives were of a type ('nominal' co-operatives) which 'usually experienced a very poor development of collective production. . .and an extensive privatisation of collective property. . .frequently well in excess of the 5% of the cooperative's cultivated acreage' (Ibid, p. 15).

These accounts have important implications for our analysis. Firstly, they indicate that despite central government and party directives to the contrary, petty commodity production in agriculture involving co-operative members continued to operate to a significant degree. It can be argued, therefore, that the policy reforms of the early 1980s, associated with subcontracting and free trade, did not introduce new relations of production and exchange in any qualitative sense, but essentially legalized and expanded a *de facto* situation. Secondly, the conflict of interests which existed at the level of the co-operative posed a serious obstacle to policy implementation. Perhaps more seriously, however, this conflict extended to the party structure itself. Fforde, for example, points out that 'Party members do not seem. . .to have always agreed on the correct roles they should play in local conflicts. The various cadres within a cooperative were often far from united in their interests and aims' (Ibid, p. 13). In addition to conflicts and divisions at the local level, what emerges clearly from Fforde's analysis is the extent of the rift between central and local levels of the party structure as the 'autarky' of the co-operatives impeded the implementation of central-level directives. 'The old dynastic maxim,' writes Fforde, 'that "the writ of the Emperor bows to the customs of the commune". . .was probably replaced by something close to "the order of the Party Centre bows to the customs of the commune's Party Committee"' (Idem., 1985, pp. 12–13).

This rift was likely to be exacerbated during difficult crop years, such as those experienced during the latter half of the 1970s. As Post explains:

> the co-operatives have developed in such a way as to give a sort of collective security to members even against the Party and the state, given expression in particular in times of bad harvests by a sort of silent struggle over tax payments (in kind) and sales of rice to the state at fixed prices. . .From the point of view of the leadership, the weak link in its control has always been the local Party and state cadres who, resident among the peasants and often literally related to them, have frequently tacitly sided with members of co-operatives rather than with their superiors in times of adversity. (Post, 1982, p. 34)

On the basis of these observations there are grounds for supposing that rich peasant interests found expression within the party itself. Important changes had also taken place in the social composition of the party and the central administrative apparatus of the state. During the 1970s and 1980s, the number of cadres and civil servants with training in economics and direct experience of economic management grew and assumed a more prominent role. Within industry also there was a considerable increase in the number of technical and managerial personnel. As White points out, such groups realized that excessive state control could interfere with economic growth and that a degree of economic liberalization and greater reliance on material incentives could make a positive contribution to the development process (White C., 1983, p. 263). By the beginning of the 1980s, Vietnam's intelligentsia, consisting of scientific, technical and pro-

TABLE 3.7   *Employment structure in the SRV, 1980*

	Millions	*%*
Economically active population[1]	24.9	100.0
In agriculture[1]	16.8	67.5
Working class[2]	3.1	12.5
'Productive' (blue collar)	(1.9)	(7.6)
'Non-productive' (white collar)	(1.2)	(4.8)
Intelligentsia[2][4]	0.8	3.2
Other groups (residual)	4.2	16.8

SOURCES   [1] *FAO Production Yearbook*, 1985, vol. 39.
[2] Post, 1982, pp. 25–6.
[3] Refers to wage labourers in industry and construction.
[4] Refers to scientific, technical and professional workers with university and vocational training.

fessional workers, numbered 776 700. This was a very different situation from that which had existed in the North two decades earlier when there existed just 18 400 technical and professional workers (Post, 1982, p. 26).

An analysis of the employment structure in the Socialist Republic of Vietnam reveals that those sectors of the economically active population classified as 'intelligentsia' and 'non-productive' (roughly equivalent to 'white collar') workers expanded to such an extent that by 1980 they were as large as those groups comprising industrial wage labourers and construction workers. Table 3.7 presents a rough approximation of the employment structure in Vietnam in 1980.

Data on employment in North Vietnam show that the number of 'scientific, technical and economic management cadres' increased from 18 400 in 1960 to 429 500 in 1975. The rate of growth experienced by this group far exceeded that of the industrial working class, which increased from 124 100 to 405 000 over the same period (Fforde and Paine, 1987, pp. 144–6).

CONCLUSION

The above analysis of the reform process in Vietnam indicates clearly that the policy changes introduced since the late 1970s should not be interpreted simply in terms of pragmatic or tactical adjustments to economic problems which arise in a particular conjuncture. Neither should the determinant arena of struggle be reduced to the upper echelons of the party/state apparatus. Our discussion has highlighted five key aspects or areas of analysis which any adequate explanation of the reform process in Vietnam must take into account.

Firstly, the policy changes occurred in the context of a crisis of the party/state which related to the limited capacity of the latter to mobilize and appropriate surplus, plan and implement policies, and exercise hegemony. Secondly, the key constraints that restricted production and productivity were to a certain extent conjunctural (war, levels of aid, adverse climate/harvests, and so on) but were also systemic (extractive mechanisms, subsidies, accumulation/heavy industry bias), and structural (state–commune dichotomy). Thirdly, in the context of these constraints and conditions, specific forms of class practices or struggle ('avoidance and non-cooperation strategies') manifested themselves, which undermined the type of socialist development strategy associated with the state-centred accumulation model. Fourthly, changes in the balance of social forces, favouring in particular the rich peasantry and a technical/professional stratum, saw these groups increase their control over economic and administrative resources. These groups were opposed to, or critical of, many of the types of policies which characterized orthodox socialist development strategy. Fifthly, the interests of these groups found expression at different levels within the party/state structure.

Notes

1. The official party position regarding the respective roles of the different economic sectors was stated in the following terms at the Third Party Congress in 1960: 'to build a balanced and modern socialist economic structure, to co-ordinate industry with agriculture, and take heavy industry as the base, to give priority to the rational development of heavy industry, at the same time striving to develop agriculture and light industry, with a view to transforming our country into one country endowed with a modern industry and a modern agriculture' (see Post, 1982, p. 16).
2. There appear to be considerable differences of opinion among researchers regarding the extent to which profits from state-owned industries contributed to budgetary revenues. White, for example, states that 'the overwhelming majority' of domestic budget revenues derived from state industrial sector profits during the mid-1960s and 1970s (White C., 1985, p. 98). Spoor, on the other hand, when analysing an earlier period, claims

that the contribution of industry to state revenues increased from 20 to 31 per cent between 1959 and 1961 (Spoor, 1985, p. 343) and maintains (in correspondence with the author) that industry's subsequent contribution was considerably below the levels indicated by White.

3. Although limited research has been carried out on this aspect, it is apparent that considerable regional variations exist in the levels of living of the rural population. It is possible that statements regarding the relatively favourable position of the rural population *vis-à-vis* urban dwellers, are based on a comparison of the situation in Hanoi with that of adjacent or 'model' rural areas, where levels of living are thought to be higher than in many other rural areas.

4. Between 1961 and 1965 the number of non-industrial state employees doubled, reaching approximately 970 000 (Fforde and Paine, 1987, p. 59).

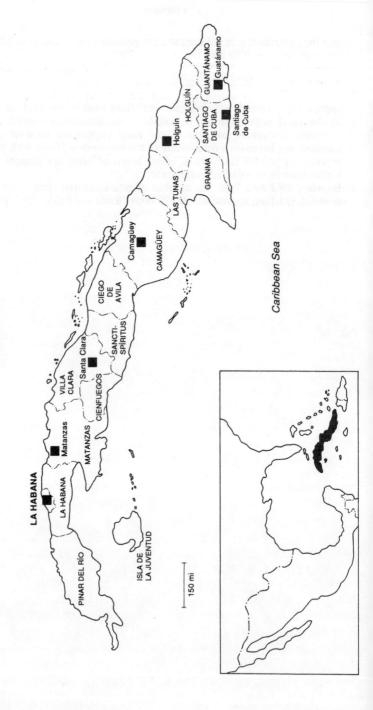

CUBA

Caribbean Sea

150 mi

PINAR DEL RÍO

LA HABANA

LA HABANA

Matanzas

MATANZAS

VILLA CLARA

Santa Clara

CIENFUEGOS

SANCTI-SPIRITUS

CIEGO DE AVILA

ISLA DE LA JUVENTUD

CAMAGÜEY

Camagüey

LAS TUNAS

GRANMA

Holguín

HOLGUÍN

SANTIAGO DE CUBA

Santiago de Cuba

GUANTÁNAMO

Guantánamo

4 Cuba

INTRODUCTION

At the time of the revolution in 1959, the Cuban economy had an extremely narrow productive base centred primarily on sugar-cane production and processing. Sugar-cane accounted for half the total crop area while raw sugar and its by-products made up more than 80 per cent of the country's exports (Benjamin *et al.*, 1984, pp. 9–10). A capital goods industry was virtually non-existent. Most industrial activity centred on the processing of sugar-cane, the production of textiles and a limited number of food products. Tertiary-sector activities, including those associated with tourism, constituted a relatively important area of economic activity.

The economy was highly dependent on the United States market for merchandise trade, capital and tourists. United States' companies directly controlled some 40 per cent of sugar production and a large proportion of the public utilities, communications, mining and petroleum sectors (Brundenius, 1984, pp. 8, 11). Approximately 80 per cent of all imports were from the United States. The country had to import a large proportion of its food and raw materials requirements (Dumont, 1970, p. 12). Food imports amounted to $140 million in 1954, or a quarter of total imports (Benjamin *et al.*, 1984, p. 8).

Although there had been some growth in the non-sugar manufacturing sector following the Second World War, the economy as a whole had stagnated, particularly after 1952 (Brundenius, 1984, pp. 12–13). While many Latin-American countries were experiencing relatively high rates of growth during the 1950s, the Cuban economy grew at a per capita rate of just 1 per cent (Mesa Lago, 1971, p. 278). In agriculture, there was some growth in agro-export sectors such as tobacco and coffee, as well as in the production of rice and certain fruits and vegetables. There was stagnation, however, in the major sugar-cane and cattle sectors (MacEwan, 1981, pp. 6–7).

Apart from an extremely narrow product range, agriculture was also characterized by low productivity and the underutilization of land. Only a fifth of all farm land was actually cultivated (Ibid., p. 17). Nearly half the total farm area was poor quality pasture used for extensive grazing. A largely non-mechanized, low-yield sugar-cane sector accounted for between 60 to 70 per cent of the total crop area, while much of the remainder consisted of subsistence production of maize and root crops (Benjamin *et al.*, 1984, p. 9; MacEwan, 1981, p. 6). Surplus from the large sugar and cattle estates was often invested, not in agriculture, but in more profitable 'non-productive' urban sector activities (Ibid., p. 19).

In comparison with many Latin-American countries, the social structure of pre-revolutionary Cuba had two distinguishing characteristics which have important implications for the analysis which follows. Firstly, the vast majority of the rural population was made up not of peasants but of 570 000 landless labourers (*guajiros*) and their families. An estimated 100 000 tenants, sharecroppers and squatters also depended on agriculture for their livelihood (Benjamin *et al.*, 1984, p. 4). The number of small-farm owners amounted to just 20 000. Secondly, there was a large urban population which accounted for an estimated 53 per cent of the country's seven million people. The urban working class numbered approximately 400 000. Unionization had improved job security and the incomes of this sector. There was also a large urban informal sector which serviced the upper-income groups and the tourists (Benjamin *et al.*, 1984, p. 5).

Income and wealth were highly concentrated in the hands of a relatively large urban-based bourgeoisie and 'middle-class' sector, which included technicians and managerial personnel, public functionaries, and those engaged in the liberal professions (Dumont, 1970, p. 14). An estimated 62 per cent of the land was owned by just 9 per cent of all landowners.

Average figures on per capita income and consumption in pre-revolutionary Cuba indicate relatively high levels of living compared to many Latin-American countries. Such figures conceal, however, the extreme income inequality which existed and the situation of an estimated 1.5 million landless agricultural labourers, poor peasants and the unemployed (Benjamin *et al.*, 1984, p. 2). Large sectors of the rural population remained underemployed for much of the year. Given the seasonal nature of demand for labour in the sugar-cane sector and restricted access to land, up to a quarter of the rural population found themselves without employment for most of the non-harvest season (Mesa Lago, 1971, p. 279). As a result, much of the rural population lived in extreme poverty and suffered from ill-health and malnutrition (Brundenius, 1984, p. 14). Some reports during the early 1950s claimed that over 60 per cent of the rural population and between 30 and 40 per cent of the urban population were malnourished (Benjamin *et al.*, 1984, p. 13).

When the revolutionary government assumed power it was confronted with a serious situation of food insecurity. At the national level it was imperative to produce more of the country's food requirements; at the level of the Cuban family, it was necessary to raise consumption levels. Agriculture and food consumption patterns, as well as industry and foreign trade relations, all needed to be diversified. It was imperative to provide rural workers and peasants/tenant farmers with secure employment and tenure, respectively. Prospects for achieving these goals seemed reasonably good. The movement to overthrow the extremely corrupt and repressive Batista regime gained the support of diverse social groups. There was no immediate large-scale flight of capital or expertise, and excess capacity in agriculture and industry meant some gains in output could be achieved without major investments (MacEwan, 1981, p. 32). This scenario, however, was soon to change, as structural transformations took effect. Private farmers decapitalized their enterprises, problems of labour shortages in agriculture arose, managers and technicians left the country, and the United States mounted military, diplomatic and economic actions to topple the revolutionary government (Ibid., pp. 33–5).

POST-REVOLUTIONARY FOOD AND DEVELOPMENT POLICY

Economic policy during the first five years of the post-revolutionary period focused on structural transformations which radically altered the distribution of income and wealth and diversified the productive base of the economy (Turits, 1987, p. 168).

Agrarian Reform and Nationalization

The first agrarian reform law of 1959 eliminated most large-scale private agricultural enterprises and rent payments for tenants and sharecroppers. The size of the capitalist farming sector was further diminished following the implementation of the second agrarian reform law of 1963 which imposed a ceiling of 67.1 ha. on the size of landholdings. Control of expropriated lands passed to both the state and small producers. While the state acquired 63 per cent of all cultivable land, the redistribution of land to individual producers led to a tenfold increase in the number of small-farm owners. By 1970, this group numbered 235 000 (Lehmann, 1985, p. 252; MacEwan, 1981, pp. 49, 84; Rodriguez, 1987, 24).

The early 1960s had seen most other sectors of the economy nationalized. By the end of 1963, all banking and foreign trade; 95 per cent or more of industry, construction and transport; and 75 per cent of local commerce was controlled by the state (MacEwan, 1981, p. 70).

The Decline of Petty Commodity Production

Towards the end of the 1960s there was a shift in state policy regarding petty-commodity producers. Agricultural producers came under increasing pressure to sell or lease their lands to the state, and private sales of agricultural produce were abolished. Between 1967 and 1970 some 24 000 small farms were purchased by the state (Deere, 1986, p. 112). Even state farm workers were deprived of the plots allotted to them for self-provisioning (Zimbalist and Eckstein, 1987, p. 9).

During the late 1960s and early 1970s the amount of land controlled by the private sector declined as approximately 750 000 ha.[1] were absorbed into the state sector through different types of arrangement (Rodriguez, 1987, p. 29). Gradually the state sector increased its land area and by the early 1980s it controlled 80 per cent of all cultivable land. The rate of expansion of the state farm sector, however, stabilized from the late 1970s onwards, when more emphasis was placed on co-operative development (Deere, 1986, p. 112).

The decline of petty-commodity production was even more dramatic in urban areas following the government's attempt in 1968 to eradicate a flourishing black market by expropriating private retailers, artisans and small manufacturers (Petras and Selden, 1981, p. 194). During the so-called 'Revolutionary Offensive' of that year, 55 600 small private enterprises, accounting for up to one-third of all retail sales, were nationalized (Brundenius, 1984, p. 55).

Redefining Dependency and the Accumulation/Consumption Balance

The economy fared badly during the 1960s with gross material product – GMP[2] – growing annually by just 0.2 per cent. While some writers reduce the poor performance of the economy to problems associated with ideology and the non-pragmatic character of the party/government leadership (Mesa Lago, 1978, pp. 25–6), others focus on constraints and distortionary effects arising from the process of rapid structural change itself. As Ghai *et al.* point out:

> The poor performance is not hard to explain. There were major institutional changes as more than 80 per cent of the economy was transferred to state control; there was the imposition of an economic boycott, observed by almost all of the Western hemisphere, which enforced a complete reorientation of trade and capital flows; there was a massive outflow of skilled professionals and technicians; a substantial increase in defence spending; a comprehensive shake-up of development priorities, economic planning and management methods; and towards the end of the decade, the virtual abolition of internal accounting methods and material incentives. (Ghai *et al.*, 1986, p. 27)

In response to the economic trade boycott spearheaded by the United States, the Cuban economy came to rely increasingly on trade with, and aid from, Eastern Europe and, in particular, the Soviet Union. The increasing integration of the Cuban economy with the Eastern bloc economies was reinforced in 1972 when Cuba was admitted as a full member of the CMEA. Relations with the CMEA did little to transform Cuba's traditional insertion in the world economy as a sugar producer, although Eastern bloc assistance was used to expand the industrial base.

Considerable emphasis was placed on the development of a capital goods industry, which was virtually non-existent prior to the 1960s. This centred primarily on the manufacture of machinery and equipment for agriculture. According to one estimate, annual growth in this industry averaged in excess of 15 per cent between 1965 and 1985, with the engineering goods industries increasing their share of total industrial production from 2.4 to 13.2 per cent over the same period (Brundenius, 1987, p. 98). Major investments were also undertaken in such areas as thermoelectrical and nitrogenous fertiliser plants, a nickel processing complex, a glass-container factory and lubricants plants (*Granma Weekly Review*, 29 June 1986, p. 1). Between 1974 and 1979 the percentage share of investment accounted for by industry doubled from 19 to 38 per cent (Ibid., p. 101).

TABLE 4.1 *Marketed production of selected food crops, 1958–75 (in 000s of tonnes)*

Year[1]	Yuca	Boniato	Malanga[2]	Beans	Rice	Potatoes
1958	207.8	168.1	185.6	19.8	218.9	82.6
1963	108.7	117.3	49.5	29.2	185.7	87.1
1968	46.5	75.2	40.0	10.1	122.0	106.3
1973	69.3	79.5	23.7	4.2	261.6	73.1
1975	84.8	91.7	32.5	5.0	338.0	116.8

SOURCES In Lehmann, 1985, p. 257, based on Ritter, 1974, p. 188 and JUCEPLAN *Anuario Estadistico*, 1975, p. 81.
[1] Three-year averages except for 1958.
[2] Taro.

The growth of industry accelerated following the *rapprochement* with Western countries and international lending agencies during the early and mid-1970s. Imports from the West, consisting largely of machinery and equipment, increased sharply from a yearly average of 373 million pesos in 1971–73 to 1348 million in 1975–78 (Turits, 1987, p. 166).

Developments such as these implied high levels of accumulation. As a percentage of Global Social Product (GSP),[3] gross investments doubled between 1970 and 1977 (Brundenius, 1987, pp. 98–9). During the latter half of the 1970s, levels of investment averaged 29.3 per cent of GMP per annum compared, for example, to 16.9 per cent in 1962 and 25.3 per cent in 1967 (Zimbalist and Eckstein, 1987, p. 16).

While agriculture's share of total investment declined significantly during the latter half of the 1970s (from 27 per cent to 16 per cent between 1974 and 1979), high levels of investment were nevertheless sustained. During the previous decade agricultural production had stagnated.[4] Particularly affected was food crop production. The poor performance of this sector is indicated in Table 4.1, which presents data on marketed production for six basic food products. In an attempt to boost agricultural production, levels of investment in agriculture increased considerably. Much of this was accounted for by a large irrigation programme. Between the mid-1970s and 1980 the area under irrigation nearly doubled, from 593 000 ha. to 962 000 ha. (FAO, 1986, p. 59).

Procurement and Consumption

A crucial component of the state-centred accumulation model was the national procurement system that was quickly established after the revolution. The state controlled the marketing and distribution of virtually all agricultural produce through an extensive network of depots and vehicles. Certain quantities of crops, other than key agro-exports such as sugar, coffee, tobacco and beef, could be retained for local consumption. In addition to the state collection centres, the state-controlled Select Fruits Enterprises organized the marketing of high-quality perishables (Ghai *et al.*, 1986, p. 49).

As mentioned earlier, government policies during the first decade focused on the redistribution of wealth and income. Important in this respect were programmes intended to improve people's access to essential goods and social services. In order to ensure an equitable allocation of scarce consumer goods, a comprehensive rationing system was introduced in 1962. Apart from certain changes in the composition of the products allocated on the *libreta*, this system has operated ever since. In Table 4.2 it can be seen that significant quantities of food and other products were obtained at very low prices. Benjamin *et al.* present data showing that the ration alone provided each person with approximately 1900 calories a day – a figure not far below recommended minimum intake levels (Benjamin *et al.*, 1984, pp. 94–5).

This system enabled the vast majority of Cuban families to obtain the necessary minimum of essential food products at just a fraction of their household income. The monthly cost of basic food products obtained on the rationing card in 1983 was less than 10 pesos per adult. Average basic monthly incomes of agricultural, non-agricultural workers and technical staff were in the region of 100, 150 and 200 pesos respectively (Ghai *et al.*, 1986, p. 40). Nationally, it has been estimated that in 1980 approximately 30 per cent of consumer spending was on rationed goods (Zimbalist and Eckstein, 1987, p. 14).

Food and other goods could also be obtained via two other markets controlled by the state: the so-called 'free' and 'parallel' markets. The former operated through the same retail outlets used to distribute products on the *libreta*. Goods could be purchased in unlimited quantities at relatively high but fixed prices. In contrast, prices on the state-controlled 'parallel' market bore more relation to demand and

TABLE 4.2 *The adult monthly ration, 1983*

Product	Quantity	Price (pesos/lb)	Value (pesos)
Bread	15lb	0.15	2.25
Rice	5lb	0.24	1.20
Beans	20oz	0.24	0.30
Oil	8oz	0.40	0.20
Lard	1lb	0.30	0.30
Sugar	4lb	0.14	0.56
Milk*	3 cans	0.30 (/can)	0.90
Beef	20oz	0.65	0.81
Chicken	27oz	0.70	1.18
Potatoes	6lb	0.12	0.72
Tomatoes	3lb	0.20	0.60
Oranges	1lb	0.08	0.08
Sub-total			9.10
Others (salt, tomato sauce, soap, tobacco, etc.)			2.72
Total			11.82

SOURCE Based on Benjamin *et al.*, 1984, p. 36.
* Evaporated/condensed milk.

supply and tended to reflect black-market prices. As Ghai *et al.* observe this 'helped to push the black market in food onto the sidelines' (Ghai *et al.*, 1986, p. 52).

Given the poor performance of national production and the impact of redistributive policies on effective demand and consumption levels, the country continued to depend heavily on imported foods. Major changes in consumption patterns occurred away from locally-produced root crops and pulses towards imported wheat and rice, as well as national dairy products. It has been estimated that between 1970 and 1975 some 23 per cent of export earnings were spent on food imports (Lehmann, 1985, pp. 256–7).

ECONOMIC AND FOOD POLICY REFORMS

Economic policy reforms were introduced very gradually from the early 1970s onwards. In this section I will summarize the nature of the reforms introduced since that time, concentrating particularly on a set of policy changes which occurred during the first half of the 1980s when measures associated with the liberalization of domestic trade in foodstuffs, material incentives and changes in the accumulation–consumption balance were implemented. I will also refer to subsequent developments involving the introduction of a series of new policies and programmes which brought to an abrupt halt several of the reform initiatives.

Reform Initiatives in the 1970s

During the first half of the 1970s the government attempted to correct the chronic imbalance between demand and supply, reflected in problems of shortages and low labour productivity. As explained by Petras and Selden:

In the case of Cuba, economic dislocations and shortages that accompanied the supposed revolutionary offensive of 1968. . .and the failure of the targeted ten million ton harvest resulted in a shift in emphasis from mass mobilization to economic planning and programming, from a stress on moral exhortation to greater emphasis on material incentives, from a focus on revolutionary ascetism to expanded consumer rewards. (Petras and Selden, 1981: 194)

The government reduced the rate of investment (which fell from 33 per cent of GMP in 1970 to 28 per cent between 1971 and 1972), and allocated certain quantities of consumer durables and housing materials to work centres as incentive goods to be distributed according to criteria of merit and need by the workers themselves (Zimbalist and Eckstein, 1987, p. 11). Throughout the 1970s there was a significant expansion in the quantity and variety of consumer goods available, while the proportion of consumer spending associated with rationed goods fell considerably from 95 per cent in 1970 to about 30 per cent in 1980 (Ibid., p. 14).

Monetary incentives were also partially restored, the prices of non-food consumer goods raised, and wages of certain groups reduced (Griffin and James, 1981, pp. 92–3). A number of restrictions related to the hiring of labour by peasant producers and the private sale of agricultural produce were also lifted (Deere, 1986, p. 135).

Planning and Participation

During the 1970s, and particularly from the middle of the decade, a system of centralized directive planning took effect, which at the same time was characterized by a considerable degree of consultation and popular participation (Zimbalist and Eckstein, 1987, p. 12). Under the Economic Management and Planning System (SDPE) the principle of 'centralised pluralism' was put into effect (Stubbs, 1989, p. 48), whereby draft plans were drawn up by the central co-ordinating agency, JUCEPLAN, on the basis of priorities determined by the party, as well as information and requests for resources submitted by the ministries. The draft was then passed down to ministers, enterprises, mass organizations and the regional and local organs of Popular Power (the elected government apparatus) for comments and counter-proposals. These were then sent back to be considered in a reformulated version of the plan, which was ultimately approved by the party leadership and became law once ratified by the National Assembly of Popular Power (White G., 1985b, pp. 4–5).

While the planning system was highly centralized, important measures were introduced in 1975 to decentralize economic management. Lowy outlines the content of these measures as follows:

in the struggle against bureaucratization. . .a new and original solution, without precedents in any other state in transition, was to be implemented: popular power.

The essential principle of popular power is that all production or service units which supply goods or services to the community should be under that community's management and control. This meant that schools, medical centers, stores, eating places, factories, movie theaters, entertainment centers, and so on were all to be managed by the community in each location. (Lowy, 1986, pp. 269–70)

By the mid-1980s, an estimated 34 per cent of all Cuban enterprises were controlled by the local organs of Popular Power (Zimbalist and Eckstein, 1987, p. 12) while the share of the total state budget assigned to the latter increased from 21 to 33 per cent between 1978 and 1984 (Zimbalist, 1989, p. 74).

Other measures were introduced during the 1976–80 period which encouraged further decentralization and greater local initiative. In 1976, certain private-sector activities were legalized, as licences were issued to promote self-employed or co-operative service activities involving traders, carpenters, electricians, car mechanics and builders. During the month immediately following legalization, some two thousand people were reported to have taken out licences to become street peddlers in Havana (Zimbalist and Eckstein, 1987, p. 13).

During the 1970s, then, the reform movement gradually gathered pace and culminated, in the early 1980s, in a series of policy changes which liberalized trade in certain foodstuffs, increased the availability of consumer goods and provided a greater role for material incentives in the workplace.

Material Incentives in the 1980s

The decade began with the introduction of reforms in the wage system. In 1980, the minimum wage increased by 14 per cent while the average monthly wage in agriculture rose by 30 per cent (Jiménez, 1987, p. 135). Two new forms of productivity bonus were introduced in 1979 and 1981: the '*prima*', distributed to individuals, and the '*premio*', distributed collectively (Ghai *et al.*, 1986, p. 42). Other incentive schemes relating, for example, to the sale of vehicles to certain employees, also came into effect and gradually expanded well beyond the scale originally envisaged by the planners.

From 1980 onwards, labour was increasingly organized in work brigades which would enter into contracts with enterprises. The terms of the contracts provided for economic incentives and allowed the brigade members to organize their own work process. By 1985, over 1200 brigades had been formed, primarily in agricultural enterprises (Zimbalist and Eckstein, 1987, p. 12). Certain enterprise managers were also given the right to retain a small percentage of their annual profit to pay individual and collective bonuses.

Macroeconomic Policy Changes

Tentative steps were taken towards greater reliance on credit as opposed to budgetary grants to finance both working capital and (since 1985) investment (White G., 1985b, p. 11). Reforms relating to the official price system were also introduced in an attempt to curb the growth of excess demand. At the end of 1981, retail prices of many food products and other basic consumer items such as textiles, were increased for the first time since 1962 (Jimenez, 1987, p. 135). Food price increases averaged between 10 and 12 per cent but, as indicated in Table 4.3, were much higher in certain product lines.

Food prices in restaurants also increased by between 11 and 30 per cent, although prices in certain establishments increased far more as

TABLE 4.3 *Retail price increases for selected food products, 1981*

Product	Percentage Increase
Pasteurized milk*	25
Rice*	20
Potatoes*	71
Beans**	56
Beef**	61
Sugar/soft drinks**	100

SOURCES   * Jimenez, 1987, p. 135.
** Benjamin *et al.*, 1984, p. 57.

they were upgraded in the restaurant classification scale. However, these price increases immediately sparked off a public outcry to which the government promptly responded by reversing the measures a few days later (Benjamin *et al.*, 1984, p. 57).

The 1981 price rises increased average family expenditure by an estimated 8 pesos per month and contributed to a significant reduction in the food subsidy. Wage increases, however, had provided the average family with an extra 36 pesos a month (Jimenez, 1987, p. 135). To deal with the problem of excess demand the government also announced measures to encourage savings. More important, however, were measures designed to increase the supply of consumer goods and services (Benjamin *et al.*, 1984, pp. 63, 83).

Increasing the Availability of Consumer Goods

Imports of canned and bottled goods increased while the relaxation of export quotas had the effect of expanding domestic supply of certain products, such as citrus fruits and juices. The quantity and variety of goods sold on the state-controlled parallel market expanded considerably while the market in second-hand products assumed a more open face through media advertising.

Trends towards increased consumption were reflected in a decline in the investment ratio, which fell from the level, indicated earlier, of 29.3 per cent of GMP during 1976–80, to a projected level of 18 per cent in 1984. Table 4.4 presents data illustrating the rise and fall of the accumulation rate during the 1970s and early 1980s.

TABLE 4.4 *Gross investment (GI) ratio, 1971–83 (GI as a percentage of GSP)*

1971	1974	1977	1980	1983
10.7	13.0	18.7	15.6	14.0

SOURCE Brundenius, 1987, p. 99, based on official statistics.

Freeing the Market

One of the most important measures affecting the distribution and consumption of consumer goods related to the partial elimination of controls on the private sale of certain goods such as handicrafts and, in particular, food products. During 1980 and 1981, 'free peasant markets' sprang up in each of the country's 169 municipalities, selling mainly vegetables, fruits, pork, cheese and live animals, staples such as rice, beans, taro and plantains. Benjamin *et al.* outline the content of this policy reform in the following terms:

The 1980 decree establishing the markets set the following ground rules:

● Private individual farmers and producer cooperatives were authorized to sell. Also authorized was anyone who held any sort of land, including those with backyard plots and farmers who had leased their land to the government but had kept a few acres for home production. State farms were authorized to sell only the surplus from their self-provisioning land with the proceeds going to a common recreational and development fund for the farm employees.

● Vendors were required to be producers; reselling was strictly prohibited.

● Prices were 'free,' that is, to be determined between buyer and seller with no government interference.

● The sale of beef, tobacco, sugar, coffee and cocoa was prohibited – beef to avoid jeopardizing building up the national herd, and the others to preserve valuable foreign-exchange earners.

● Farmers had to provide their own transportation.

● The markets were placed under the authority of People's Power,

Cuba's elected government apparatus, which would assign each market an administrative staff responsible for checking all documents, assigning space, and allocating a nominal daily seller's fee. (Benjamin *et al.*, 1984, pp. 63–4)

Before selling in the peasant markets, however, farmers had first of all to meet the quotas established by the government for sale of produce at official prices to the state. Such quotas were generally fixed at relatively low levels given the difficulties of monitoring the production levels of private farmers – difficulties which resulted from the lack of state personnel and the fact that private farmers were not obliged to keep detailed accounts (Ghai *et al.*, 1986, p. 90). This meant that a significant proportion of a farmer's output could be channelled towards the peasant markets once the self-provisioning of the family had been accounted for.

While the peasant markets provided farmers with an opportunity to increase their income considerably, they accounted for the majority sales of very few products and for only a small percentage of national food sales. One estimate for the first quarter of 1981 put the figure at 6.5 per cent of the national total. Another estimate for 1984 cited the figure of 5 per cent, while in 1985 the value of foodstuffs sales in the peasant markets was estimated at approximately 7 per cent of the value of goods sold on the state-controlled 'parallel' market (Benjamin *et al.*, 1984, p. 67; Ghai *et al.*, 1986, p. 53). Further incentives to agricultural producers were introduced in 1981, when agricultural prices increased by an average factor of 1.6 to 1.7 (Ibid., p. 48).

Reasserting Social Control or 'Rectification'

Cuba's experiment with liberalization in the shape and form of the free peasant markets soon ended. For reasons which will be analysed below, trading in these markets was suspended temporarily in 1982 and 1983, and abolished indefinitely in 1986. The closure of the peasant markets was one of the first significant measures in what the government referred to as the 'process of rectification of errors and eradication of negative tendencies'. This process sought to reassert social control over the economy, both through the centralization of certain planning mechanisms and the more active participation of party members and organized social groups at the local level – in the work-place, the neighbourhood committees, and so on.

The policy changes and initiatives associated with the rectification process were essentially concerned with four major aspects, namely the economic and 'moral' decline of certain institutions that characterized Cuban socialism; the need to reduce trade and budgetary deficits; improvements in housing conditions and the expansion of social infrastructure; and national food security.

There was an attempt to overhaul and strengthen certain 'socialist' institutions including co-operatives, state enterprises and the state administrative and planning apparatus. Numerous measures were introduced intended to reduce inefficiency in state enterprises and corruption in both enterprises and the bureaucracy. There was an attempt to increase the number of hours effectively worked during the day, reduce manning levels on new projects, link wage and salary levels more closely to productivity, reduce wage differentials, and encourage the more efficient use of resources in production. During the latter 1980s somewhat hesitant steps were taken to reduce state financing of enterprise deficits and encourage firms to cover their costs (Mesa Lago, 1989, pp. 109–10). The attempt to put the socialist house in order also involved measures to deal with the misuse of state resources. Numerous enterprise managers as well as party and government officials were dismissed or demoted while, in 1988, several new crimes relating to administrative offences were added to the Penal Code (Ibid., pp. 115–16).

As part of the drive to increase labour productivity and reaffirm the importance of moral incentives, special construction contingents were set up in 1987; by 1989 these claimed over ten thousand members (Ibid., p. 117). Working up to fourteen hours a day, six days a week, these workers were assigned to priority projects, for example in the tourism industry, in order to reduce the construction phase rapidly. By the end of the decade such contingents were being organized in several other sectors, notably industry and state telephone repair services (Díaz, 1990).

During the latter half of the 1980s the government clamped down on private-sector activities, not only closing down the free peasant markets but also suppressing the activities of private manufacturers, street vendors, builders and others engaged in self-employed service activities (Mesa Lago, 1989, pp. 108–9). Following the decision to eliminate the peasant markets, two measures were taken which aimed to strengthen both the co-operative sector and the state procurement system. These included an increase in the allocation of incentive goods, such as building materials and motorbikes, to co-operative members. Farm workers also benefited from an expanded quota of construction materials for houses. Regarding procurement, there was an attempt to substitute the role performed by the peasant markets by increasing the capacity of the state collection system and the Select Fruits Enterprise (*Granma*, 9 July 1987, p. 2).

A prominent feature of the rectification process, from 1987 onwards, was the reactivation of the so-called minibrigade movement which had operated during the early 1970s. This involved the mobilization of tens of thousands of people to work on construction projects associated primarily with social infrastructure. The minibrigade movement provided a way of reviving public-sector social programmes that had stagnated over the years. In 1987 the minibrigades constructed 600 family doctor home/offices, fifty-four infant day-care centres, and had begun work on eleven special education schools (GWR, 10 January 1988, p. 3).[5] Particular emphasis was placed on the construction of housing units in Havana, where housing conditions had deteriorated over the years. By the end of 1989, some reports claimed that the movement had built 35 000 such units (Díaz, 1990).

To reduce both trade and budgetary deficits, the government introduced policy measures and programmes to boost export production, cut imports and reduce domestic consumption. The level of investment was increased and priority was given to projects in a number of sectors which were potentially high foreign exchange earners or savers, including, for example, nuclear power, tourism, biotechnology, pharmaceuticals and microelectronics.

The increase in the accumulation rate during 1985 and 1986, however, intensified the squeeze on consumption. This tension is clearly illustrated in the following excerpt from a report, published in *Granma*, on the opening of the January 1987 session of the National Assembly. Juxtaposed we find references to progress on the heavy investment front and shortages of basic manufactured goods.

Work is under way on the first and second reactors of the three-billion peso nuclear power plant, the first reactor is scheduled for operation by 1990 and the second by 1992. The two remaining reactors will be operational in 1994 and 1996. . .

Deputy Diosdado Hernandez wanted to know what could be done to produce more frying pans and buckets, etc. and Minister Lage acknowledged that sufficient resources had not been devoted to this. (GWR, 11 January 1987, p. 2)

Both to save foreign exchange and to promote internal budgetary equilibrium, the government launched an austerity drive. During 1987 some twenty-eight measures were implemented, designed to restrict people's access to certain basic goods and services such as textiles, public transport and energy, as well as non-essential items. The latter included, for example, cuts in expense accounts of public functionaries, and currency allocations for trips abroad, as well as controls on the private use of state vehicles.

Many of the measures affected the access of certain social groups to food. Social consumption in particular was restricted. Reductions were announced in the quota of milk assigned to intermediate-level students and to worker dining rooms. The amount of milk and beef assigned to people on supplementary dietary rations for medical reasons was also reduced and measures were taken to control the number of people qualifying for special diets. The afternoon meal in child day-care centres was replaced by a 'good snack'. Snack breaks in central government agencies and local People's Power bodies were eliminated. Sugar and rice quotas assigned to the food processing industry and certain work places, respectively, were also reduced for a specific period. The quantity of food allocated through the central administration to worker dining rooms in the Ministries of the Sugar Industry and Agriculture was reduced (except for the cane sector during the harvest period), on the assumption that more could be obtained through self-provisioning. Price increases were announced for certain goods sold on the state-controlled parallel market, including milk, rice and yogurt, as well as for produce from local market-garden areas.

There was some attempt to alleviate the impact of the crisis and the austerity measures on the more vulnerable groups. No reduction, for example, was announced in the substantial milk quota of a litre a day allocated to younger children. Lower-paid pensioners, health workers and agricultural labourers received pay increases. Despite serious problems of overmanning in state enterprises, the decision was taken not to lay off people. When the supply of certain food products was reduced, attempts were also made to provide substitutes, as occurred, for example, when domestically-grown potatoes replaced imported rice.

Towards the end of the decade, the government launched a food security programme which aimed to diversify national food production and reduce Cuba's dependency on imported food by rapidly increasing the production of pork, chicken, eggs, dairy products, rice, root crops and plantains (*viandas*), fruit and vegetables (Díaz, 1990). The programme became necessary following the poor performance of domestic food production in 1986 and 1987, and absolutely vital when events in Eastern Europe and the Soviet Union (which accounted for approximately 40 per cent of food supply) threatened to seriously disrupt or reduce food imports (*Pensamiento Propio*, August 1990, pp. 16–18).

EXPLAINING THE REFORMS

The reforms dating from the early 1970s emphasized different measures at different times, but essentially consisted of policy changes involving decentralization of economic management, the increasing use of material incentives, increased reliance on market mechanisms, and the increased availability of consumer goods. It is clear, though, that the reform process in Cuba was very partial and piecemeal. Even during the early 1980s, the predominant tendency was still, as White points out, to rely heavily on administrative directives as opposed to economic mechanisms or incentives associated with fiscal, credit or price policy (White G., 1985b, p. 9).

Economic and Systemic Constraints

While most writers agree on these aspects of the reform process, there are considerable variations in their accounts of why the reforms took place. For some, the reform process of the 1970s was essentially a response to economic crisis conditions which derived from world market conditions and the type of systemic constraints (referred to in Part I) associated with the state-centred accumulation model.

In explaining the reform movement of the 1970s, Zimbalist and Eckstein argue that the shift in strategy reflected a response to an economic and political crisis which had emerged as a consequence of the failure of an accumulation strategy based on external resources. This strategy had become ineffective during the late 1960s as a consequence of unfavourable world sugar prices, slow- or low-yielding investment projects, and the limits to which the working class would accept material sacrifices. In response, the government was obliged to shift to a domestically-based accumulation strategy. This required increased worker motivation and productivity, which would be achieved through measures relating to decentralization,

privatization, reform of the wage system, and the increased availability of consumer goods and services. Changes which had occurred
in the employment structure were, according to these authors, also
important in accounting for the reforms: 'the government's more
permissive stance towards private economic activity, in both the cities
and the countryside, undoubtedly partly results from the decline in
the need for labor in the sugar sector', which had arisen due to
mechanization (Zimbalist and Eckstein, 1987, pp. 10, 14).

Petras and Selden also see the change in policy as a response to the
crisis of the late 1960s. Here, however, the rationale involved is
somewhat different. They argue that the problems of shortages and
black market activities, which intensified during these years, highlighted the inability of the state to effectively control and manage the
economy and substitute the activities of private agents expropriated
during the Revolutionary Offensive. It was this situation that prompted
moves towards decentralization (Petras and Selden, 1981, p. 193).
Economic dislocations and the failure of the *Gran Zafra* in 1970 also
highlighted the need to develop the productive forces rapidly. This
could only be achieved through increased reliance on foreign technology and increased penetration of competitive foreign markets,
which in turn implied expanded relations with the world capitalist
system. Hence 'pressures built up internally to give greater scope to
market forces and technical specialists, and to view with increasing
distrust the demands of an internally divided party' (Ibid., p. 196).

It was this very process of development of the productive forces,
combined with certain demographic changes, which permitted, according to some writers, a relaxation of the accumulation rate and
further reforms in the 1980s. Turits, for example, argues that: 'As the
sugar industry approached nearly full mechanization, and large infrastructural needs were met, these capital investments could be tapered
off. Similarly, the rapid decline in the birth rate. . .meant that
education and other social investments could be decreased' (Turits,
1987, pp. 172–3).

Another account emphasizes more debates among planners and
political leaders regarding the efficacy of different planning methods.
White, for example, sees the 'very tentative steps towards decentralization of economic decision-making power and the use of "economic" mechanisms over the past decade' (White G., 1985, p. 4) as a
response of planners and leaders to the types of problem characteristic of centralized directive planning systems in general. These include:
'systemic "scarcity". . .widespread waste, absenteeism, "unemploy-

ment on the job", weak incentive systems, inefficient use of investment, "storming" to meet targets by the end of the month or some
politically significant date. . .and so on' (Ibid., p. 10).

While analyses such as these identify a series of conditions and
constraints arising from relations with the world economy, the domestic
model of accumulation and the planning system that are highly
relevant for understanding the reform process, there is little analysis
in the literature of the extent to which changes in the balance of social
forces and social pressures influenced the policy process.

Consumer and 'Middle Class' Interests

Benjamin *et al.*, referring more specifically to the emergence of free
peasant markets, emphasize the role of consumer discontent and
demands associated with non-essential consumption. According to
these authors, the increased availability of food products expected
to result from the measures would, the government assumed, cater to
consumer demands and also render more effective the system of
material incentives intended to boost labour productivity (Benjamin
et al., 1984, p. 62).

Also illuminating in this respect are the speeches of Fidel Castro in
1986/87, where he explained the need to halt the trend towards
liberalization. As we will see later, Castro implied that policy errors
or planning imbalances associated with an excessive emphasis of
material incentives, economic growth and investment, reflected the
increasing strength of bureaucratic and technocratic interests in the
state apparatus and the ongoing pervasiveness of 'petty-bourgeois'
ideology, particularly that associated with the urban population of
Havana.

What emerges clearly from an analysis of the socioeconomic conditions that prompted the food policy reforms in Cuba, is that they
did not reflect a response to a situation of serious shortages of
essential food products or a 'food crisis', but to a set of problems
characteristic of a more advanced stage of development, notably
problems of diversity and quality of agricultural output, diet and of
consumer goods in general. In this respect, it is interesting to note the
observation made in one study of the food situation in Cuba, that
when price increases were announced in 1981, the measure that
caused most public concern was not that related to increases in the
prices of basic food products but that which caused a rise in restaurant prices (Benjamin *et al.*, 1984, p. 57). Remarks in Castro's

TABLE 4.5   *Official average annual growth rates of gross social product (GSP) 1962–85*

	1962–65	1966–70	1971–75	1976–80	1981–85
GSP	3.7%	0.4%	7.5%	4.0%	7.3%
GSP per cap.	1.3%	–1.3	5.7%	3.1%	6.4%

SOURCE   See Zimbalist and Eckstein, 1987, p. 8.

speeches in later years relating to problems of distribution and shortages of consumer goods also appear to support this idea. Even in 1986, when the economy faced serious difficulties, one finds few references to problems associated with essential food products; rather, the commentary tended to focus on products such as beer, rum and even 'coconut-flavoured buffalo yogurt'.

During the 1970s, Cuba resolved many of the problems of food supply and basic needs which had characterized the pre-revolutionary development model, some of which had persisted into the 1960s (Benjamin *et al.*, 1984; Brundenius, 1984; Ghai *et al.*, 1986; Griffin and James, 1981). The decade had seen the performance of the Cuban economy improve significantly. Official figures, presented in Table 4.5, record an annual growth rate of 7.5 per cent during the first five-year plan (1971–75) and 4 per cent during the second five-year plan (1976–80). While several commentators have argued that these figures are inflated (Brundenius, Zimbalist, Mesa Lago) they clearly reflect an improvement on the preceding quinquennium. Dissatisfaction with the variety and quality of goods was, it seems, prevalent during the late 1970s. As Benjamin *et al.* explain:

Consumer aspirations were heightened by the return visits of Cubans who had left in the 1960s. After the Cuban government had granted emigres permission to visit their families in 1979, they started returning at the rate of about a hundred thousand a year, bringing with them an array of goods not available in Cuba. This sudden direct exposure to the world's foremost consumer society – on top of the barrage of advertising Cubans received through Miami-based radio and television stations – made the Cuban lifestyle seem austere by comparison. Certainly many of the over 120,000 Cubans who left their homeland in the 1980 boatlifts were seeking greater material comfort. Dissatisfaction with the limits of

TABLE 4.6   *Changes in the composition of the labour force by sector,*
1970–79 (in 000 of workers and percentage)

Sector	1970		1979[1]	
	No.	%	No.	%
Agriculture[2]	790.4	30.0	716.0	21.9
Industry/Construction	690.4	26.3	908.4	27.8
Services	622.0	28.6	934.0	28.6
Commerce	306.0	11.6	265.5	8.1
Transport/Communication	161.4	6.1	202.7	6.2
Others	63.2	2.4	243.7	7.4
Total	2 633.3	100.0	3 270.3	100.0

SOURCE   Brundenius, 1984, p. 133.
[1] Occupied labour force.
[2] Includes fishing and forestry.

consumption in Cuba might well have been more widespread than most party officials had realized. (Benjamin *et al.*, 1984, pp. 62–3)

During the 1970s there was a significant rise in what could be labelled 'middle-class' groups, which included technical and managerial staff in state enterprises, public functionaries and other 'service' sector workers. Of the categories used in the official statistics on employment, that of 'non-productive services' (comprising public administration and financing: health and social security; education, culture and research; housing; and sports and recreation (Mesa Lago, 1981, p. 115)) is particularly relevant. In 1979 this sector employed nearly a million people of a total labour force of 3.27 million. Moreover, the size of this sector had increased by 50 per cent between 1970 and 1979 (see Table 4.6).

Participation and Pressure From Below

While consumer discontent appears to have been rife, there is little indication in the literature of how consumer pressures actually manifested themselves, or how they might have influenced the policy process. Referring to the initial wave of popular discontent that emerged during the late 1960s, Zimbalist and Eckstein point out that discontent tended to manifest itself more in the form of 'foot-dragging' and absenteeism rather than in political activity (Zimbalist and Eckstein, 1987, p. 10).

Presumably, by the late 1970s, the three main institutional channels for expressing demands associated with greater availability of goods and basic services were mass organizations such as the Committees in Defense of the Revolution (CDR) which, according to Lowy, 'have managed to organize and mobilize the masses more effectively and more broadly than any other institution' (Lowy, 1986, p. 274); the Confederation of Cuban Workers; and the local organs of People's Power, whose elected representatives hold periodic meetings with their constituents. According to Zimbalist and Eckstein: 'Available information suggests that local meetings are concerned primarily with discussions of bureaucratic deficiencies, including consumer scarcities and complaints about urban services' (Zimbalist and Eckstein, 1987, p. 12). The close links between these organizations and institutions, on the one hand, and the party on the other, provided a channel through which decision-makers could keep in touch with popular sentiments and demands. On the question of the extent to which the party was responsive to 'popular opinion' it should also be remembered that the party itself was a mass-based organization with a membership that exceeded half a million people.

There is, however, considerable debate over the degree of participation of the mass of the population in the planning and policy process (LeoGrande, 1981). While most writers stress the hierarchical and centralized nature of the Cuban political and planning system, they differ on the degree of participation. It would seem, however, that processes of consultation were institutionalized at different levels and became more effective throughout the late 1970s and early 1980s. While pointing out a number of limitations in the democratic character and economic role of Popular Power institutions. White claims that:

> Poder Popular does give some expression to regional and local interests within the planning process, as well as providing outlets for citizen complaints on mundane matters. . .In comparison with other state socialist economies there may be a relatively high degree of consultation and discussion at all levels of the Cuban planning system. (White G., 1985b, pp. 7–8)

Pressures favouring liberalization were also brought to bear by the

National Association of Small Farmers (ANAP), representing virtually all the country's peasant producers and agricultural cooperative members. Given the nature of the reform measures, however, it would seem that the influence of small commercial farming interests on the policy process was limited. The reforms were restricted essentially to the opening of the free peasant markets for above-quota surplus. We do not see a comprehensive package of pro-peasant reforms including increased availability of production inputs, investment goods, vehicles or consumer goods, or of technical assistance.

The Decline of Rich Peasant Interests

In order to understand the limited nature of the pro-peasant reforms and the subsequent volte-face regarding policy on the free peasant markets, it is important to refer to the position of rich peasant producers in the social structure. The small commercial producers represented by ANAP did not constitute one of the country's major social forces. As indicated in the Introduction to this chapter, the key distinguishing characteristics of Cuban social structure were the relatively large proportion of the population which lived in urban areas and worked as agricultural wage labourers.

While the sector of small private farmers had expanded as a consequence of the agrarian reform measures of the 1960s, it still numbered less than a quarter of a million by 1970. It did, however, control a significant share of the land, estimated at between 25 and 30 per cent in 1965, and an estimated 42 per cent of arable land. The importance of this social group in rural social structure was to diminish considerably thereafter. During the 1970s, an estimated 100 000 producers, or 42 per cent of all peasant farmers, abandoned farming by either selling or renting their land to the state.[6] The decline of this sector is indicated in Table 4.7. It can be seen that the number of self-employed farmers fell from 235 000 to 136 000 between 1970 and 1981 (Ghai *et al.*, 1986, p. 91).

This decline continued in subsequent years as small farmers joined the co-operatives (Ramirez, 1984, p. 8). By 1985, the private sector controlled just 8 per cent of the land.

It is also important to refer to changes occurring within the producers' association. During the early 1980s it was the co-operative movement that came to dominate ANAP. When the decision was taken in 1980 to establish the peasant markets, the vast majority of

TABLE 4.7   *Composition of agricultural labour force, 1970–81 (number of workers and percentages)*

	1970		1981		Growth per annum
	No.	%	No.	%	%
State farms	495 073	63	598 762	76	1.7
Collective farms	1 800	—	30 223	4	25.6
Private farms					
Self-employed	235 001	30	135 926	17	–5.0
Wage workers	24 139	3	19 658	2	–1.9
Family workers[1]	34 289	4	6 300	1	–15.4

SOURCE   Ghai *et al.*, 1986, p. 111, based on official statistics.
[1] Unpaid.

ANAP members were private farmers. At that time, the co-operative movement had only approximately 30 000 members (Ibid., p. 6), about a fifth of the total number of small farmers. Moreover, the co-operatives only controlled 12 per cent of the land held by the non-state sector. By 1985, however, this balance of forces had changed considerably. The co-operative movement had more than doubled in size, growing to 72 597 members (Ghai *et al.*, 1986, p. 29), while the amount of land controlled by the co-operatives represented 61.3 per cent of the total held by the non-state sector, or 12 per cent of all farm land (Rodriguez, 1987, p. 29).

Given the considerable material benefits received from the state and increased participation in political and planning processes, it may be assumed that the demands of this group did not centre on those associated with the free market. In explaining the relative absence of pressure for changes in economic policy from the private sector, it is also relevant to refer to the generally favourable situation it had experienced during nearly three decades of rule by the revolutionary government. In this context, Lehmann refers to the situation of the Cuban peasantry as one of under- as opposed to over-exploitation:

it is fairly clear that the smallholding farmers, or the private sector of agriculture, have had a good deal: they have gained or preserved access to land ownership in far larger units than they could ever have expected but for the Revolution. They have also enjoyed unparalleled opportunities for social mobility. . .They enjoy the same rations as everyone else, in addition to consuming their own production. (Lehmann, 1985, p. 268)

Contradictions Which Prompted the Closure of the Peasant Markets and the 'Rectification' Drive

The limited strength of private farming interests was reflected all too clearly in 1982 when the free peasant markets were temporarily closed. While there is some evidence to show that production of certain crops increased in response to the opportunities for higher profits provided by the markets and that a significant proportion of the population visited the markets at least once a month (Benjamin *et al.*, 1984, p. 68), the markets soon generated a new set of problems for the government. These included the illegal diversion of products from state channels, the charging of extremely high retail prices and the rapid expansion of a *nouveau riche* sector of small farmers and middlemen.[7]

A major clampdown on market activities, centering particularly on the capital's twelve markets, led to many arrests and the confiscation of large quantities of produce. Until October 1983, little trading took place in the markets. In the ANAP Congress of May of that year, the farmers had pressured the government to allow free market mechanisms to operate and criticized a government proposal to impose a 50 per cent tax on sales. The government settled for a figure of 20 per cent and sought to curtail the scale of the markets by competing through the state's own parallel market, where the volume and variety of produce sold expanded rapidly. Procurement prices for above-quota produce increased and taxes on private sales to the state were set at just 5 per cent – well below the level operating in the free peasant markets (Ibid., pp. 77–9).

By the mid-1980s, however, the same problems had re-emerged. Moreover, the markets and the income opportunities they provided for private farmers were seen as having a debilitating effect on the co-operative movement. Leaders of co-operatives, which now dominated ANAP, apparently called for the closure of the markets at the Second National Meeting of Agricultural Production Co-operatives in May 1986. The party immediately responded but, according to some accounts, had turned up at the meeting with proposals merely to increase taxes in the markets, convinced that their eventual elimination would take longer (Castro, 1986b, p. 3).

The process of 'rectification', outlined earlier, represented an attempt to reverse trends towards liberalization and to reassert administrative controls over the economy, as well as the roles of both moral incentives and popular mobilization in social and economic development. Increased reliance on market mechanisms and material incentives had generated a number of negative effects, which contradicted basic socialist principles and goals in three major areas.

Firstly, the reforms were seen as weakening the socialist sector of the economy. This occurred in several ways. Productivity in state enterprises was affected through pilfering to obtain supplies for private sale, and absenteeism, which enabled workers to devote more time to private-sector activity (Zimbalist and Eckstein, 1987, p. 13). Basic problems in the planning system and the implementation of the system of material incentives had created a situation where many workers and technicians were being paid wages or salaries which bore little relation to the work they performed. Despite the introduction of more and better machinery, work norms remained unchanged in many enterprises, as did the levels of manning. Central marketing channels were increasingly bypassed as bartering developed between enterprises or between the latter and co-operatives. An increasing number of instances of outright corruption were also reported.

The development of the co-operative sector was also affected by the operation of the free peasant markets. As income and profits of private farmers rose, so the numbers of producers joining co-operatives declined. Leaders of the co-operative movement assembled for their Second National Meeting expressed concern at these developments. Castro summed up their views as follows: 'the cooperative peasants insisted: "Put an end to it: they're fooling us, making a mockery of all of us who belong to the cooperatives. They're buying up the world with all the money they make and try to demoralize us"' (*GWR*, 28 September 1986, p. 3).

Moreover, the free peasant markets had affected relations between the co-operative movement and other sectors of the population, weakening in effect the worker–peasant alliance. The party/government viewpoint was outlined by Castro at the 2nd National Meeting of Agricultural Production Co-operatives:

we couldn't have the cooperatives involved in the free peasant market, for it is a matter of ethics, of principle, dignity and morality not to get involved in that commercialism and speculation. The Revolution had tried to create ideal conditions for the cooperatives and a number of measures were taken which really benefitted them in every respect. . .There was no need for the cooperatives to go to the free peasant markets, nor was there any need for cooperatives to be discredited, because I want to tell you that although the people bought certain produce out of need and had to pay high prices, they had a very, very bad opinion of the free peasant market. . .The people would buy but they felt they had been robbed. I was really upset at the idea that the cooperative movement, with the prestige it had acquired, could become the target of the population's rejection, repudiation and hostility. (Castro, 1986b, p. 3)

Secondly, the increased emphasis on material incentives (and certain social programmes) resulted in a number of unintended effects which manifested themselves in several fairly widespread abuses of bonus schemes and social programmes,[8] as well as outright corruption, which weakened the party's position. Castro summed up his thoughts on the nature of these problems in the following terms:

In the search for economic efficiency, we've created the breeding ground for a heap of vices and deformities, and what's worse, corruption. . .All that can dull the revolutionary feelings of our people, our workers, our farmers. And that's really bad because it weakens the Revolution. . .If we have a working class that lets itself be influenced by money alone, that starts being debased by money, whose actions revolve only around money, then we're in bad shape. . . . (Castro, 1986b, p. 4)

Perhaps it is our idiosyncracy, or individualist and anarchic spirit, a legacy of centuries of colonialism and neocolonialism, that any measure adopted here rapidly degenerated. . .Material incentives were introduced and were used to extremes and people were corrupted. (Idem., 1987a, pp. 4–5)

Thirdly, the peasant markets had facilitated the formation of what Castro referred to as 'newly-emerged neo-capitalist elements', which were seen as threatening basic principles associated with equality and the need to plan the use of resources. Moreover, the economic power of this sector was expanding through accumulation. Not only were farmers and middlemen enriching themselves in the peasant markets and engaging in luxury consumption, they were using this money to accumulate through, for example, the urban housing market by building, buying and selling houses (Castro, 1986a: p. 3).

Such a situation might have been tolerated during a period of high economic growth and relative prosperity as existed, for example, at the beginning of the 1980s when the reforms were introduced. The party would not tolerate it, however, during the mid-1980s when the economy was severely hit by a sharp reduction in hard currency earnings and the government was forced to implement a major austerity programme. In 1986, the country's foreign exchange earnings plummeted. Export revenues and import spending were seriously affected by the drop in oil prices which meant a loss of $300 million (which would have been obtained through the re-export of Soviet oil) and the decline in the value of the US dollar, which increased spending on imports by approximately $150 million. Agro-export revenues declined and imports of food and raw materials increased as a consequence of the prolonged drought conditions that had affected agriculture since 1981 – the impact of which was all the more dramatic given the poor performance of the hydraulics works programme, which had deteriorated since the late 1970s. Agricultural production had also been affected by Hurricane Kate which hit the island in November 1985, damaging banana plantations and the sugar crop. In 1986, the growth rate of GSP fell to 1.2 per cent, while negative growth of 3.8 per cent was recorded the following year (Mesa Lago, 1989, Table 1, p. 119). As a consequence of these conditions, Cuba was unable to meet international financial obligations relating to interest repayments for the first time in twenty-seven years (Castro, 1987a, p. 2).

The rectification process in general, and the minibrigade movement in particular, represented an attack on technocratic and bureaucratic planning methods which, the party leadership believed, had prioritized economic growth at the expense of social development and had wasted one of the country's most valuable resources, namely labour. More specifically, such methods had failed to recognize the contribution to development that voluntary labour could make. The party leadership vehemently criticized the bureaucrats and technocrats that had 'given up on the people' and established a false dichotomy between the economic management and planning system, on the one hand, and the minibrigade movement and politically motivated work campaigns on the other.

This form of exclusion of the working class in the development and planning process was, the party believed, a reflection of the growing pervasiveness of what Castro called the 'petty bourgeois spirit' that existed, particularly in the capital, Havana:

The capital is characterized by a strong proletarian spirit and also a strong petty bourgeois spirit. This is historic. The bureaucracy, all the top posts, a whole series of responsibilities and privileged social groups live in our capital. . .In a spirit of historical justice, we must say that generally speaking the petty bourgeoisie in our country. . .supported and still supports the Revolution. . .But the petty bourgeoisie has left a legacy of petty bourgeois spirit in the capital. (Castro, 1987b, 2)

The rectification process was clearly an attempt to reassert the dominance of the 'proletarian spirit'. The bottom line of this new approach was the need to mobilize the energies of the people by, as Castro put it, developing people's consciousness through political work and 'realistically using material incentives without such incentives being the driving force behind man's efforts' (Castro, 1987a, p. 5). This involved revitalizing a party whose position had weakened considerably in previous years and reasserting its 'vanguard' role in directing the evolution of the economy and society.

CONCLUSION

The reform process in Cuba stands in sharp contrast to that of Mozambique and Vietnam from the point of view of (a) the underlying conditions that prompted the reforms; (b) the content of the reform 'package'; and (c) the direction the reform process took during the latter half of the 1980s.

In common with the other experiences were a series of systemic constraints associated with inefficiency and waste in state sector enterprises and projects, as well as accumulation bias and its indirect effects on labour productivity via shortages of consumer goods and limited material incentives. World market relations also played an important role. Conditionality arising from increased links with Western governments and international lending agencies during the 1970s does not, however, appear to have been an important factor. Nevertheless, greater reliance on foreign technology and penetration of competitive foreign markets no doubt intensified the need to boost domestic efficiency and productivity. The constraints imposed on the development model from the decline in world sugar prices during the late 1960s, have been identified as a key factor prompting the need to define an alternative accumulation strategy based to a greater extent on the mobilization of domestic resources through a degree of decentralization, privatization and increased reliance on material incentives.

We have identified, however, another set of conditions, related to pressures 'from below' and changes in the balance of social forces, which played an important role in the Cuban reform process. While there is limited information available regarding these aspects, I have referred to a number of elements which seem important. Firstly, there was the question of growing discontent among large sectors of the population and increasing consumer demands for improved variety and quality of goods. The emergence of these 'middle-class' demands was related partly to the fact that important basic needs associated with food, education and health had, to a large extent, been met. Also, increased links with the 'world's foremost consumer society' revealed the considerable gap in material living standards between Cuba and the United States.

The rise of such demands, though, was also linked to the changes which had occurred in Cuban social structure. Here, we saw that 'white-collar' workers, and technical and professional personnel associated particularly with the 'non-productive service' sector of the economy, expanded rapidly during the 1970s. This period also saw the growth of a technocratic group within the state apparatus interested in applying new economic management and planning methods to resolve the country's economic problems.

Consumer discontent found both economic and institutional channels for influencing the policy process. Regarding the former, class practices associated with absenteeism, 'foot-dragging', and so on contributed to serious problems of low labour productivity, which eventually called into question the validity of the existing accumulation model. The development of participatory structures during the latter half of the 1970s provided institutional channels through which discontent was heard and demands could be both articulated and channelled upwards.

Whereas the reforms which were implemented in Mozambique and Vietnam brought about significant changes in property relations and the organization of the labour process, with a reduction in the scale of the state sector (Mozambique) or a decline in the effective control of the co-operatives (Vietnam), such was not the case in Cuba. Neither do we see in Cuba significant changes in the allocation of inputs and goods to peasant producers, as occurred in the other countries. Rather the emphasis in Cuba was on the increased availability of consumer goods to the working class, the bureaucracy and, more generally, a growing 'middle class' sector. Key issues were those associated with enterprise efficiency, material incentives, and the variety and quality of food/consumer products, rather than how to boost basic food production and procurement levels.

The Cuban reforms were also far more partial and piecemeal than those of the other countries. In accounting for these differences it is important to refer not only to such factors (usually emphasized in journalistic accounts or inside the covers of certain Western political science journals) as the ideological purity or rigidity of the party leadership – read Castro – but also to two other conditions, specific to the Cuban social formation. The first concerns the very different social structure of Cuba, where the majority of the population is urban-based and employed as wage or salaried workers by the state. Unlike the other countries, the small-scale farming population (whether organized in co-operatives or operating as private farmers) represents only a small percentage of the economically-active population and does not constitute a major social force. Moreover, the size of the private farming sector was to diminish considerably during the 1970s.

The second condition relates to the level of development of the productive forces and the nature of the so-called 'crisis' facing the Cuban state. We do not see in Cuba the same scale of problems or distortions, reflected in chronic shortages of food and other *basic* consumer goods, inflation and the proliferation of black market activities, as occurred in Mozambique or Vietnam. Not only had important basic needs been met, but the country's industrial base had also expanded. Moreover, the capacity of the state to plan resource allocation and accumulation was far greater. The implications of this situation for our analysis are threefold. It relieved the pressures on sustaining high rates of accumulation in both economic and social areas and permitted a partial 'freeing' of consumption. It also affected the content of the reforms. During the 1970s, fundamental problems affecting Cuban society related to the limited availability of non-essential consumer goods or lack of material incentives. The crucial issue was not how to resolve a food crisis by mobilizing agricultural resources and motivating rural producers to produce basic food products, but how to expand the production and supply of manufactured consumer goods and diversify the family diet. Finally, the fact that the 'crisis' was qualitatively different and not so acute, helps explain not only some of the differences in the content of the reforms and their restricted pro-peasant orientation, but also why several of the reforms – notably the free peasant markets – were abandoned once new contradictions arose.

Notes

1. The FAO records a total arable and pasture area of 6.7 million hectares in the mid-1970s (FAO, 1986, p. 50).
2. GMP is the gross value of production of agriculture, forestry, fishing, industry, construction, transport, communications and trade, minus the value of intermediate inputs.
3. GSP is the gross value of production of agriculture, forestry, fishing, industry, construction, transport, communications and trade. It excludes certain services: health, education and others (Brundenius, 1987, p. 111).
4. Between 1961 and 1970 total agricultural production (including forestry and fishing) registered an annual average growth rate of 1.5 per cent, while zero growth was recorded for non-sugar production. During the latter half of the 1960s (1966–70), agriculture recorded a growth rate of 0.4 per cent.
5. It was estimated that the minibrigades would contribute approximately 300 million pesos to the GSP in 1988 through an ambitious construction programme concentrated primarily in the capital. This would involve the building of health and educational facilities, some 13 000 housing units (approximately three times the annual home construction capacity of the Ministry of Construction), more than fifty day-care centres and twenty-eight bakeries intended to improve people's access to high-quality bread. Longer-term plans existed to expand the number of bakeries and the network of retail outlets in the capital, as well as to extend the work of the brigades from community projects to industrial and agricultural projects.
6. It has been argued that this was due not so much to coercive measures imposed by the state or to excessive restrictions on the allocation of essential goods and services, but more to social change and mobility promoted through the education system. As Ghai *et al.* explain: 'Indeed, of all the factors hastening the decline of small private farming, it seems that educational opportunity is the most powerful. Small private farmers today are generally elderly. Their offspring only rarely choose to take over the lands on which they were born, and work them in the old style. . .The children typically leave home in their early teens to attend secondary school, and usually go on to establish their lives elsewhere.' (Ghai *et al.*, 1986, p. 89).
7. Rough estimates regarding the size of the population that would make regular purchases at the free peasant markets were obtained from three sources for the study of the Cuban food system conducted by Benjamin *et al.* They ranged from 'somewhere under 50 per cent' to 80 per cent of the population (Benjamin *et al.*, 1984, p. 68).
8. The following examples were reported in the Cuban press:
   State vehicles were often used by employees for personal use (going to

beaches and recreational centres), while a scheme which was to enable a restricted number of technicians in key posts to buy cars on the condition that they would then place their cars at the service of the agencies they worked for resulted in some 20 000 workers and technicians obtaining vehicles.

Agricultural enterprises had been encouraged to produce food for their own workers' dining rooms. In many enterprises a surplus was produced and sold to workers at the subsidized ration book prices, some of which was later resold at the higher parallel market prices.

The number of special diets, supposedly issued for medical reasons and which provided the beneficiary with an increased quantity and variety of food, had reached as many as 1.2 million 'patients' out of a total population of 10.2 million in 1986.

Part III

Economic and Food Policy Reform in Nicaragua

Introduction

From the preceding discussion of the reform process in Mozambique, Vietnam and Cuba, it emerges that the shift from orthodoxy to reform occurred in the context of a crisis of the post-revolutionary state, which was associated with problems of surplus mobilization and appropriation, planning and hegemony. I have insisted throughout, however, that economic reforms were introduced in these countries not just because planners and leaders suddenly saw the errors of their ways or felt they had no alternative because of the state of the economy, public opinion or external pressures. Neither was it simply the case that 'moderates' came to dominate the 'hard-liners'. Rather, I have stressed the need to integrate in the analysis additional elements associated with developments at the level of civil society and the way in which different social groups were able to influence the policy process via forms of 'class struggle' or 'survival strategies' as well as institutionalized participation in decision-making processes.

Here in Part III I examine, in a more systematic and detailed manner, the process of economic and food policy reform in Nicaragua. This study follows the structure of the three previous chapters by (a) identifying the main features that characterized development policy during the pre-reform period; (b) describing the types of reforms that were introduced during the 1980s; and (c) analyzing the nature of the crisis which prompted a major shift in policy approach. Unlike the other case studies, however, an additional chapter is presented which focuses specifically on changes which occurred in the balance of social forces. Particular attention is paid to transformations in state–society relations and the forms and effectiveness of participation by different social groups in the policy process.

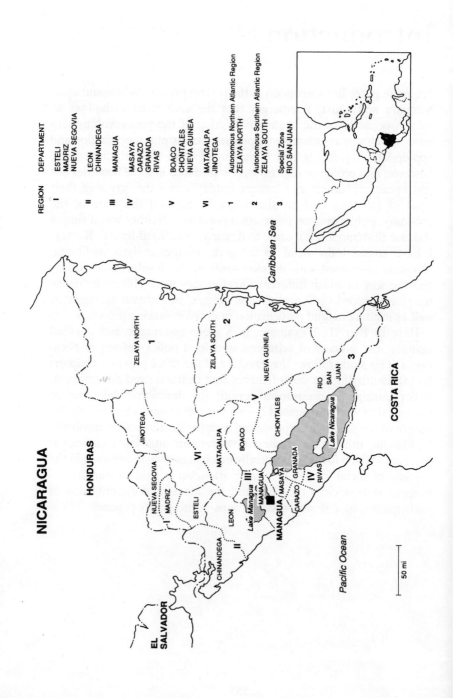

NICARAGUA

EL SALVADOR

HONDURAS

Caribbean Sea

ZELAYA NORTH

CHINANDEGA

NUEVA SEGOVIA

MADRIZ

ESTELI

JINOTEGA

LEON

MATAGALPA

Lake Managua

MANAGUA / MASAYA

MANAGUA

CARAZO

MASAYA

GRANADA

BOACO

CHONTALES

ZELAYA SOUTH

NUEVA GUINEA

RIO
SAN
JUAN

Lake Nicaragua

RIVAS

Pacific Ocean

COSTA RICA

50 mi

REGION	DEPARTMENT
I	ESTELI
	MADRIZ
	NUEVA SEGOVIA
II	LEON
	CHINANDEGA
III	MANAGUA
IV	MASAYA
	CARAZO
	GRANADA
	RIVAS
V	BOACO
	CHONTALES
	NUEVA GUINEA
VI	MATAGALPA
	JINOTEGA
1	Autonomous Northern Atlantic Region
	ZELAYA NORTH
2	Autonomous Southern Atlantic Region
	ZELAYA SOUTH
3	Special Zone
	RIO SAN JUAN

5 Post-Revolutionary Food and Development Policy

On seizing power in July 1979, the Sandinista government embarked on an ambitious reconstruction and development programme which sought to rebuild a war-torn economy, eradicate extreme poverty and transform an economic structure that concentrated resources in an agro-export sector controlled by a relatively small group of capitalist farming enterprises, agro-industrial processors, and finance and trading companies. The inherent logic of what has been called a 'repressive agro-export model' (IFAD, 1980) has been summed up by Fitzgerald in the following terms:

> Essentially, the model had been a dualistic one where the capitalist export sector generated the realised surplus and concentrated investment, serving also as the 'Department I' of the economy through exports to finance imported producer goods. . .[The] peasant sector was. . .doubly exploited: both as a source of cheap labour and as a supplier of cheap food. Reproduction of the labour force was thus achieved at a minimum cost and released a maximum of surplus as work intensity on the estates was kept high by various forms of coercion. Moreover, much of the surplus was strictly speaking differential rent generated at an international level by the fertility of Nicaraguan soils and its favourable geographic location. (Fitzgerald, 1985a, 209)

This interpretation over-simplifies somewhat certain structural features of the model which are relevant for the analysis which follows on crisis and reform. The classic dualist image of rural Latin America – a few *latifundistas* controlling the majority of the land and a vast mass of *minifundistas* eking out a living on small subsistence plots – does not depict accurately rural social structure in Nicaragua.

The peasantry was, in fact, a highly differentiated sector. Pressure on the land had been reduced through a number of historical processes – starting with the elimination of much of the indigenous population during the colonial period, and continuing in the twentieth century through migratory processes associated with agro-export development that opened up the large agrarian frontier and concentrated much of the population in the cities.

From the 1950s onwards, there emerged in Nicaragua a relatively large sector of middle and rich peasant producers with access to sizeable tracts of land, much of which was used for extensive cattle grazing in the interior regions of the country. Moreover, many peasant producers were producing not only labour and food, but also agro-export crops: 50 per cent in the case of coffee; 20 per cent of cotton.

What is important to note in this context is not only the presence of this middle sector in rural social structure but also that the pattern of resource allocation promoted by the *Somocista* state tended to constrain the process of social differentiation from peasant to capitalist producers by restricting the access of this group to vital resources such as credit, infrastructure and support services, as well as through the price system.

Another important feature of rural social structure related to the presence of an extremely large poor peasant or 'semi-proletarian' sector comprised of families which engaged in direct production on the land for a part of the year but which also worked as wage labourers for a number of months, often during the coffee and cotton harvests.

As indicated above, migratory processes also led to rapid urbanization. At the time of the revolution, nearly 30 per cent of the population lived in the city of Managua (CIERA, 1984e; Massey, 1987). From the middle of the twentieth century, the food system was increasingly shaped by the needs of the capital for large quantities of cheap food, as well as imported non-essential food products consumed by a growing middle-class sector. Much of the peasant population produced maize and beans not only for self-provisioning but also for the market. Cheap food for the urban masses was guaranteed via a highly exploitative set of social relations which left the mass of basic grain producers handing over part of their crops to merchants and landowners for little return.

During the 1960s and 1970s, a number of large capitalist producers, including the Somoza family, had also taken up intensive rice and sorghum production for the internal market. These and other agro-export producers, as well as local agro-industries, were highly dependent on Western markets for inputs and machinery. In 1970, approximately 60 per cent of total imports came from the OECD countries (36 per cent from the United States), while the Central American

Common Market accounted for a quarter of imports. Export markets were somewhat more diversified, with Western European countries purchasing nearly 30 per cent of all exports in 1977 (CIERA, 1981b, p. 22).

The agrarian and food problem facing the new revolutionary government centred on four main questions: firstly, how to reactivate production quickly on the large estates that had been abandoned and decapitalized by the *Somocistas*; secondly, how to proceed with a land redistribution and co-operativization programme that did not antagonize capitalist producers and rich peasants and did not starve the agro-export sector of harvest labour; thirdly, how to convert a relatively large sector of middle and rich peasant producers, historically deprived of essential resources, into a more dynamic sector; and fourthly, how to continue to supply urban areas with cheap food while trying at the same time to eliminate the highly exploitative exchange relations that had impoverished peasant producers.

BASIC DEVELOPMENT PRINCIPLES AND GOALS

Post-revolutionary development strategy sought to promote an integral process of socioeconomic change, involving major structural transformations affecting patterns of distribution of income, wealth and power; a rapid process of accumulation to expand the productive base of the economy and modernize agriculture; as well as a new pattern of insertion in the world economy. The basic principles underlying the new development strategy were those of mixed economy, the satisfaction of basic needs, participatory democracy, and autonomous and integrated development.[1]

The principle of 'mixed economy', as initially conceived, referred to an economy in which diverse forms of property coexisted but where the state enterprise sector – known as the Area of People's Property (APP) – was considered the 'engine of growth'; and where the central administrative apparatus was to intervene, in an attempt to regulate patterns of resource allocation and use in accordance with national priorities associated with the provision of basic needs, accumulation and defence.

The so-called 'reformed sector' of the economy, which included both the APP and co-operatives, was given priority in resource allocation controlled by the state. State intervention was exercised through direct control of the banking system, much of foreign trade and of numerous large-scale agricultural, mining, fishing, industrial, construction and service enterprises previously owned by the Somoza group. A comprehensive planning system was established. The Ministry of Planning (MIPLAN) elaborated annual economic plans which established production targets and guidelines governing the sectoral allocation of resources. Economic policies affecting prices, domestic marketing, credit, wages and conditions in the work-place were instrumental in regulating the economic activities of producers and merchants, and of transforming social relations of production; while development programmes associated with the agrarian reform and investment were intended to bring about major changes in social and economic structures.

Large sectors of the population soon became organized in a variety of 'mass organizations'; representing industrial workers (CST); agricultural labourers (ATC); women (AMNLAE); youth (JS19J); agricultural producers (UNAG); and urban neighbourhood dwellers (CDS). These organizations participated to varying degrees in the policy process. Such participation was fundamental to the notion of democracy in Nicaragua and gave the democratic process a dimension often absent from the political systems of many post-revolutionary societies. Participatory democracy entailed the active participation of the mass of the population in the tasks of economic, social and cultural development and change, as well as in activities associated with defence. As such a key feature of the post-revolutionary period was the repeated mobilization of thousands of people in campaigns to eradicate illiteracy; immunize children; promote adult education; harvest agro-export crops; grow food crops; and organize civil defence. These forms of popular participation were to be combined with many of the practices, rights and institutions associated with representative democracy, including a multi-party political system, periodic legislative and presidential elections, and freedom of association and expression.[2]

The notion of autonomous development expressed the nationalist character of the revolution and the struggle against the economic, geopolitical and cultural domination of the United States in Central America. What was central here was the need to modify the historical form of insertion in the world economy. This had left the national economy dependent on the export of just a handful of primary products and with an extremely narrow industrial base. It was also highly dependent on the United States' market or on US trans-nationals based in Central America. Transforming this pattern of insertion did not involve, as it did in Cuba, for example, overtly hostile actions towards United States' capital. There was little nationalization of foreign or US enterprises. Rather, attention was focused on strengthening economic and political ties with a broad range of OECD, socialist bloc and Third-World countries; developing new trade and aid relations involving concessionary credit lines, preferential prices, grants and barter; and embarking on an ambitious public investment programme to expand capacity in energy, agriculture and the industrial transformation of raw materials.

The principle of integrated development related to two key problems associated with dependency and underdevelopment in Nicaragua: firstly, the disarticulation of agriculture and industry, which manifested itself in the fact that the economy depended on the export of largely unprocessed raw materials, while the small industrial sector that existed was highly dependent on imported raw materials; and secondly, the isolation of the Atlantic Coast region (approximately half the country's land area) and its various ethnic populations, which were linked more to Caribbean and US markets than to the Central and Pacific regions of Nicaragua.

It was these principles that formed the basis of three programmes or sets of policies associated with food and agriculture that were to play a crucial role in the attempt to transform social relations of production; redistribute income; develop the productive forces; and reduce external vulnerability. The programmes/policies involved were those relating to agrarian reform, 'cheap food' policy and agro-industrial development.

AGRARIAN REFORM

The commitment of the Sandinistas to develop agriculture and transform the agrarian structure and social relations to benefit the peasantry and rural labourers was explicitly outlined as early as 1969 with the publication of the *Historical Programme of the FSLN* ten years before the overthrow of the Somoza regime. The document called for an immediate and massive 'land to the tiller' redistribution programme; the elimination of *latifundia*; an agricultural development plan to diversify and intensify peasant production; improved access of peasant producers to credit, technical assistance and markets; compensation for 'patriotic landowners' affected by the agrarian reform; the organization of peasant producers in co-operatives; the

abolition of informal debt; and the creation of improved employment
opportunities for the rural population, to overcome the problem of
seasonal unemployment (FER, 1972).

Many of these points shaped the broad agrarian reform programme initiated by the new revolutionary government in 1979.
Important differences in emphasis arose, however, regarding the
pace of redistribution and the relative importance assigned to different forms of property in resource allocation. Farms confiscated from
the Somoza group were generally retained as large-scale units dependent on salaried labour, with property rights and managerial control
passing to the state. The confiscation of some two thousand farms
enabled the state to take control of 1.2 million ha., or approximately
20 per cent of the total cultivable area (Nuñez O., 1987, p. 169). This
process saw the size of the large landowning sector (properties above
350 hectares) fall from 36 per cent to 18 per cent of the total
cultivable area, which amounted to an estimated 5.7 million ha.

In other sectors of the economy the extent of state control was
generally greater. The APP controlled 25 per cent of manufacturing
production, 70 per cent of construction, 95 per cent of mining, and 55
per cent of tertiary sector activities. In 1980, some 41 per cent of
GDP was accounted for by the state sector (MIPLAN, 1980). In
resource allocation, priority was clearly given to APP enterprises,
which were regarded as 'superior' forms of production.

The actual process of land redistribution to the peasantry started
relatively slowly. The first Agrarian Reform Law of 1981 established
generous limits (350 ha. in the Pacific region and 700 ha. elsewhere)
regarding how much land someone could own before being liable to
expropriation. Criteria for expropriation related to land that was
idle, underutilized or rented. Smaller limits (of 35 ha. in the Pacific
region and 70 ha. elsewhere) were established for land being exploited on the basis of pre-capitalist relations associated with share-
cropping and labour-service agreements. All land which had been
abandoned was liable to confiscation (Deere *et al.*, 1985; p. 33).
During 1981 and 1982 only one per cent of all land was actually
redistributed, to approximately eight thousand families. At the same
time, the area under state control increased from 20 to 23 per cent of
the total cultivable area (IHCA, 1985, p. 9c). Between 1981 and 1985
only 396 000 ha. (7 per cent of the total) had been expropriated or
confiscated from the private sector on the basis of the criteria contained in the law. Moreover, between 1981 and the end of 1984,

TABLE 5.1   *The land reform process*
A   *Changes in agrarian structure, 1978–84 (as percentages of total cultivable area)*

	1978	1981	1984
Private sector:	100	69	64
350 or more ha.	36	18	13
140–350 ha.	16	13	13
35–140 ha.	30	30	30
7–35 ha.	16	7	7
less than 7 ha.	2	1	1
Co-operative sector	0	11	17
Production co-operatives	0	1	7
Credit and service co-operatives	0	10	10
State sector	0	20	19
Total	100	100	100

B   *Land redistribution and legalization, 1981–84 (in 000s of hectares and peasant families)*

	Land-redistribution	Legalization[1]	Total
Area	478	944	1422
Beneficiaries	31.5	32.3	63.8

SOURCE   Ministry of Agricultural Development and Agrarian Reform.
[1]Refers to land titling and small areas of land incorporated under the Indigenous Communites Programme.

approximately two-thirds of the expropriated land was acquired by the state (Nuñez O., 1987, p. 171).

During 1983 and 1984 the land reform programme focused less on land redistribution and more on the question of property rights. Peasant producers who had never held title to the land they farmed were provided with security of tenure through an extensive titling programme. It can be seen in Table 5.1 that while some 63 000 peasant families had benefited from the government's land reform programme, only 31 000 families had actually received new lands by the end of 1984.

Of a total rural population of approximately 1.7 million in 1984 (some 240 000 families) there were an estimated 150 000 families

TABLE 5.2   *Rural class structure in Nicaragua, 1984 (as percentages of agricultural economically-active population)*

Social category	%
Agricultural bourgeoisie[1]	2
Middle and rich peasantry[2]	24
Co-operatives[3]	13
Poor peasantry and seasonal workers[4]	43
Permanent wage and salaried labour[5]	18
Total	100
Total rural population[6]	1.7 million
Total national population[6]	3.6 million

SOURCES   Based on CIERA, 1985b; Barraclough & Scott, 1987; Fitzgerald, 1987b.
[1] Refers to agricultural producers with over 200 manzanas (141 ha.)
[2] Refers to agricultural producers with less than 200 manzanas who do not sell their labour power to any significant degree.
[3] Refers to producer co-operatives (CAS) in which most land, means of production and profits are collectivized.
[4] This category includes persons who may have access to some land but whose livelihood depends primarily on the sale of labour power.
[5] Also included in this category are farm technicians and administrators.
[6] Population estimates presented here are based not on official statistics provided by the Nicaraguan Institute for Statistics and Censuses – INEC – which are based on projections of 1971 census data, but on a 1987 census carried out by the Ministry of Health. This data has been adjusted for 1984 on the basis of INEC demographic growth rate data of 3.3 per cent nationally and 2.5 per cent for the rural population.

which could be regarded as potential beneficiaries of the land redistribution programme (CIERA, 1985b).[3] This meant that the first five years of the post-revolutionary period had benefited approximately 21 per cent of the potential number of beneficiaries. Although poor peasants and seasonal labourers no longer constituted the majority of the agricultural economically active population,[4] Table 5.2 shows that this group still constituted the largest category in rural class structure in 1984, accounting for 43 per cent of the agricultural EAP.

In order to transform social relations and develop the productive forces in rural areas, the agrarian reform programme focused particularly on the provision of cheap credit as well as the organization of the peasantry, both at the level of co-operatives and trade union organization.

The credit system was radically transformed in two important respects. Firstly, the sectoral allocation of credit changed. Priority was given to agriculture and industry, or the so-called 'productive' sectors of the economy. Between 1977 and 1982, the share of total credit accounted for by agriculture increased from 36 to 48 per cent, while that of commerce and housing declined from 42 to just 9 per cent (CIERA, 1984a; p. 39). Secondly, the access of the peasantry to credit improved markedly, breaking the historical constraint of scarce and expensive credit for this social group (CIERA, 1986). Before the revolution (1977), only ten per cent of the agricultural/livestock bank loans went to small producers. In 1980 this figure had nearly trebled, to 27 per cent, reaching 31 per cent in 1985. The number of peasant families receiving bank credit increased from 28 000 before the revolution to an average of 86 000 between 1980 and 1983 (Enriquez and Spalding, 1986, pp. 113–14). In addition, preferential and highly subsidized rates were offered to small producers, particularly co-operatives, while the banks adopted a flexible attitude towards loan repayment, announcing in 1984 a moratorium on the repayment of much of the peasant debt accumulated during the early years of the revolution.

Access to cheap credit was a crucial mechanism for transforming the type of exploitative social relations that had characterized the *Somocista* development model. These had rendered the peasant producer extremely vulnerable to large landowners and merchants who lent money, often at usurious rates, and engaged in futures purchases of harvests at very low prices, or in share-cropping arrangements whereby certain means of production were provided in return for a considerable share of the harvest. The new credit system enabled many producers to bypass these types of relationship.

This period also saw the organization of much of the peasant population. The co-operative movement was virtually non-existent before the revolution. There were in 1978 an estimated 42 credit and service co-operatives, with 9270 members. By the end of 1982 over 2800 agricultural co-operatives of different types had been formed under the government's agrarian reform programme. Four years later, this sector controlled 21 per cent of the land, 35 per cent of production for the internal market, and 21 per cent of agro-export production (IHCA, 1987b, p. 15).

Some 76 000 families, or a third of all rural families, were organized in co-operatives, which were generally of two types: production co-operatives (CAS) – accounting for 45 per cent of land held by co-operatives – where most land, means of production and profits were collectivized and controlled by a board elected by the members; and credit and service co-operatives (CCS), where the land was worked on an individual basis but producers organized their credit requirements and occasionally certain other services on an associated basis.

Production co-operatives were assigned a high priority in resource allocation, and it was probably this social group that made the most significant advances in terms of levels of living. Increases in production, though, were less than expected – a fact which contributed to a major reassessment of state policy towards the co-operative movement in later years (Kaimowitz, 1988). As pointed out by the Minister of Agricultural Development and Agrarian Reform in his annual evaluation of the performance of the agricultural sector in 1986, the 'humanistic' content of the agrarian reform had exceeded the economic by overemphasizing 'hand-outs' of land and credit while neglecting aspects of economic organization related to the provision of essential goods and services, the use of family labour, and the training of co-operative members in basic administrative and accounting procedures, as well as investment (MIDINRA, 1987, pp. 17, 20).

A key feature of the immediate post-revolutionary period was the organization of both low-income rural and urban social groups at the national level and their participation in the policy process. As indicated earlier, organizations representing industrial workers and public employees, agricultural labourers, women, youth, and urban dwellers, expanded rapidly following the revolution. Initially, however, peasant producers had little direct representation. This situation changed abruptly in 1981 with the formation of the National Union of Farmers and Cattlemen (UNAG) which grew to incorporate more than half the country's agricultural producers and become one of the most powerful mass organizations. As we will see later, the UNAG emerged as an effective pressure group able to influence the policy process to benefit the mass of rural producers. The CDS, for its part (representing primarily urban neighbourhood dwellers), played a major role in both shaping and implementing policies which brought improved food security for much of the low-income population of the towns and cities.

CHEAP FOOD POLICY

The marketing and price system for basic grains and essential goods underwent several major transformations. Following the revolution, the government introduced a 'cheap food policy' intended to ensure that the mass of the population had easy and regular access to low-priced basic food products. Food pricing policy had three broad objectives: to correct the historical inequities of a marketing system that had left the peasant producer receiving minimal prices for produce sold to merchants; to minimize the adverse effects of major price fluctuations on both the small producer and the consumer; and to improve the access of the low-income consumer to basic food products through reduced prices.

There were seven major components to this policy.[5] Firstly, guaranteed producer prices, calculated on the basis of average production costs plus a stable mark-up, were set for most peasant (and agro-export) products, with the notable exception of perishables such as fruit, vegetables and plantain. Secondly, the state established an extensive procurement network, notably for basic grains and coffee. State procurement levels for peasant products increased rapidly following the reorganization, during late 1979, of the National Institute of Foreign and Domestic Trade (INCEI) as the Nicaraguan Basic Foodstuffs Company (ENABAS). Unlike its predecessor, which accounted for no more than 5 per cent of the national grain market, ENABAS intervened heavily in the local procurement, import, wholesaling and retail distribution of maize, beans, rice and sorghum, with the objective of not only guaranteeing 'fair' prices to producers, but also of ensuring that consumers enjoyed secure lines of supply at low prices (Saulniers, 1986; Deve and Grenier, 1984; MICOIN, 1983). Grains purchases increased from approximately 180 000 tonnes in 1980 to nearly 340 000 in 1983. Purchases of beans reached 28 000 tonnes in 1983, which was the equivalent of approximately half of national production and roughly 80 per cent of marketed production. In 1984, ENABAS purchased nearly 59 000 tonnes of maize, or 27 per cent of the national crop and roughly half of marketed production (ENABAS, 1984, 1985).

A third component of 'cheap food policy' consisted of large-scale food imports, the prices of which were kept low via an exchange rate which overvalued the córdoba in relation to the dollar. Food imports soared in 1980 and reached 131 million dollars in 1981, nearly 16 per cent of the value of total imports. Although reduced in subsequent

TABLE 5.3   *Trends in food imports, 1978–84 (in millions of US dollars)*

	1978	1980	1981	1982	1983	1984
1 Food imports	23.8	88.4	131.5	64.8	72.8	76.2
2 Total imports	593.9	887.2	999.4	775.5	806.9	826.3
1/2 %	8.3	14.1	15.6	10.8	9.9	11.1

SOURCE   Ministry of External Trade.

years, they still averaged around 10 per cent of total imports, and reached 24 per cent of the value of exports in 1984 (see Table 5.3).

Another feature that these figures conceal is the strict prioritization introduced, which favoured essential, as opposed to non-essential, food imports. Whereas before the revolution (1978), 48 per cent of all food imports consisted of basic food products, the latter accounted for 84 per cent of total food imports during the 1980–84 period (Utting, 1987, pp. 137–8). This prioritization formed part of a broader policy to restrict imports of non-essential items. Such a policy contributed to the dramatic fall in private consumption of 'non-essential' goods and services, which fell by 73 per cent between 1980 and 1985. Over the same period, private consumption of 'essential' goods and services fell by 17 per cent, although this was compensated to some degree by an increase in public consumption (socialized services), which more than doubled (see Table 7.12 on page 222).

Fourthly, a planned distribution system was implemented which established family and/or regional quotas for essential food products such as grains, sugar, vegetable oil, flour and salt. Two additional features of cheap food policy consisted of official retail prices which were set for many basic products, and food subsidies. Retail prices for grains were generally set below producer prices. Moreover, the gap between the two gradually widened. Between 1980 and 1983 there were periodic increases in official producer prices while retail prices for most subsidized products remained frozen. Subsidies on basic grains, milk and sugar, increased throughout the early 1980s, and in 1984 accounted for 6.3 per cent of total government expenditure, or 3.7 per cent of GDP (Utting, 1985).

While, in practice, the sale of subsidized food products tended to be concentrated in urban areas, subsidy policy assumed a fairly non-discriminatory character. There was no intention to target, for example, the working class or the very poor. Certain social programmes, however, did assist specific social groups, either by providing subsidized meals in the workplace or by donating a specific quantity of food products to nutritionally vulnerable families. By 1984, nearly 2000 work-place cafeterias were providing subsidized meals in state enterprises and institutions as well as in some private establishments (Collins, 1985, p. 217). Various state institutions, including the Ministries of Health (MINSA) and Education (MED), the Social Welfare Institute (INSSBI) and the Nicaraguan Food Programme (PAN) operated nutritional programmes (Utting, 1987, p. 144).

Finally, the state distributed products through an extensive network of state and private retail outlets selling at official prices. The state experimented with a variety of retail systems. Initially, attention focused on a network of state-run 'people's shops' (*tiendas populares*) located in the urban neighbourhoods, or *barrios*, work-place commissaries, and small outlets operated by the local residents' organizations (CDS). By 1982, however, it was apparent that the state could not directly operate a highly decentralized marketing system, and that a more effective alternative would be one based on the traditional privately-owned neighbourhood retail outlet – the *pulperia* – which enjoyed a number of advantages associated with infrastructure, marketing experience and cultural integration with the local community. An increasing number of *pulperias*, while retaining their private status, were transformed into 'people's stores' (*expendios populares*) that sold ENABAS-supplied goods at official prices. Although profit margins on these goods were very low, this system provided store owners with a large fixed clientele that had to buy at a particular store in order to acquire the products sold on the quota system. The retailer could then sell other goods, the prices of which were not regulated to these consumers. In 1984 this network expanded considerably and by the end of the year some 6000 outlets were operating throughout the country (Ibid., p. 144).

As will be analyzed in more detail later, policies and programmes associated with the distribution of basic goods tended to be more effective in urban areas. There was during this period, however, the establishment of an extensive network of state stores selling agricultural inputs and implements in rural areas.

AGRICULTURAL MODERNIZATION AND AGROINDUSTRIALIZATION

By 1981, the Sandinista government had embarked on an ambitious investment programme centred on agriculture and agroindustry; the development of economic infrastructure; notably, roads, port facilities, and geothermal and hydroelectric energy stations; as well as social infrastructure. The fixed investment–GDP ratio increased from an annual average of 16.3 per cent during 1970–78 to 19.3 per cent between 1981–85 (SPP, see Fitzgerald, 1988b). Between 1980 and 1985 the share of agricultural and agroindustrial investments in the public investment programme increased from 12 to 50 per cent. The quantitative increase in agricultural investment was reflected in the rise in the value of imported capital goods for agriculture, which increased from an annual average of 10.4 million dollars between 1970 and 1978 to 54 million a year between 1980 and 1984. The emphasis placed on investment in general and agriculture in particular becomes apparent when viewed in the regional context. The early 1980s saw most countries in the region reducing levels of investment in agriculture. In Guatemala and Costa Rica, for example, imports of capital goods for agriculture fell from approximately 36 million to 12 million dollars between 1978 and 1982, whereas in Nicaragua they increased from 13 million to 45 million dollars (CIERA, 1986).

By the mid-1980s, the agricultural and agro-industrial investment programme centred on 38 large-scale projects (Wheelock, 1985, p. 129), associated primarily with sugar, intensive dairy production, vegetable and fruit processing, oil-seed plantations and processing, tobacco cultivation, and irrigated basic grains production. Several large integrated rural development projects, involving peasant and co-operative producers, were also implemented in more marginal areas of the country (CIERA, 1984a).

The industrial transformation of the country's natural resources into products with a higher value-added than traditional semi-processed agro-exports, and which substituted imports, was the basis of the growth strategy. As indicated by the Minister of Agricultural Development and Agrarian Reform:

> in the future, Nicaragua should cease to export raw materials but rather sell them in a semi-processed or processed form. Neither should we have 'final touch' (*toque final*) industries. Therefore, we have to install industries to process our raw materials. That, we

consider, should be the basis of our economic development. As a consequence, agriculture constitutes the central pivot in this stage of development. (Wheelock, 1985, p. 50 – author's translation)

A medium- and long-term development plan drawn up through 1982/83 (entitled *Marco Estrategico de Desarrollo Agropecuario* – MEDA) emphasized the need to industrialize not just products associated with agriculture but also those derived from other primary activities, such as fishing, forestry and mining (MIDINRA, 1983). The geographical location of the war, however, imposed a serious constraint on the development of these sectors. With regard to agricultural production, the plan prioritized investment in capital-intensive enterprises, where it was considered that quick returns in terms of output per hectare (or head of cattle) could be achieved. When discussing the technological choices the government faced to develop the cattle sector and deal with the historical problems of low yields and levels of consumption, Minister of Agriculture Wheelock stated:

we had two choices: work with a herd of two million head. . .which are dispersed anarchically all over the place (and often in the hands of those who are not responsive to new and different techniques. . .). This would mean the country would have to become involved in a campaign on a scale similar to that of the Literacy Crusade so that these producers might produce an extra half litre. . .or we opt for intensive methods, which while not substituting the former completely, will enable us. . .to produce in ten years an additional fifty million litres. (Wheelock, 1985, p. 59 – author's translation.)

The development strategy formulated for agriculture stressed also the need to reorder the geographical location of crop and livestock production in accordance with conditions associated with soils, water and climate. This meant concentrating livestock production in the hilly areas of the interior of the country and annual crops such as cotton and grains in the fertile Pacific coastal region. The introduction of sophisticated irrigation systems on a massive scale was proposed, not only to increase yields but also to enable the dry Pacific region to be used all year round to produce both food and export crops. In the large Atlantic Coast region, agricultural development would focus on permanent and perennial crops such as African palm, coconut, rubber, cocoa, plantains and root crops (MIDINRA, 1983).

In addition to the scale of the public investment programme in general and its emphasis on large-scale capital intensive projects associated with food and agro-export production, agro-industry and economic infrastructure, there were two other features of the accumulation process that should be mentioned. These are pertinent to the discussion which follows regarding the nature of the crisis which beset the Nicaraguan economy from 1983 onwards. Firstly, many projects were slow-yielding, often taking between five and ten years before coming on stream. Secondly, investment tended to be concentrated not only on a sectoral basis but also institutionally and geographically, in the state sector and the Pacific coastal region, respectively.

Certain features described above, notably the prioritization of the state sector and the emphasis on accumulation, have led several writers to employ the label 'state-centred accumulation' to describe the development model which emerged in Nicaragua during the first half of the 1980s (Irvin, 1983; Kaimowitz, 1988). Such a label conceals the extent to which government strategy also emphasized programmes associated with social development and food security. This broad basic-needs approach, however, was also characterized by some imbalances, in that certain policies and programmes associated, for example, with consumer subsidies and food rationing, tended to favour the urban population. In this respect not only 'state-centred accumulation' but also 'urban-centred consumption' was an important feature of the early post-revolutionary development model.

Notes

1. These ideas regarding basic development principles were originally outlined by the author in a paper prepared jointly with Solon Barraclough entitled 'Transition and Development in Nicaragua: Promise, Reality and Prospects', which was prepared in 1987 for a United Nations University project on alternative development experiences in the Third World.
2. Following the escalation of the war and the imposition of a State of Emergency in 1981, rights associated with freedom of expression were restricted.
3. Estimates presented here of the size of the rural population are based on a census of rural (and urban) households undertaken by the Ministry of Health in 1987. Figures have been adjusted for 1984, applying the demographic growth rate for the rural population used by the official statistics office (INEC).

4. A 1981 CIERA study (CIERA, 1981a) estimated that these groups accounted for 53 per cent of the economically-active agricultural population in 1978.
5. These components of 'cheap food policy' have been outlined by the author in Utting, 1987.

6 Economic and Food Policy Reforms

Development strategy in Nicaragua underwent several important changes during the mid-1980s which were to have far-reaching economic, political and social implications. Less emphasis was placed on 'development', 'growth' and 'modernization'. Rather, the government stressed the need to create a 'survival economy' geared towards defence and the production and provision of basic goods. This involved not only important changes in the structure of resource allocation but also in the composition of the dominant alliance; more specifically in relations between the state, on the one hand, and the peasantry and the ethnic groups of the Atlantic Coast on the other – relations which had become increasingly strained. Neither was the emphasis any longer on the rapid elimination of poverty and improvements in levels of living of the population in general. Instead, attention shifted towards defending the levels of living of *specific* social groups.

While the first significant policy changes were introduced in 1984 (on the basis of guidelines drawn up in late 1983), it was not until February 1985 that a comprehensive package of reform measures was announced. These were designed to contain growing macroeconomic disequilibria; boost agricultural production; curb parallel trading activities and the rapid growth of the urban 'informal' sector; and protect the levels of living of workers and peasants. Specific measures included a reduction in consumer subsidies; a freeze on government employment and expenditure levels in certain areas; the introduction of tighter controls on levels of public investment and the types of projects implemented; a 64 per cent devaluation of the córdoba (from 10 to 28 to the US dollar); significant increases in agricultural producer prices; productivity incentives for industrial and agricultural workers; considerable wage rises for the working-class and state sector employees; the imposition of a number of controls on informal sector trading; and new taxes on merchants and self-employed professionals (Pizarro, 1987; CIERA, 1984b; Avendaño, 1988).

DEALING WITH THE PEASANT QUESTION

To achieve the twin objectives of increasing food production and strengthening the dominant class alliance it was crucial to resolve the so-called peasant question. When analyzing the nature of the latter in Nicaragua and the response of the state, it would seem useful to identify two sets of problems. The first related to the peasantry in the war zones and the more isolated areas of the country. The second concerned peasant households (including co-operative members), whose reproduction was highly dependent on commodity relations. Somewhat different approaches were adopted to deal with these two situations.

The problem of the peasantry in the interior of the country where the war was being waged could not be tackled by economic policy reforms alone but required a far more integrated approach. In mid-1985 a special plan was drawn up to deal specifically with the peasant question in the two northern interior regions of the country (Regions I and VI) where much of the peasant population was located and which at that time were the main theatres of war.

The importance which the Sandinistas attached to resolving the peasant problem in these regions was reflected in a decision to assign on a full-time basis one member of the party's nine-man National Directorate to oversee the formulation of the plan. The latter contained seven specific objectives:[1]

1. To satisfy the increasing demands of the poor peasantry for land.
2. To improve the supply and distribution of agricultural inputs, work implements and certain basic consumption goods to rural areas.
3. To transform the role of state agricultural enterprises from entities that competed for resources with other local producers to agents that provided services to stimulate production.
4. To reorganize procurement and distribution networks by expanding the role of the state in wholesale activities and encouraging greater participation of private agents in retail activities.
5. To improve the transportation system to facilitate the movement of people and goods.
6. To resettle populations affected by the war.
7. To reorganize defence activities on a territorial basis in order to increase the capacity of each locality to defend itself.

TABLE 6.1   *Land redistribution in Nicaragua, 1981–86 (area in 000s of hectares)*

Beneficiary	Oct. 1981–1982	1983	1984	1985	1986	Total
Co-operatives	78.2	189.8	173.4	127.3	139.8	708.5
Individuals	16.4	9.2	11.1	100.7	97.5	234.9
Total	94.6	199.0	184.5	228.0	237.3	943.4
No. of Beneficiaries*	9 141	9 962	12 384	15 470	15 741	62 698

SOURCE   Ministry of Agricultural Development and Agrarian Reform.
* No. of families receiving new lands.

Considerable emphasis was placed on accelerating the agrarian reform programme, particularly in the northern-interior departments of Matagalpa and Jinotega, where land redistribution had been slow. By mid-1985 it was estimated that 40 per cent of the peasantry in that region still encountered serious problems of land (Carrion L., *Barricada*, 10 July 1985). At the national level, the number of families receiving new lands increased from an annual average of 10 000 between 1982 and 1984, to 15 600 in 1985 and 1986. Particularly important was the new emphasis on redistribution to individual producers and not just production co-operatives. The amount of land distributed to individual families increased from an annual average of approximately 11 000 ha. between 1982 and 1984 to 99 000 ha. in 1985 and 1986.

As indicated in Table 6.1, between 1984 and 1986 the number of families receiving new lands doubled, from 31 000 to 62 000. By the end of 1986 nearly a million hectares (of a total agricultural area of 5.6 million hectares) had been redistributed to the peasantry.

In order to accelerate the redistribution process it was necessary to amend the 1981 Agrarian Reform Law. The revised law of January 1986 expanded the potential pool of land available for redistribution by effectively eliminating the exemption clauses that had permitted inefficient landowners to retain large areas of land. In practice, however, large private landowners were not significantly affected by the new law. Both in the interests of national unity and in response to a redefinition of the role of the state sector in the economy (discussed below), particular emphasis was placed on the redistribution of farming land controlled by state enterprises. As lands were handed over to co-operatives and individual peasant families, the size of the state farm sector decreased from 1.2 million ha. in 1983 to 761 000 ha. by the end of 1986; that is, from 20 to 13 per cent of the total agricultural area.

To treat the problem of the peasantry dependent on commodity relations, more specific policy changes were required. These attempted to correct a number of planning imbalances, indicated above, that had characterized development strategy during the early 1980s, and which had restricted the access of the peasantry to goods, services and infrastructure.

ALTERING THE DOMESTIC TERMS OF TRADE

Measures were introduced which intended to shift the terms of trade in favour of agricultural producers. Particularly important were changes in pricing policy, which sought to alter the relative prices of basic grains and manufactures that had deteriorated between 1980 and 1984 from the point of view of the peasant producer (see Table 6.2).

Large increases in official producer prices were announced in early May 1984 and again the following year. Data presented in Table 6.3 indicate an improvement in the terms of trade from the point of view of the peasant producer during the 1984–85 agricultural cycle. The above figures, however, probably overstate the benefits to the peasantry, since they are based on prices for manufactures in urban areas, which are generally lower than in the countryside. During 1984 and 1985 the access of the peasantry to such goods was still restricted.

It was probably not until 1986 that a more significant change in relative prices occurred. This was possible both because of substantial increases in the price of beans and maize (official prices rose by approximately 450 and 750 per cent respectively, that year), and the increased supply of manufactures to rural areas through outlets which sold at regulated prices (CIERA and DGRA, 1987).

Table 6.3 indicates that producer price increases for maize, beans and milk during the 1985–87 period were more than double those of certain basic manufactured products. This situation contrasted sharply with that of the previous period (1978–85) when price increases for articles such as clothing far outstripped those of food.

The above calculations are based on official producer prices for beans and maize, which by 1986 tended to be fixed midway between

TABLE 6.2 *Evolution of agricultural price index and terms of trade,*
1980–87

	1980–81	1981–82	1982–83	1983–84	1984–85	1985–86	1986–87
Official producer prices							
Domestic consumption	100	108	131	167	543	1526	4662
Export products	100	105	124	150	270	1099	2541
All agriculture	100	106	127	156	367	1251	3292
	1980	*1981*	*1982*	*1983*	*1984*	*1985*	*1986*
Domestic terms of trade[1]	100	84	83	88	154	186	162
Real export prices[2]	100	107	102	110	109	149	105

SOURCE SPP, INEC (see Fitzgerald, 1988b, Table 8.11).
[1] Agricultural producer prices for food deflated by the urban price index for clothing and household goods and services.
[2] Agricultural producer prices for exports deflated by the GDP deflator.

TABLE 6.3 *Evolution of relative prices: agricultural products versus basic*
manufactures, 1978–87

Product	Unit	Price (córdobas)[1]			Increase[3]		Maize equiv. (lb)[4]		
		1978	*1985*	*1987*	*1978/85*	*85/87*	*1978*	*1985*	*1987*
Maize	quin.[2]	45	1 000	50 000	22	50	n.a.	n.a.	n.a.
Beans	"	110	2 300	85 000	21	37	n.a.	n.a.	n.a.
Milk	gal.	5.8	162.5	6 500	28	40	n.a.	n.a.	n.a.
Machete	1	22	400	8 000	18	20	49	40	16
Rubber boots	pr.	18	500	7 700	28	15	40	50	15
Shirt	1	22	2 300	35 000	105	15	49	230	70
Trousers	pr.	10	1 400	19 000	140	14	22	140	38

SOURCE Based on data from the Centre for Research and Studies of the Agrarian Reform (CIERA).
[1] Prices of food products correspond to official producer prices; prices of manufactures correspond to retail prices.
[2] 1 quintal = 100 lb.
[3] Number of times prices increased over the period indicated.
[4] Value of manufactured item expressed in pounds of maize.

officially-calculated costs of production and the open market price (see Table 6.4). As such, the positive movement of the terms of trade was generally greater for those producers which sold a larger proportion of their produce on the open market.

TABLE 6.4   *Maize and beans: costs of production, official and open market prices, 1986 (córdobas/quintal)*

Product	Costs of production	ENABAS price	Open market
Maize	1 700*	8 360**	15 000**
Beans	6 632*	15 855**	35 000**

SOURCE   CIERA/DGRA, 1987.
* Refers to costs associated with the use of intermediate technology.
** Prices correspond to late 1986 harvest period (*postrera*).

LIBERALIZING TRADE

Trade in basic grains was partially liberalized for the 1985/86 agricultural cycle, enabling private merchants to buy grain, normally at around double the price paid by ENABAS (see Table 6.4). The 'free trade' measure was first applied in the three interior regions of the country, where the dispersed character of grain production, the extremely poor state of both the ENABAS fleet and roads as well as war conditions, had prevented the marketing board from organizing an effective procurement system.

This marked the beginning of a new principle that would guide government policies regarding the procurement and distribution of essential goods. Rather than attempting to control the marketing and distribution of all essential products, the state would only intervene in the case of those products where experience had shown that effective control could be achieved. This meant, first and foremost, in those product sectors where production was concentrated in relatively few enterprises. The free trade measure was subsequently extended to other regions although very different interpretations as to what 'free trade' actually meant could be found at the regional level.[2]

The inability of ENABAS to compete with private merchants led the state marketing agency not only to announce significant price increases, but also to offer producers who turned up to sell grain at the agency's procurement depots the possibility of buying cheap manufactures. Regional governments were also free for the first time to set their own official producer prices in response to local costs of production and market conditions. Ministry officials, in unison with UNAG, mounted community, municipal and regional assemblies to encourage producers to continue to sell a significant proportion of their surplus grain to ENABAS, stressing the need to supply grain to the army and the harvest workers. Producers were also encouraged to retain the quantities they needed to cover the self-provisioning requirements of the household in what related to food, animal feed and seed.

During 1985 and 1986 the government sought to restrict the activities of private merchants through a series of controls. In the major cities, particularly Managua, the Ministry of Internal Trade reduced the size of some market-places and closed a number of others. Licences were issued to a certain number of traders and periodic police operations sought to remove illegal vendors from the main market-places. By 1987, some 40 000 traders or trading establishments, of a national total estimated to be in the region of 130 000, had been issued with licences (Cabrales, 1987).

In an attempt to promote regional self-sufficiency and stem the flow of grains and other food products from the interior of the country to cities like Managua, roadside control posts were set up to restrict the interregional movement of grain by merchants or producers. Given, however, the unpopularity of this measure (even ordinary travellers on intercity buses sometimes had certain provisions confiscated), and the difficulty of actually controlling interregional flows outside official marketing channels, these controls were eliminated in April 1987.

During that same year, the government adopted a new approach for dealing with intermediaries and informal sector traders (Ibid.). Instead of attempting to suppress the activities of these agents, the government sought to integrate them into the 'formal' economy. Licences were to be issued to another 40 000 traders. This meant they would contribute to state revenues through both licence fees and taxes. Regional governments sought to work with licensed merchants to organize the procurement of basic grains. In some regions, merchants were assigned specific procurement areas, notably those where the state marketing agency ENABAS had a limited presence. These merchants were encouraged to sell directly to retail outlets so as to reduce the number of links in the commercial chain.

Rather than attempting to control all trade, government strategy stressed the need to intervene selectively in the principal sites of accumulation of commercial capital, notably the import trade and wholesale activities. Intervention in the retail trade was limited primarily to direct control of a network of supermarkets, which expanded rapidly from the mid-1980s to number thirty-six in 1987 (Ibid.).

FROM BASIC NEEDS TO SELECTIVE PROVISIONING

Attempts to control macroeconomic disequilibria which undermined planning, as well as to channel more resources towards the peasantry, involved a significant change in the broad basic-needs approach that had characterized early development strategy and which tended to identify the 'popular sectors' in general as the intended beneficiaries of government basic-needs-related programmes. From the mid-1980s onwards, the army and the so-called 'productive sectors' (namely the working class and agricultural producers) were identified as priority groups. State employees were placed at an intermediate level in the scale of priorities, while the urban informal sector was relegated to last place. As President Ortega said, when outlining the 1986 Economic Plan:

The decision to favour the salaried sector as opposed to the informal sector, combined with the priority given to the countryside [over the city], inevitably implies a significant reduction in the standard of living of that half of the urban population outside of the formal sector. (Ortega, 1986, p. 12)

Particularly important in this process were a series of measures affecting the distribution of basic goods. In 1984, measures were implemented to reduce the quotas of basic products assigned to some of the more 'urbanized' regions of the country, notably Managua (Region III), in order to increase allocations to regions in the interior of the country, particularly the war zones (CIERA, 1986). To take one example, the quantity of powdered milk assigned to the region of Managua was reduced by a third in 1984 (CIERA, 1984b). The government radically reduced its commitment to supply the mass of the urban population with a wide range of essential consumer products. As the Minister of Internal Trade explained in 1987:

In 1982 we stated that we would acquire as many goods as possible to supply the people. In 1983–84 we talked of something in the region of 50 products; by mid-1984 we said the [consumer] basket would be reduced to 25 products but on analyzing the situation we reduced it to 17. Again it was revised and reduced to 8. Then we ended up with five and now we are guaranteeing 2 [products]. (Cabrales, 1987, p. 4)

Between 1985 and 1987, the government attempted to supply the national network of official price stores (*expendios populares*) with five basic products: sugar, vegetable oil, rice, soap and salt. It could not, however, guarantee regular or sufficient supplies.

The supply of so-called 'peasant (consumer) goods' increased significantly during this period. Through the Peasant Supply Programme, the Ministries of Agricultural Development and Agrarian Reform (MIDINRA) and of Internal Trade (MICOIN) gave priority to the supply of thirty-eight basic means of production and consumption goods to rural areas. The latter included batteries, maize grinders (to make maize meal for *tortillas*), kerosene lamps, torches, lighters, matches, razor blades, cotton thread, sewing needles, machetes, files, cloth and rubber boots (INIES/SPP, 1987, p. 128). The number of privately-owned rural retail outlets working within the MICOIN system was expanded, notably in the main cattle-producing region (Region V) where approximately 120 such stores were operating by the end of 1987 (DGFCDC, 1988c).

Concern about the state's limited capacity to supply rural areas prompted the UNAG to involve itself directly in the task of supplying the countryside (Barraclough *et al.*, 1988, pp. 109–13). This process began in 1984, when an emergency programme supported by the Swedish government and NGO aid, was implemented in Region VI where much of the peasant population had been affected by the war. In 1985 the 'temporary' programme was extended to Region V, and in the following year the decision was taken to establish a permanent network of peasant stores (*tiendas campesinas*). With increased external support, the network of co-operative retail outlets extended to 183 by the end of 1987 while another 34 outlets were supplied by the UNAG company ECODEPA. An estimated 65 000 peasant families, located primarily in areas of the interior of the country affected by the war, benefited from this project (Serra, 1988, p. 33).

The differential impact of these measures on urban and rural groups was confirmed through a series of personal interviews with leaders of the major mass organizations. Whereas the rural-based UNAG and ATC claimed that the situation regarding the supply of certain basic goods had generally improved, notably during the latter

half of 1986, leaders of the CDS in particular, but also the CST, complained of shortages.[3]
As one UNAG representative explained:

> In relation to other years, considerable advances were achieved in 1986 in the supply of production inputs. The supply of basic consumer goods also improved. The state is now importing the traditional products we need – like shovels, hammers, etc.. Also these products are now arriving directly to the producer, without middlemen, and this helps reduce the flow of products to the speculative market. (Gustavo Toruño, UNAG)

According to the head of the ATC:

> In 1985 and the first half of 1986 the supply of food and other goods to the workers' canteens and shops was restricted. Towards the end of the year, however, the supply of food and other products like clothing, footwear, and basic household products improved. (Edgardo Garcia, ATC)

These comments contrast sharply with the evaluation of the CDS:

> In a meeting held not long ago we reached the conclusion that the standard of living of the urban population had deteriorated during 1986. The prices of basic products had shot up and supplies to the workplace canteens were reduced. While the territorial distribution network now works reasonably well, the variety and quantity of products supplied through these outlets are too restricted. (Ronald Paredes, CDS)

According to the CST:

> Although the concept of worker prioritization existed, this was not put into practice in 1986. The worker canteens, for example, were poorly supplied. In 1987 efforts have been made to correct this situation. (Ronald Membreño, CST)

From 1985 onwards, an increasing number of the state-controlled supermarkets were converted into 'workers' supply centres' (*centros de abastecimiento de los trabajadores* – CATs) to which only the families of 'formal sector' workers and state functionaries had access. An agreement signed by the Ministry of Internal Trade and the main industrial trade union conferation, the CST, obliged the former to supply these outlets with sixteen basic manufactured products. In 1986, the terms of this agreement were modified somewhat, when only workers and state functionaries, and not their families, had the right to a specific quota of these goods, and at the same time industrial and agricultural workers were given priority over others (INIES/SPP, 1987, p. 123). These categories were abolished, however, the following year.

In 1987, attention shifted away from attempting to guarantee the supply of essential goods, towards controlling the distribution of a group of fifty-four products, the importation, production and distribution of which was largely in the hands of state enterprises. This group of products, however, included many non-essential items. Price movements of these products were monitored closely and used as a basis for negotiating wage rises.

Subsidies on basic products which had benefited primarily the urban population were also reduced. In mid-1984 it was announced that the price differential on basic grains (official retail prices having been below producer prices) would be eliminated. The government continued, however, to subsidize ENABAS's administrative and operational costs. Further reductions in food subsidies were included in the February 1985 package of reforms, when it was also announced that they would eventually be eliminated. The change in subsidy policy, combined with the devaluation of the córdoba, plus the increase in official producer prices, contributed to an increase of 362 per cent in the retail price index of a basic consumer basket of twelve food and three non-food products between May 1984 and May 1985.

The government was unable to eliminate food subsidies altogether. The milk subsidy, for example, experienced a fourfold increase in 1986 in current terms. What did change, however, was the way in which subsidies were financed. Instead of relying exclusively on direct budgetary transfers, subsidies were financed from the extraordinary profits obtained in state commercial enterprises, from the sale of certain basic products (such as rice and sugar) at high prices on the official 'parallel' market, or of certain luxury items such as electrical appliances (Cabrales, 1987, p. 5).

ALTERING THE ACCUMULATION–CONSUMPTION BALANCE

Liberating resources for peasant production also required altering the accumulation–consumption balance in favour of the latter. At the end of 1984, stricter priorities were established for investment projects. From 1985 to 1987 the number of new projects initiated each year was progressively reduced and an attempt was made to rationalize ongoing investment projects. Several projects in non-priority areas were delayed or postponed. Rather than expanding capacity, the emphasis shifted to using existing capacity more effectively, with particular attention being paid to repair and maintenance.

To achieve significant reductions in the level of investment, however, was difficult, given both the economic and social costs involved in halting numerous large-scale projects that were already at a reasonably advanced stage, and the strength of interests behind such projects. These included, for example, technocratic elements within the central state apparatus which favoured rapid modernization; local government and party leaders concerned with regional development; and foreign donors providing development assistance for large-scale projects. While the 1986 Plan had intended to reduce the fixed investment/GDP ratio from 19 per cent to 15 per cent, the real figure was 18 per cent (see Table 6.5).

During this period there was also a shift in the composition of imports, away from investment goods and towards so-called 'operational' resources, namely inputs, raw materials, spare parts and consumption goods (Barraclough *et al.*, 1988, p. 64). The 1987 Economic Plan set the goal of reducing the share of investment goods to just 19 per cent of total imports (INIES/SPP, 1987) in comparison with over 40 per cent during the early 1980s. By mid-1987 it was apparent, however, that the accumulation/consumption balance was still too heavily weighted in favour of the former. This was made clear by the President when he announced a series of midyear adjustments to the 1987 Plan:

The investment programme will be subject to a more drastic rationalization in order to guarantee that resources are available for agro-export, food and basic goods production, as well as to maintain health services and programmes to attend the war victims (Ortega, *Barricada*, 7 June 1987).

TABLE 6.5   *Fixed investment, 1980–86 (in millions of córdobas at 1980 prices)*

	1980	1981	1982	1983	1984	1985	1986
Fixed investment (FI)	3032	4854	3920	4104	4194	4241	3983
FI/GDP (%)	14.5	22.2	18.0	18.0	18.7	19.8	18.7

SOURCE   SPP.

REDEFINING 'MIXED ECONOMY'

A key feature of the mid-1980s reforms were a series of measures that aimed at redefining the way in which the 'mixed economy' operated in Nicaragua. These measures attempted to correct the type of planning imbalance, identified earlier, that had prioritized state-sector enterprises in the allocation of production inputs and investment goods.

A new role for the APP enterprises was proposed which implied a different form of articulation of the various property sectors engaged in agriculture. The process of redefining the role of the state enterprises began in earnest in 1985 and continued throughout 1986 and 1987, when a number of pilot projects were implemented in different regions. According to this new conception, the key concern of the APP would not rest solely with the growth of production in state agricultural and agro-industrial enterprises but rather with what was referred to as the 'territorial organization of production and exchange' (OTPI), that is, with the growth of production of the major property forms that existed in the territory where the enterprise was located (MIDINRA, 1986).

State enterprises attempted to stimulate production in a given territory by improving the distribution of inputs, capital goods, certain consumer products and technical assistance, as well as marketing, repair and maintenance services among the different types of producers, be they co-operatives, capitalist enterprises, state farms or individual peasant producers. Through measures such as these, an attempt was made to incorporate the different forms of property more effectively in the development process and to rearticulate production and marketing circuits that had been disrupted for a variety of reasons which are analyzed below. By centralizing these activities at the level of the state enterprise, the government also sought to overcome problems which had been caused by the dispersion of agricultural support services among numerous state institutions and agencies. Increased emphasis was also placed on the incorporation of co-operatives and private producers in the public investment programme.

ECONOMIC STABILIZATION AND ADJUSTMENT: 1988 AND 1989[4]

While the reforms of the mid-1980s served to increase basic food production, serious problems continued to afflict the economy. Agricultural exports declined from $316 million to $230 million between 1984 and 1987, while total export revenues remained below the $300 million mark. Levels of external development assistance fell sharply in 1986 and 1987 and sources of Western aid virtually dried up. The war effort continued to sap the economy of vital human and material resources. Official estimates indicated that the direct economic cost of the war had increased to $1.8 billion in 1987[5] (INEC, 1989, p. 58). Government price controls and a highly overvalued córdoba led to major distortions in relative prices, large foreign exchange losses, microeconomic inefficiency and waste, and the ongoing proliferation of black market activities. The distortion in the exchange rate was such that by January 1988 the official rate was 70 córdobas to the US dollar, while the black market rate was 60 000. Inflation continued to increase and reached 1347 per cent in 1987.

To contend with this situation the government introduced a series of radical stabilization and adjustment measures during 1988 and 1989. Attempts to regulate the economy through selective policy interventions and administrative controls, such as guaranteed prices, differential exchange rates, centralized allocations of foreign exchange and the rationing of basic products, gave way to the use of more traditional macroeconomic policy instruments and the reestablishment of market mechanisms to determine patterns of resource allocation (Arana, 1988, 1990; Fitzgerald, 1989).

Briefly, the major economic policy measures adopted during 1988 and 1989 are summarized below (from Arana, 1990; CIERA, (ed) 1988; Gutiérrez R., 1989; Stahler-Sholk, 1990; Stahler-Sholk and Spoor, 1989; Utting, 1990b). In February 1988 a new currency was introduced which resulted in a 20 per cent reduction of the money supply. At the same time the national currency was devalued by 99 per cent[6] in relation to the US dollar and the system of differential exchange rates was abolished. A tighter credit policy was also introduced by reducing the credit ceiling, particularly on long-term credit. In an attempt to reduce budgetary outlays by 10 per cent, the state administrative apparatus was rationalized. A number of government departments and ministries were absorbed by other agencies and several thousand public-sector employees were laid off. Differentials between workers at the top and bottom of the official salary scale increased from 8:1 to 15:1.

The rationalization of the state sector also involved the amalgamation of numerous state agricultural and agro-industrial enterprises into several large vertically integrated corporations organized on a product sector basis (cotton, coffee, tobacco, beef, milk, sugar and poultry). This new organizational structure, combined with the new-found concern for cost-efficiency and profitability of state sector enterprises, was considered incompatible with the notion that such enterprises should concern themselves with the well-being of other local production units. As a result, the OTPI, referred to above, died a sudden death.

The multi-service principle, however, was not abandoned and a new type of centre emerged in 1988 known as the Peasant Development Centre (CDC). In its original conception, the role of the CDC went beyond that envisaged for the state territorial enterprise in that apart from providing a variety of services for local producers, the latter were expected to actively participate in the CDC's major decision-making processes. By the beginning of 1990 some 41 CDCs were in operation throughout the country. In practice, however, many CDCs had great difficulty in providing the types of services originally envisaged. Moreover, considerable tensions developed between the CDCs and the UNAG which undermined the role of the CDCs as participatory structures (MIDINRA, 1990).

A second package of measures was introduced in June 1988. The currency was again devalued, this time by 85 per cent[7] while producer prices and workers' salaries were further deregulated. A radical change in credit policy emerged when the government announced its intention to index interest rates to inflation. In practice, however, real interest rates remained negative (Spoor, 1989).

The recessive impact of the 1988 stabilization measures was severe. Both GDP and agricultural output fell by 11 per cent. Industry was particularly affected, with the value of industrial output declining by 28 per cent *in 1988* (ECLAC, 1990).

While basic grains production fared reasonably well during this period, consumers were affected by changes in food marketing policy, which altered the role of ENABAS in the national food system. Many 'people's stores' were closed when ENABAS refused to grant further credit to store owners. The rationing system was effectively terminated although certain 'priority groups', including the army, 'strategic' enterprises, harvest workers and health centres were assigned quotas (Stahler-Sholk and Spoor, 1989, p. 32). ENABAS attempted to regulate prices by selling stocks when prices began to rise excessively. The grain marketing board announced its intention to purchase reduced quantities of grains and substituted its policy of reaching producers dispersed widely throughout the country by one which required that producers deliver their grains to the agency's procurement depots.

Eliminating the chronic distortions in relative prices that had arisen through price controls led, of course, to major increases in production costs. Devaluations fuelled the inflationary spiral and during the second half of 1988 hyperinflation set in. This had resulted also from the sudden relaxation of budgetary expenditures and credit policy that followed in the wake of Hurricane Joan, which devastated large parts of the country in October. During 1988, inflation totalled more than 33 000 per cent.

To deal with this situation, the 1989 Economic Plan introduced major cuts in government spending, which declined by 49 per cent in 1989. The goal was set to reduce the global public-sector deficit from 52 per cent of GDP in 1987 to 11.3 per cent in 1989. As a percentage of government spending, the fiscal deficit was reduced from 54 per cent in 1988 to 13 per cent the following year. To cut spending, the government laid off an additional 30 000 public functionaries.

In line with the 1988 decision to index interest rates to inflation, sharp increases were announced in interest rates, which reached 60 per cent a month for agriculture and industry and 90 per cent for commercial activities during early 1989. In order to increase government revenues, there was a proposed 10 per cent increase in the number of tax contributors. Taxes paid by agricultural producers were also increased.

The public investment programme was cut, causing fixed investment to fall by nearly 20 per cent in 1989. Strict priority was given to quick-yielding, export-generating or import-substituting investments, as well as those associated with repair and maintenance of machinery and equipment. Agricultural investment declined sharply and work on a number of major development projects virtually ground to a halt.

Although agricultural investment had fallen in 1988, the state-centred bias which had been a feature of the post-revolutionary development model persisted. The 1989 economic plan sought to reduce the state sector allocation from 60 per cent to 15 per cent of total agricultural investment and prioritize long-term credits for private coffee and cattle producers. The percentage of total credit allocated to cooperatives and projects associated with the agrarian reform was expected to increase from 5 per cent to 20 per cent (IHCA, 1989b, p. 37).

During the first half of 1989 the córdoba was devalued on twenty occasions. In March, parity was achieved on all three exchange rates (official, parallel and black market) while greater exchange rate stability was achieved in June. The rate of inflation slowed considerably, falling from 127 per cent in December 1988 to around 16 per cent a month during the latter half of 1989.

An important development in 1989 was the attempt by the government to stimulate private-sector confidence by engineering a social pact with the private sector and engaging the latter in a national dialogue about the state of the economy. Expropriations of private holdings declined sharply during 1987 and 1988 and were virtually halted during 1989. The government announced that a third Agrarian Reform law would be drafted, with the intention of restoring private-sector confidence by guaranteeing property rights. Producer commissions were set up in most major product sectors to review the problems affecting each of them and to make policy recommendations. On these commissions sat private producers, representatives of the main agricultural producers' association (UNAG), and state enterprise and government agency representatives.

Another distinguishing feature of the 1989 stabilization programme was its 'human face', which manifested itself in two important respects. Firstly, a series of concessions was granted to agricultural producers which relaxed much of the technocratic tightness and toughness that characterized the 1989 stabilization programme. Following the sharp rise in nominal interest rates in January 1989, an array of forces coalesced in favour of a relaxation in policy. These included the main producer organizations, certain divisions within the Ministry of Agricultural Development and Agrarian Reform more directly concerned with peasant production, as well as the FSLN and other newspapers. Two concerns, in particular, motivated this opposition: (i) that the recession which had dealt a severe blow to industrial production in 1988 would spread to agriculture; and (ii) that the social impact of the measures on peasant producers would be too extreme.

In April 1989 the indexation principle was substantially modified when the decision was taken to fix interest rates for four-month periods and impose a ceiling of 20 per cent on monthly interests rates. The debts of basic grains producers were wiped out and concessionary interest rates were introduced for peasant and co-operative producers of basic grains as well as for producers wanting to invest in coffee renovation and the purchase of cattle. As Stahler-Sholk and Spoor point out, these measures went some way towards reducing the insecurity which characterized the producers' economic calculations, but also threatened government deficits and the objectives of the stabilization programme (Stahler-Sholk and Spoor, 1989 pp. 27–8).

The UNAG also called for a revision in ENABAS's pricing policy, more specifically the reintroduction of guaranteed prices for basic grains on the basis of 'border prices'. A policy was eventually formulated whereby ENABAS would announce at the beginning of each month procurement prices, calculated on the basis of a formula which took into account border and local market prices and costs of production, as well as the agency's financial costs and profitability.

Secondly, in order to alleviate the social impact of the stabilization programme, the government introduced a series of 'compensatory' measures to protect certain groups. One group particularly affected by cuts in public spending were state-sector employees on the central government's payroll. As real incomes fell, the government began to pay employees partly in kind. Public functionaries received a monthly food package consisting of 10 lb of both rice and red kidney beans as well as 5 lb of sugar. In 1989, 170 000 people (including people on state pensions) received the food package. Certain groups such as teachers, who were at the bottom end of the pay scale managed to negotiate (following strike action) an expanded food package which included powdered milk, vegetable oil and tins of sardines.

Other protective measures were also taken during 1989 which included the introduction of a school milk programme. By the beginning of 1990, some 125 000 first- and second-year children received a glass of milk each day. During mid-1989, the state once again established a system whereby ENABAS would supply basic products to a network of private retail outlets at official prices in low-income neighbourhoods. While ENABAS provided short-term credit to shopkeepers on favourable terms, the system involved no direct consumer subsidies. In July, some sixty fair-price stores were set up in Managua, each receiving supplies of fourteen basic products from ENABAS which included both food and household goods. By early 1990, some 270 stores were in operation. Prices in these stores were generally 10 per cent to 25 per cent below normal retail prices (MIDINRA, 1990).

As pressure for land grew, a special plan was announced which doubled the amount of land distributed through the agrarian reform programme. Those demanding lands included not only poor peasant producers located in areas where the person/land ratio was extremely high, but also people who had been laid off as a result of cuts in government spending and industrial recession. Another group claiming lands consisted of so-called semi-proletarian agricultural workers, who traditionally worked several months in the agro-export harvests and the remainder of the year were engaged in informal sector activities. Petty trading and service sector activities, however, were also seriously affected by the collapse in effective demand. In May 1989, the government announced a special 'Land Plan' which aimed to distribute 88 000 ha. to nearly 12 000 families. A land bank was established, consisting primarily of areas which had been abandoned due to the war: land belonging to state enterprises as well as land held by co-operatives, which had a very low person-to-land ratio. The Land Plan attempted to accommodate demands for land without expropriating private holdings.

While more stringent than many Latin-American stabilization programmes, the Nicaraguan programme did not receive special assistance packages from the major international lending institutions such as the IMF. The concessions made to agricultural producers alone (in April 1989) were expected to cost an estimated $40 million. Rather than resort to printing money, the government approached a number of European governments and at the Stockholm donors' conference, organized by the Swedish government in May 1989, obtained $50 million. While providing some relief, this was far less than was required.

The levels of living of large sectors of the population declined sharply during 1988 and 1989. By the end of the decade an estimated 32 per cent of the work-force was officially classified as unemployed or underemployed, while basic food consumption levels (per capita calorie intake) were down 30 per cent on 1985 levels.

There did not occur, however, the outbursts of social discontent experienced in many Third-World cities when economies have been subjected to shock treatment. A small number of strikes did occur, notably one in 1989 involving teachers. On such occasions, the government tended to move quickly, opening negotiations and making limited concessions. A considerable degree of communication and dialogue between government leaders and the mass organizations, as well as with the population in general via the media, was an important factor which prevented social tensions from boiling over. Nevertheless, social discontent intensified throughout 1989 and, on 25 February 1990, 59 per cent of the electorate seized the opportunity of free and fair elections to oust the Sandinistas from government.

Notes

1. The content of the 'Plan General Unico' was outlined by Comandante Luis Carrión, Vice Minister of the Ministry of the Interior, in an interview published by *Barricada*, 10 July 1985.
2. When participating in food policy evaluations in the different regions of the country, I found that 'free trade' was interpreted by the state authorities in three different ways:

   freedom for ENABAS to set a procurement price which did not adhere strictly to the traditional formula based on costs of production but which also took into account open market prices;

   freedom for private merchants to operate in the grain trade once they were licensed with the authorities. In some areas merchants were expected to co-ordinate their procurement activities with the state authorities so that ENABAS and the merchants would not compete in the same area; and

   freedom for peasant producers to sell a portion of their crop at open market prices, on the understanding that they would also sell a portion to ENABAS.

3. These interviews were conducted in 1987 with Ronald Paredes (CDS), Gustavo Toruño (UNAG), Edgardo Garcia (ATC), and Ronald Membreño (CST).
4. This section on economic stabilization and adjustment draws heavily on a series of reports and seminar papers I prepared for UNRISD for its projects on 'Food Policy and the World Recession' and 'Participation and Reform in Socialist Contexts' (see Utting, 1989, 1990a, 1990b).
5. Direct economic costs include the value of material damages (production and infrastructure) caused by fighting; lost credits, loans and trade resulting from the economic boycott of Nicaragua by the United States and

certain international finance agencies; and excess defence expenditures, that is, those that exceed the cost of maintaining an army in peacetime.
6. The córdoba was devalued from 0.07 'new córdobas' (70 old córdobas) to the dollar to 10.
7. The córdoba was devalued from 12 to the dollar to 80.

7 The Nature of the Crisis

The policy reforms of the mid-1980s are generally explained in terms of a response on the part of the state to a new set of economic, social, political and military circumstances which emerged during the 1983/84 period. Until then the prospects for economic and social development had been fairly positive.

EARLY POST-REVOLUTIONARY PERFORMANCE

Following the sharp decline in economic growth during the insurrectionary period of 1978 and 1979, high rates of economic growth were recorded during the early 1980s. As can be seen in Table 7.1, the performance of the Nicaraguan economy contrasted sharply with that of other economies in the region, which generally experienced negative growth during the 1980–83 period.

While production levels of a number of important agricultural products remained fairly static (maize, sugar-cane) or fluctuated widely (beans, sorghum), the performance of agriculture in general was fairly positive. With the exception of maize and major agro-exports like cotton and coffee, it can be seen in Table 7.2 that production levels in 1983/84 tended to be above pre-revolution levels.

During this same period inflation remained relatively stable at around 25 per cent per annum, while annual export revenues fluctuated within the $400 million band, averaging $447 million between 1980 and 1983.

Improvements were achieved in the levels of living of large sectors of the population. Social services expanded rapidly. Between 1978 and 1983 the number of teachers increased from 14 209 to 24 638, while the number of people in education doubled, from 477 000 to 941 000 (MED, 1987). The same period also saw a sharp rise in the number of health centres, which increased from 43 to 532. The literacy 'crusade' of 1980 had reduced illiteracy from 50 to 12 per cent of the national population. Some 43 000 homes were built in Managua alone in the four-year period dating from July 1979, while electricity and drinking water services were extended in both urban and rural areas (Barraclough *et al.*, 1988, p. 38). Table 7.3 shows that

193

TABLE 7.1   *Gross domestic product in Central America, annual growth rate, 1980–86 (per cent)*

Country/area	1980	1981	1982	1983	1984	1985	1986
Nicaragua	10.0	5.4	–0.8	4.6	–1.6	–4.1	–0.4
El Salvador	–8.7	–8.3	–5.6	0.8	2.3	2.0	0.6
Honduras	0.6	1.0	–2.6	1.1	3.0	3.2	2.7
Guatemala	3.7	0.6	–3.5	–2.6	0.5	–1.0	0.5
Costa Rica	0.8	–2.3	–7.3	2.9	8.0	1.0	4.6
Region average	1.5	–0.8	–4.2	0.3	2.4	0.1	1.6

SOURCE   See Timossi, 1989, Table 7, based on ECLAC.

per capita consumption levels of most major food products in 1983 generally exceeded pre-revolution levels.

ECONOMIC DECLINE

This generally favourable scenario was to change in 1983. During that year serious problems of shortages of basic food products emerged, while inflation (as measured by the retail price index) increased to 33 per cent. During 1984 and 1985 the economic situation deteriorated sharply. Negative rates of economic growth were recorded in both these years. Inflation increased to 334 per cent in 1985 and reached 747 per cent the following year. Table 7.4 shows that the rate of inflation was even higher in sectors associated with 'popular' consumer goods such as food, drinks and tobacco. Equally dramatic was the collapse of export revenues, which fell from $431 million in 1983 to $298 million in 1985. As indicated in Table 7.5, the balance of trade deficit rose from $375 million to $594 million over the same period.

Between 1983 and 1985, production levels of food and agro-export products fell in ten of the twelve product sectors for which data were presented in Table 7.2 (see page 195). State procurement levels of beans, rice, sorghum, coffee and milk fell during or following the 1983/84 cycle. This was particularly evident in the case of beans which represent for the peasant producer more of a cash crop than maize. ENABAS procurement levels for beans (for two of the three main harvest periods) collapsed by 83 per cent, from 15 000 to 2 600 tonnes

TABLE 7.2 *Trends in agricultural production (1974–78, 1980/81 – 1985/86)*

Product	Unit		1974/78*	1980/81	1981/82	1982/83	1983/84	1984/85	1985/86
Maize	Quintal**	000s	4568	3995	4200	3603	4517	4581	4242
Rice	"	"	1209	1377	1947	2134	2233	1943	1774
Beans	"	"	1215	625	905	1030	1226	1260	1008
Sorghum	"	"	1373	1940	1951	1151	2224	2354	3346
Cotton	"	"	8149	4879	4081	5070	5691	4609	3350
Coffee	"	"	1115	1285	1328	1568	1070	1115	769
Sugar cane	S. tons	"	2703	2672	3116	2992	3133	2584	2789
Bananas	Boxes	"	6258	6501	6309	4478	6895	6051	5950

			1974–78	1980	1981	1982	1983	1984	1985	1986
Beef[1]	Lb.	mill.	103	104	79	113	115	112	98	62
Milk[2]	Gal.	"	11.2	7.5	15.1	19.3	18.8	17.7	17.6	18.1
Chicken[3]	Lb.	"	9.8	14.5	16.1	22.3	23.6	20.9	22.6	22.6
Eggs[3]	Doz.	"	4.4	11.7	15.4	18.1	18.7	17.1	21.3	22.2

SOURCES   MIDINRA, 1990; CIERA, 1989d.
* Annual average.
** 1 quintal = 100lb.
[1] Includes clandestine slaughter.
[2] Pasteurized milk only.
[3] Does not include peasant production.

TABLE 7.3 *Per capita food consumption levels, 1976–78, 1980–86*

Product	Unit	1976–78	1980	1981	1982	1983	1984	1985
Maize	Lb.	158	123	124	149	129	135	123
Rice	"	37	81	64	70	73	76	71
Beans	"	35	31	28	38	40	33	28
Wheat flour	"	31	59	42	34	38	32	42
Sugar	"	97	90	102	104	100	119	102
Veg. oil	Lt.	8.5	12	10	15	11	9	11
Beef	Lb.	26	20	21	22	26	24	17
Chicken	"	7	9	10	10	7	9	11
Pork	"	5	10	10	10	9	9	6.7
Eggs	Doz.	10	11	14	13	13	14	10
Milk	Lt.	90	61	74	85	88	85	81
Calories	Kcal.	2053	2232	2112	2395	2232	2266	2161
Protein	gm.	52	53	51	56	56	54	45

SOURCE   PAN (See MIDINRA, 1990).

TABLE 7.4 *Annual increase in the retail price index, 1982–86 (percentages)*

	1982	1983	1984	1985	1986
General price index	22	33	50	334	747
Food, drinks and tobacco	24	45	59	389	956

SOURCE INEC.

TABLE 7.5 *Evolution of trade deficit, 1974–77, 1980–86 (in millions of US dollars)*

	1974–77*	1980	1981	1982	1983	1984	1985	1986
Imports	593.2	887.2	999.4	775.5	806.9	826.2	892.3	761.2
Exports	483.7	451.0	499.8	405.4	431.3	384.8	298.5	252.0
Deficit	109.5	436.2	499.6	370.1	375.6	441.4	593.8	509.2

SOURCE Ministry of External Trade.
* Yearly average.

between the 1983/84 and 1985/86 agricultural cycles (CIERA and DGRA, 1987). The sale of milk to processing plants producing pasteurized and powdered milk, primarily for urban markets, also fell sharply during this period. Although the figures for maize procurement shown in Table 7.6 indicate a slight increase in maize purchases by the state agency ENABAS in 1984/85, this was largely accounted for by a substantial increase in large-scale irrigated maize production. It is probable that procurement levels of maize produced by peasant producers fell significantly during that year.

State surplus appropriation was also affected by the fall in production of certain agro-export crops, the procurement and export of which was monopolized by the state. Most important in this respect were coffee and beef which were produced to a significant extent by rich peasant and capitalist producers. Coffee production was dependent on the poor peasantry or 'semi-proletarians' for harvest labour. As real wages fell and access to land increased, many traditional coffee pickers failed to turn up for the harvests and the state had to rely increasingly on inexperienced voluntary pickers from the city. Additional problems associated with smuggling and the sale of raw coffee beans and beef, for internal consumption outside the state marketing channels, reduced the government's foreign exchange revenues from these sources.

TABLE 7.6   *Evolution of state procurement levels of grains,* coffee* and milk,** 1980–87 (* in thousands of quintals; ** in millions of gallons)*

Product	1980/81	1981/82	1982/83	1983/84	1984/85	1985/86	1986/87
Beans[1]	212.7	389.6	613.3	535.8	312.7	131.4	197.9
Maize[1]	554.4	848.2	802.8	953.4	1169.0	1056.9	715.0
Rice[1a]	420.0	1196.1	1556.7	1773.6	1319.3	820.1	1221.6
Sorghum[1]	1110.8	1454.4	866.5	1584.2	1256.8	2005.3	1680.4
Coffee	1237.0	1168.7	1451.9	919.7	973.5	768.9	852.9
	1980	*1981*	*1982*	*1983*	*1984*	*1985*	*1986*
Milk[b]	9 946	13 149	13 678	9 626	8 571	8 668	7 263
Index							
Beans	100	183	288	252	147	62	93
Maize	100	153	145	172	211	191	129
Rice	100	216	281	320	238	148	220
Sorghum	100	131	78	145	113	181	151
Coffee	100	94	117	74	79	62	69
Milk	100	132	138	97	86	87	73

SOURCES   ENABAS, ENCAFE, ENILAC.
[1] Although ENABAS's annual grain procurement data correspond to the calendar year, the data presented here cover the period from June to May. I have selected this period since it corresponds more closely to the agricultural cycle (April to March) as well as the policy cycle (that is, the announcement of new prices etc.).
[a] Paddy rice has been coverted to milled rice using the coefficient of 1.6.
[b] Includes milk purchased by the three state-owned Managua-based processing plants and the Nestlé subsidiary, Prolacsa.

During this period there were also significant changes in the employment structure. High levels of unemployment were not a prominent feature of the crisis. Rather, there was a considerable rise in informal sector employment, as many salaried labourers, peasants, bureaucrats and the previously unemployed took up urban-based, self-employed or family-based service and trading activities. While reliable data is lacking, it has been estimated that the size of the urban informal sector increased from 238 000 in 1980 to 395 000 in 1985, that is, by 66 per cent (Fitzgerald, 1987b, p. 36). According to this calculation, the sector increased from 27 to 38 per cent of the total economically-active population in just five years.

It can be seen from Table 7.7 that non-agricultural 'formal' sector employment declined by 6 per cent while the size of the agricultural

TABLE 7.7   *Structure of economically-active population, 1980–85 (in 000 and percentages)*

	1980	%	1985	%	% change 1983–85
Agricultural EAP	380	43.5	412	39.4	8
Non-agricultural EAP	493	56.5	635	60.6	29
Formal sector[1]	255	29.2	250	23.9	–6
Informal sector	238	27.3	395	37.7	66
EAP total	873	100	1047	100	20

SOURCE   Fitzgerald, 1987b, based on INEC, CIERA.
[1] Refers to people employed in enterprises of five or more workers.

EAP remained virtually static, rising by little more than one per cent a year despite an annual population growth rate of 3.3 per cent.

Labour instability was further exacerbated by the high rate of rotation of personnel from one enterprise to another or within the bureaucracy. Labour productivity declined in both industrial and agricultural enterprises. This process had begun during the initial post-revolutionary phase. As Deere *et al.* point out:

> Throughout the country [the workers] took their 'historic vacation'. Absenteeism, tardiness, three-hour work days, and low productivity became endemic as the old structures of oppression were stripped away by the revolution. (Deere *et al.*, 1985, p. 80)

In certain branches of agriculture and industry productivity continued to decline in subsequent years. In the rice and sugar-cane sectors, for example, traditional work norms had fallen by 25 and 40 per cent respectively by the mid-1980s (Wheelock, 1985, p. 107).

DECLINE IN THE LEVELS OF LIVING

The years 1984 and 1985 also saw a reversal of the positive trends of earlier years relating to basic-needs provisioning. The coverage and quality of health and education services deteriorated. Illiteracy and child mortality rates began to rise again. Table 7.3 on page 195 shows that per capita consumption levels in seven of the eleven food product sectors fell between 1983 and 1985. There was a sharp decline in real wages. When measured in relation to two different basic consumer baskets, purchasing power declined by 40 and 75 per cent between 1979 and mid-1985 (Stahler-Sholk, 1985; also see Vilas, 1986a).

Particularly affected were the levels of living of significant sectors of the peasant population. With the escalation of the war in the interior of the country and border areas, rural social services, which had expanded rapidly between 1980 and 1982, were disrupted. Many schools and health centres had to be closed. By the end of 1984 it was estimated that the suspension of social services had deprived 36 775 students of primary and adult education, while 225 000 rural inhabitants were deprived of access to health services (Fitzgerald, 1987a, pp. 204–5).

Social infrastructure became one of the main targets of 'Contra' attacks. Between 1980 and 1985 it was estimated that as a consequence of the war, twenty health centres had been destroyed and ninety-nine abandoned; forty-eight schools were destroyed and another 502 were closed; 840 adult education groups had ceased to function (Vergara *et al.*, 1986, p. 55).

Restrictions on the availability of basic goods in rural areas, and the deterioration of the domestic terms of trade from the standpoint of the rural producer, in addition to declining levels of production and marketed surplus, all contributed towards a general deterioration in living levels for many peasant families and communities. As indicated earlier, many were forced to abandon their lands and homes altogether. By the end of 1986, 110 000 people had been relocated through rural settlement schemes (*Barricada*, 22 February 1987, p. 3). Although they received high priority in the allocation of material resources and the provision of social services, living conditions were rudimentary; while culturally, adaptation to a life away from traditional communities proved extremely difficult.

THE POLITICAL AND MILITARY THREAT

On the political front, we see during this period a weakening of the base of peasant support for the revolution in certain regions of the country. In large areas of the interior and the Atlantic coastal region, rural populations had little or no access to government development programmes or ideology, yet felt the effects of shortages, inflation and government military service as young men were recruited, sometimes forcibly, into the army.

Some opposition parties were able to capitalize on peasant discontent. This was reflected in the 1984 presidential and legislative elections, when the highly positive results achieved nationally by the Sandinistas were not duplicated in many rural areas with relatively large peasant populations (Kaimowitz, 1986a, p. 113). More dangerous from the point of view of the Sandinista state were the strides made by the counter-revolutionary forces in gaining support in rural areas. Assessing the correlation of military forces in 1984, the Vice-Minister of Defense explained in a Barricada interview:

> [1984] was when the mercenary forces were at their strongest, due to the political influence they had achieved among social groups in the countryside, notably in the northern areas. As a consequence they exercised influence over the principal protagonist of the war – the peasantry – in order to feed their ranks and grow. . .It was when they had the best and greatest possibilities. We, for our part, experienced a difficult situation. . .there were areas of the countryside which had not experienced the influence of sandinismo, and since they had been abandoned, the first that arrived were the counterrevolutionaries and logically it was they that had more influence. (Cuadra, *Barricada*, 2 August 1987, p. 3)

In describing the process of the rise and fall in the strength of the 'Contras' between 1981 and 1987, the Nicaraguan current affairs review, *ENVIO*, writes:

> Following a difficult beginning, the FDN [the main military wing of the Contras] made a significant comeback in 1983 and 1984. It acquired an incipient social base among the peasantry in the outlying areas of the interior regions. This, combined with the tactics of forced recruitment of the peasant population, enabled the FDN to increase its numbers from five thousand men in 1982 to 12 thousand in 1983 and to 15 thousand in 1984. (IHCA, 1987c, p. 24)

The article goes on to point out that as a consequence of these developments, the 'Contras' were able to extend the war from the border areas to the interior of the country and depend not only on supply routes from neighbouring Honduras and Costa Rica but also on internal sources.

The political problem from the Sandinistas' point of view was, however, even more complex. Sandinista ideology identified the working class and the peasantry as the 'fundamental classes' of the revolution (Chamorro, 1983, p. 17) both in terms of the latter's key support groups and as the primary 'subjects' of development. Rapid rural-to-urban migration, however, was continually depleting the ranks of the peasantry. Moreover, newcomers to urban areas were not becoming 'productive' factory workers, but what the government labelled 'non-productive', informal sector workers, largely engaged in commercial (often speculative or black-market) activities, which undermined attempts to impose a degree of social control over the economy. Attempts by the state to curb or regulate the activities of certain informal sector groups and the adoption of an 'anti-merchant' discourse by certain government leaders inevitably led to tensions and served to alienate some sectors of the population which had previously been supportive of the Sandinistas.

CRISIS AND TRANSITION

As a framework for understanding the crisis in Nicaragua it is useful to highlight a series of contradictions and constraints that are generated by three processes of change that characterize the 'macro-process' of revolutionary transformation. Elsewhere I have identified these in terms of (a) the attempt to achieve a new form of insertion in the world system or, put another way, to redefine the dependency relation; (b) the transformation of social relations; and (c) the rapid development of the productive forces (Utting, 1987, p. 128). To these may be added, of course, other conditions that tend to affect Third World countries in general: conditions associated, for example, with international market conditions, notably fluctuating commodity prices and deteriorating terms of trade, as well as the impact on agriculture of extreme climatic and pest conditions.

These latter conditions clearly contributed to the crisis in Nicaragua. It is generally recognized that one of the fundamental constraints on the development process was the severe shortage of liquid foreign exchange. This situation was partially accounted for by the deterioration in the international terms of trade and stagnation or decline in world commodity prices. According to Goldin and Pizarro:

Between 1980 and 1986, the terms of trade declined by 31.6%.

This decline roughly matches the growth in the trade deficit over the corresponding period, so that the widening of the trade deficit may be attributed to adverse price movements, rather than a growing imbalance between the volume of exports and imports. (Goldin and Pizarro, 1988)

The deterioration of the terms of trade was particularly acute during the 1980–82 period, and again in 1985. The first half of the 1980s also witnessed the disintegration of regional trade. As Weeks points out, these latter two conditions were such that 'economic decline was probably the fate of the country whatever government followed Somoza; certainly the experience of the other countries of Central America and the Caribbean during the 1980s suggests this' (Weeks, 1988, p. 25). Weather, too, played its part. Both drought and monsoon-type conditions seriously affected harvests of basic grains and cotton during a number of years (Zalkin, 1987).

This study, though, is essentially about crisis and reform in dependent transitional economies. As such we are particularly interested in specifying the nature of the relationship between the transition process and the crisis conditions outlined earlier. The link between the two is to be found primarily in the contradictory practices engaged in by imperialist interests, capitalist and peasant producers, the working class and the urban informal sector, as well as state agencies and enterprises. It is these relationships and practices that are analysed in the remainder of this chapter.

REINSERTION AND REALIGNMENT IN THE WORLD SYSTEM

As indicated at the beginning of Part III, attempts to address the underlying causes of poverty and underdevelopment in post-revolutionary Nicaragua involved a struggle to transform the historical pattern of insertion of Nicaragua in the world economy, more specifically a struggle against the traditional forms of economic and geopolitical domination by the United States in the Central American region.

The economic, military and diplomatic response of the United States' government was to have a devastating effect on the economy. As Nuñez points out, this response had a threefold purpose: to strengthen internal counterrevolutionary forces; to destabilize the economy; and to isolate Nicaragua internationally (Nuñez O., 1987, pp. 180–1).

The war seriously undermined the rural economy and in many areas agricultural production either reverted to a subsistence regime or was abandoned altogether. An estimated 16 per cent of all farming land in the three interior regions of the country (Regions I, V, VI) fell into this latter category (DGFCDC, 1988b). This was due particularly to three specific effects of the war. Firstly, as a result of Contra attacks on co-operatives, grain storage silos, health posts, electricity pylons, and so on, there was considerable physical destruction of economic and social infrastructure. Peasant stocks of grain and livestock were also depleted as a result of purchases, requisitioning or theft. Secondly, trade circuits were disrupted. The access of both merchants and state marketing agencies to production zones in the interior of the country was seriously impeded if not cut off altogether. Thirdly, the supply of labour was severely reduced as a consequence of migration, and recruitment into both armies, through death and injuries resulting from the fighting. Not only agriculture but also other important export activities such as fishing, forestry and mining, located in the interior and the Atlantic Coast regions, were disrupted by the war.

It is important to stress that such conditions not only restricted production levels and marketed surplus but also acted as a brake on the historical pattern of extensive accumulation which had been an important feature of the Somocista development model (Baumeister, 1988a). The war restricted the expansion of the agrarian frontier which historically had been an important factor underlying increases in production of key products such as maize, beans, cattle, coffee and lumber.

At the national level, the effects of the war greatly contributed to the macroeconomic disequilibria that became a prominent feature of the Nicaraguan economy from 1983 onwards. By the end of 1985, the direct cost of the war was estimated to be $901 million (see Table 7.8). If we add to this the indirect effects on GDP, the total cost of the war amounted to approximately $2 billion (more than one year's GDP) (Marchetti and Jerez, 1988). Material destruction (capital goods and stocks), production losses (*lucro cessante*), and losses due to the trade embargo imposed by the United States government produced export losses in the region of 390 million dollars during the

TABLE 7.8 *Direct economic cost of the war, 1980–85 (in millions of US dollars)*

Concept	1980	1981	1982	1983	1984	1985	Total
Material destruction	0.6	4.0	11.0	58.6	27.6	18.3	120.1
Agriculture	–	0.1	2.3	12.2	13.9	10.4	38.9
Production losses	0.9	3.4	21.1	106.6	170.0	96.4	398.4
Agriculture	–	–	0.2	37.1	54.9	22.3	114.5
Lost external credits	–	8.2	38.3	61.3	92.1	73.0	272.9
Losses due to embargo	–	–	–	14.6	16.0	79.4	110.0
Total	1.5	15.6	70.4	241.1	305.7	267.1	901.4

SOURCES ECLAC, Ministry of the Presidency (See Barraclough et al., 1988; Fitzgerald, 1988b).

first half of the 1980s, notably between 1983 and 1985. Such losses accounted for approximately one-third of the export revenues during the latter period.

The rapid increase in defence expenditures from 1983 onwards generated pressures on the government's current account deficit. As a percentage of total government expenditure, defence/security expenditure increased from 19.7 per cent in 1983 to 32.2 per cent in 1985: 19 per cent of GDP (compared to just 7 per cent in 1981) (Delgado, 1986). The extremely large fiscal deficit sustained from 1983 onwards contributed to the rapid increase in the money supply and inflationary pressures. As a percentage of total GDP, the fiscal deficit increased from an annual average of 10 per cent during the 1980–82 period to 26 per cent during 1983–85 (ECLAC, 1984, 1987; Fitzgerald, 1988b). As indicated in Table 7.9, the increase in defence expenditure also put pressure on other government programmes such as health and education. Particularly affected, though, were infrastructural investments such as roads and the real wages of public-sector-employees, which fell by 38 per cent between 1983 and 1986 (Fitzgerald, 1988b, p. 318).

As pointed out by Fitzgerald, official figures on defence expenditure do not include armaments and strictly military supplies obtained primarily from the Warsaw Pact countries. Defence expenditures, therefore:

> effectively represent a priority claim on wage-goods (directly through local purchases of food, uniforms, etc., or indirectly

TABLE 7.9 *Share of total government expenditure accounted for by defence, health and education expenditures, and fiscal deficit, 1980–82, 1983–85 (percentages)*

	1980–82	1983–85
Defence security	22.0	24.4
Health	14.8	8.0
Education	13.2	9.1
Fiscal deficit	30.9	44.1
Fiscal Deficit/GDP	10.3	26.0

SOURCES Ministry of Finance, SPP, ECLAC.

through the payroll of the armed forces) and producer goods such as fuel and construction materials. (Fitzgerald, 1988b)

The diversion of such resources towards defence activities had major implications for agricultural and industrial production levels as well as the levels of living of the peasantry and the working class. It was estimated that supplying the armed forces with boots and uniforms accounted for 45 per cent of manufacturing capacity of the shoe industry and 24 per cent of the textile industry, while army food supplies represented 10 per cent of national consumption in 1984 (Idem., 1987a, p. 207).

The war also prompted major changes in the employment structure, draining the 'productive' sectors of the economy of labour, either directly through the incorporation of peasants and workers into defence activities or indirectly through migration, which in turn contributed to the expansion of the informal sector. Labour shortages in factories, farms and development projects became a major constraint on the development process. This was partly a consequence of the fact that between 70 000 and 100 000 men (roughly the equivalent of 15 per cent of the EAP) were involved in defence activities (Wheelock, 1984; Utting, 1987).

From 1981 onwards the US government not only increased its economic and military support for the anti-Sandinista rebels but also imposed a series of economic boycott measures. Following the suspension of bilateral assistance, the Reagan Administration pressured for the suspension of loans from multilateral lending agencies such as the World Bank and the Inter-American Development Bank (Barraclough *et al.*, 1988). By the end of 1985, an estimated 273 million dollars' worth of loans had been withheld. This assistance was to have supported twelve major development projects and programmes associated primarily with food production, rural development and agro-industrial projects, the total value of which was estimated at $423 million (Delgado, 1986).

A full trade embargo was imposed by the United States' government in May 1985. This followed moves two years earlier to reduce Nicaragua's preferential sugar quota by 90 per cent. While dependency on US markets for Nicaraguan exports had been substantially reduced by 1985 (US markets acquired only 17.6 per cent of its exports over the 1982–84 period), the proximity of the North American market made it an important outlet for perishable food products such as bananas, beef and shellfish. More important was the ongoing dependency on the US market for obtaining supplies of machinery, spare parts and agricultural inputs (Goldin and Pizarro, 1988, p. 28).

The economic boycott was to have a major distortionary effect on the economy. In response to the suspension of new loans and credits from both multilateral agencies following 1983, the Nicaraguan government turned increasingly to the socialist bloc countries for assistance. This trend was accelerated in 1984 when Mexico, also allegedly under pressure from the United States' government (Kornbluh, 1987, p. 20), suspended petroleum credits (Barraclough *et al.*, 1988, p. 59). As Fitzgerald explains:

> the macroeconomic consequences of this shift were not so much a decline in imports as an increased rigidity in the composition of goods supplied, reduced foreign exchange liquidity, and above all a shortage of spare parts, chemicals and agricultural implements needed to keep production going. (Fitzgerald, 1988b, p. 317)

It has been pointed out moreover, that the easy terms associated with imports of Eastern bloc technology meant in practice that Nicaragua acquired far more tractors, trucks, buses and cars than it was capable of maintaining. As the Minister of Agricultural Development explained in his 1986 Annual Report:

> As a result of the [economic] blockade we have introduced en masse a new technology for which we do not have the necessary infrastructure. We have imported tractors, harvestors and implements of a type that demands more maintenance than that which

we had previously. . .Only 15% of the persons operating that equipment has been trained. . .Of the 3,480 units of machinery purchased from the socialist bloc, 27% are inactive as a result of these types of problems. (MIDINRA, 1987, p. 29)

The changing pattern of trade also exacerbated problems associated with the deterioration of the external terms of trade as Nicaragua relied increasingly on imports from countries in the European Economic Community (EEC) and Japan, whose currencies were appreciating against the US dollar during the mid-1980s (Goldin and Pizarro, 1988, p. 28).

An additional distortionary effect derived from the increasing need to finance the fiscal deficit through monetary emission as foreign credits from multilateral agencies were reduced. This was to be an important element behind the inflationary pressures which built up between 1983 and 1986. During 1986, however, the fiscal deficit–GDP ratio fell considerably, and other elements emerged as the principal sources of monetary and demand expansion, notably foreign exchange losses and the expansion of 'unfinanced' investment in the state enterprise sector (Fitzgerald, 1988b, p. 319).

THE TRANSFORMATION OF SOCIAL RELATIONS AND STRUCTURES OF INCOME AND WEALTH

Another set of conditions underlying the economic crisis related to a series of class practices or forms of class struggle which undermined levels of production, productivity, state procurement and investment, and which themselves constituted a response to programmes and policies that sought to transform social relations and structures of income and wealth.

Particularly important in this respect was the response of the bourgeoisie to a situation in which it retained ownership of a significant share of the means of production, but was deprived of political power and effective control of the process of reproduction of capital. The transformation of social relations of production meant in practice: (a) that the capitalist producer could no longer dictate conditions in the labour process, and now had to contend with powerful labour unions and government regulations regarding wages and work-site conditions; (b) that the terms of access to means of production such as credit, inputs and machinery were now determined to a

TABLE 7.10 *Evolution of large-scale private production, 1982/83–1986/87 (production levels in 000s)*

Crop	Concept	1982/83	1983/84	1984/85	1985/86	1986/87
Coffee	Volume	635.3	384.3	302.3	445.5	274.8
(QQ)	Index	100	60	48	70	43
	%*	40.5	35.9	27.1	41.7	27.6
Cotton	Volume	1096.4	1012.1	706.4	570.0	541.2
(QQ)	Index	100	92	64	52	49
	%*	62.5	53.7	46.9	51.6	48.0
Sugar-cane	Volume	1813.6	1817.9	1092.2	1284.8	1083.3
(ST)	Index	100	100	60	71	60
	%*	60.6	58.0	41.4	48.7	46.8
Rice	Volume	1232.5	1111.4	896.1	815.8	731.5
(QQ)	Index	100	90	73	66	59
	%*	55.9	49.3	45.0	42.8	39.8
Sorghum	Volume	493.8	1057.8	824.7	1264.2	1072.1
(QQ)	Index	100	214	167	256	217
	%*	39.6	49.1	33.8	39.9	35.1

SOURCE Based on MIDINRA data.
QQ: Quintals; ST: Short tons;
* Percentage of national production.

large extent by the state, which controlled both imports and key distribution outlets; and (c) that the capacity of the capitalist producer to realize surplus was constrained by the fact that the government established producer prices in cordobas and producers had only very limited (legal) access to US dollars (Fitzgerald, 1985c). Moreover, while the process of land expropriation proceeded slowly, certain producers, notably extensive cattle graziers, felt that property rights were threatened by the agrarian reform.

The production performance of large-scale private producers is indicated in Table 7.10, which shows production levels in five of the main crop sectors where large producers account for a significant share of total production. Between 1982/83[1] and 1984/85 agricultural production levels for this category of producers fell sharply in all crop sectors except sorghum. We see that not only did volume levels decline but so too did the percentage share of total production accounted for by this group. Particularly worrying for the state was the decline in production levels in key export sectors such as cotton, livestock and sugar-cane. Levels of insvestment also declined. It has been estimated that the accumulation rate of the non-state sector in agriculture and industry was as low as 8.8 per cent during the 1983–85 period (Arguello *et al.*, 1987). In agriculture and agro-industry, the percentage share of total sector accumulation accounted for by large-scale private enterprise fell from 21.3 to 15.1 per cent between 1980/82 and 1984/85 (Kleiterp, 1988, p. 19).

State procurement levels of food for domestic provisioning, raw materials for local processing plants, and agro-export products were affected, not only by declining production levels but also by other practices engaged in by capitalist producers. As the gap between official and black market prices widened, increasing quantities of products such as rice, sorghum, milk and beef were sold through 'clandestine' channels. Such practices gave rise to major distortions associated with waste and inefficiency. One example is that provided by Biondi-Morra:

> Typical was the case reported by MIDINRA of some private rice producers or distributors that withdrew their first grade rice from the official market at regulated prices then paid a rice mill to convert it into second grade broken rice, and finally sold it. . .through non-regulated channels at four times the price of higher quality rice. (Biondi-Morra, 1988, p. 299)

As a result of practices such as these, idle capacity in many processing plants (notably beef) increased. Biondi-Morra claims that between 1979 and 1985 idle capacity in the entire agro-industrial sector exceeded 50 per cent (Ibid., p. 371) As producers responded to the distortions in relative prices (which resulted from the operation of the parallel market and government policies that overvalued the exchange rate and fixed official producer prices on the basis of costs of production) so the proportion of total produce sold on the internal market increased, while export sales declined.

It is impossible, though, to generalize about the behaviour of capitalist producers. As Nuñez shows, the sector became increasingly divided between what became known as the 'patriotic bourgeoisie' and the 'dollar bourgeoisie'. The former continued to produce and possibly accumulate in productive sector activities. Many so-called 'medium-sized producers' also associated themselves with the pro-Sandinista agricultural producers' organization, UNAG.

The 'dollar' group tended to consist of producers associated with the major opposition parties or the right-wing producers associations. For some associated with this latter group, decapitalization was not simply a response to what was perceived as an unfavourable economic or investment climate, but constituted an important component of a broader deliberate counter-revolutionary strategy to destabilize the economy and regime (Nuñez O., 1987, p. 178).

Certain class practices engaged in by peasant producers also contributed to the crisis. Important in this respect was the tendency of peasant producers to reduce marketed grain sales and to withhold labour from the harvests. For rich peasant producers, as well as producers organized in co-operatives, the reduction in grain production and sales reflected the trend towards more diversified cropping patterns which emerged during the early 1980s – notably the shift towards more profitable cash crops (Zalkin, 1985, 1987). Labour shortages also induced producers to restrict grain production (Dore, 1988). Certain producers preferred to buy heavily subsidized grain from the state marketing agency ENABAS rather than produce it in order to feed their workers. These trends intensified towards the middle of the 1980s as relative prices shifted against grains (Utting, 1987, p. 133).

During this latter period, many rich peasants sought to bypass state marketing channels and sell-on the black or 'grey' market. This affected not only state procurement of grains but also livestock. So-called 'clandestine slaughter' accounted for an estimated 25 per cent of national production each year. As a result, state revenues were reduced and a considerable quantity of by-products obtained through slaughter in the state abattoirs were lost. As indicated earlier, coffee too was increasingly diverted away from the state procurement depots towards the black market or across the northern border to Honduras.

Poor and middle peasant producers tended to reduce marketed surpluses of grains such as maize and beans. Particularly important in the context of these groups was the elimination of pre-revolutionary tenancy, credit and exchange relations, which reduced the obligations on such producers to dispose of significant quantities of maize as payments to landlords, moneylenders and merchants (Ibid.; Dore, 1988). To the extent that the state had difficulty substituting the functions performed by such agents, the elimination of these relations also had the effect of disarticulating rural and urban markets, thereby restricting the availability of essential goods in rural areas which in turn acted as a disincentive to marketed production.

Also, the need to sell grains to obtain emergency funds for such things as medical expenses was diminished when a free health service expanded throughout the country (Zalkin, 1985). And some maize found its way to market not as grain but as pork. Although there is little empirical evidence to assess the scale of this practice, it is probable that the traditional practice of feeding grain to pigs during the rainy season, when markets could not be reached, intensified in response to shifts in relative prices.

Many peasant producers refrained from selling their labour, particularly during the harvest period. The combination of declining real wages, improved access to land and credit (which increased the capacity of the peasant household to reproduce itself on the basis of direct agricultural production) and shortages of goods, as well as fear of being recruited into the army, kept members of peasant households away from the harvests (Enriquez, 1985). The replacement of traditional pickers by inexperienced urban youth, bureaucrats and workers was to have a damaging effect on productivity per hectare in the coffee plantations.

Labour productivity was also affected by a variety of practices engaged in by both industrial and agricultural workers. The response among agricultural labourers to the relaxation of coercive labour relations has already been noted. It has been argued that the problem of low or declining labour productivity, notably in state sector enterprises, was also an effect of a wages policy that placed considerable emphasis on 'the social wage' (free or highly subsidized food and social services) and restricted increases in nominal wages. Hence Biondi-Morra argues that such a policy:

> effectively removed the monetary incentive as a managerial instrument from the hands of state administrators. Over time this policy led to a substantial fall in the purchasing power of wages and undermined worker motivation, perpetuating the considerable loss in labour productivity that followed the revolution and the nationalization of Somoza's agribusiness operations. (Biondi-Morra, 1988, pp. 372–3)

This argument, though, would seem to overstate the effectivity of nominal wage rises as an instrument for increasing worker motivation and labour productivity in the context of a shortage economy. Such aspects are crucially linked not so much to the question of nominal wage rises *per se*, but rather to that of improved access to scarce goods. It is no coincidence that the types of demand put forward by the main union organizations in Nicaragua centred far more on the question of access to goods than on wage rises.

Government distribution policy also contributed to this problem. Many industrial workers spent an increasing proportion of the working day engaged in buying cheap basic manufactured products to which they were entitled through the state supermarket network. A proportion of these products also found their way on to the black market (Cabrales, *Barricada*, 14 November 1987, p. 3). The same phenomenon occurred during 1984 and 1985 when, in order to stem the flow of productive formal-sector workers to informal sector activities and under pressure from the unions, many enterprises adopted a policy of paying a portion of workers' wages in kind. Much of this produce was subsequently sold on the black market. This involved workers taking considerable time off to engage in commercial activities.

The phenomenon of 'urban bias' also contributed to the crisis conditions outlined earlier.[2] This bias was reflected most explicitly in the implementation of a cheap food policy which benefited mainly urban consumers. The family quota system was restricted primarily to urban areas. Even the regional distribution system, which had been intended to correct the historical bias whereby distribution was centred on Managua, tended to concentrate products in the main provincial towns. Food subsidies also benefited primarily urban consumers with certain subsidized products such as milk, which were only sold in Managua and a few other cities. Official producer prices failed to keep pace with the prices of many basic manufactures purchased by rural producers for use on the farm or in the household. Also, urban bias was reflected in the selection of products assigned priority for importation and distribution. The choice of products tended to be more in accordance with urban tastes and needs.

Investment policy also tended to concentrate resources in or close to urban centres. This applied not only to many projects associated with social infrastructure but also to several large-scale development projects in the agricultural, agro-industrial and energy sectors. Several of the largest projects, notably the Chiltepe dairy project, the Tipitapa–Malacatoya sugar complex and the Momotombo geothermal project were within a 40-kilometre radius of Managua, while the largest project on the Atlantic Coast – the new port complex – was located just outside the city of Bluefields.

The phenomenon of urban bias must be understood with reference to the predominately urban character of the insurrectionary struggle, the composition of the dominant class alliance which came to power in 1979, and the national demographic structure (Nuñez O., 1987, pp. 186–7). Urban mass organizations, in contrast to their rural counterparts, assumed an active role, for example in reinforcing, state initiatives to reorganize the distribution system for basic consumption goods. From the planning point of view, the state encountered serious administrative and material limitations, which restricted the geographical spread of the system. Planners attempting to reach the maximum number of people with limited resources felt justified in focusing attention on small, densely-populated areas, namely the towns and cities where the majority of the national population resided. The focus on urban areas was reinforced by the objective difficulties of establishing a quota system among a highly dispersed and mobile population in rural areas, above all in areas affected by the war.

The relation between this urban-centred planning imbalance and the crisis conditions analysed earlier centres on three main effects. Firstly, concentrating resources in urban areas contributed to shortages of basic processed foods or manufactures in rural areas, which in turn acted as a disincentive to peasant production and contributed to the deterioration in the terms of trade from the point of view of the peasant producer. Secondly, relatively easy access to basic goods and services, as well as employment, combined with other policies (including, for example, that of allowing squatters to settle on vacant urban lots) (MIDINRA, 1984, p. 21), constituted one of a series of conditions which attracted migrants to urban areas, and particularly to the capital, Managua. Thirdly, the attempt to improve rapidly the social conditions of the mass of the population implied massive budgetary outlays on social programmes and subsidies, which contributed to the problems outlined earlier relating to the fiscal deficit, monetary emission and inflation.

THE RAPID AND 'RATIONAL' DEVELOPMENT OF THE PRODUCTIVE FORCES

A third process of change which generated a series of contradictory effects and disequilibria involved to the attempt by the state to develop the productive forces rapidly, through planning, an ambitious public investment programme, and by concentrating productive resources in state enterprises.

The Limits to Planning

There was an implicit bias towards administrative controls as opposed to the use of macroeconomic policy instruments in order to maximize resource mobilization and promote the 'rational' use of available resources. A combination of structural, material and technical conditions, however, rendered such methods highly problematic.

The openness of the Nicaraguan economy and dependency on foreign markets and aid constituted structural features of the Nicaraguan economy which restricted the extent to which the state could effectively plan the economy. As a result the state could not determine either the prices of exports or levels of aid or, in other words, its import capacity (Fitzgerald, 1986, p. 34).

As indicated earlier, the new revolutionary state found itself in direct control of a fifth of agriculture and a third of industry: these sectors of the economy remained largely in private hands. Moreover, much of this production was controlled by petty-commodity producers and the extremely small scale of the farm units and the scattered character of production acted as a major structural constraint on planning. By 1984, the government had clearly recognized the extent to which such conditions impeded planning. The criteria governing the nationalization of wholesale trade in basic products were firmly based on such a recognition. Effective control of procurement by state wholesale agencies could only be achieved, it was argued, in those product sectors where production was concentrated in relatively few large-scale enterprises. Because of this, two of the most important food products, namely beans and maize, were excluded from the nationalization measure (CIERA, 1984b). These were produced by over 100 000 small producers spread all over the country – many in relatively inaccessible areas. It was these same criteria which contributed to the decisions taken in 1986 and 1987 to liberalize trade in basic grains.

The attempts to plan the economy had also proceeded on the assumption that Nicaraguan society was composed of well-defined classes which would respond in a predetermined manner to government policies and programmes. However, planning was undermined both by the types of class practice, noted above, relating to declining labour productivity and levels of marketed surplus, and by the extreme mobility of labour. Workers not only moved from one work site to another, but also criss-crossed geographical and sectoral boundaries: factory workers became traders; peasants moved to the towns; harvest labourers became direct producers, and so on.

The intensity of this mobility derived from the impact of the economic crisis and the war, but also from the specific sociological characteristics of many Nicaraguan households, whose members frequently engaged in a variety of forms of employment involving links with both rural and urban areas, salaried and commercial activities (Torres and Coraggio, 1987, pp. 102–3). Movement from one area or sector to another was facilitated by these family networks. Programmes such as the agrarian reform also contributed towards this rapidly-changing employment structure and the problems of labour shortages in agricultural enterprises.

The institutional organization of the state apparatus also impeded planning (Bernales, 1985). Two characteristics in particular are relevant in this context. Firstly, inter-ministerial co-ordination was impeded by what became known as 'institutional feudalism'. The scope of this problem had been highlighted early on, in seminars held in 1980 and 1981 to evaluate the initial planning experience. The economic power of the state was, in effect, diffused among a number of key ministries which in some respects operated independently of one another, although their respective areas of economic activity were closely articulated. While the Ministry of Planning had responsibility for drawing up the annual economic plan, this plan was in no way binding on the other ministries. As Ruccio explains:

Therefore, MIPLAN. . .has never enjoyed anything like complete monopoly over planning activities, short-term or annual. . . Emergency economic programs, negotiations with individual capitalist enterprises, and the continual search for foreign markets and sources of external credits and loans tended to supersede the best-laid plans of prior months. In addition, independent decisions by other ministries, especially one with the weight of Agricultural Development and Agrarian Reform (MIDINRA), would change the parameters according to which the original program was drawn up. (Ruccio, 1987, p. 71)

Two areas of state regulation or intervention significantly affected by this situation were the public investment programme and producer pricing policy. For many years different ministries would design and implement new projects, often unaware of what projects were being undertaken by other ministries in related areas, and of whether the resources required by the project were really available. As a result considerable delays in project execution arose, while other social groups were squeezed of essential resources such as building materials.

In relation to pricing policy, administrative procedures for setting official producer prices tended to be lengthy and cumbersome. As one writer points out:

> In the case of beef and milk, for example, price setting procedures involved a minimum of four different ministries, seven administrative steps, and six months of negotiations among various government branches before a decision on a new price could be reached. This lengthiness and complexity was found to prevent the translation of price policy into consistent and timely operational decisions and to contribute to the perpetuation of perverse price incentives. (Biondi-Morra, 1988, p. 372)

A second problem affecting policy and programme implementation concerned the organization of state services on the basis of independent bureaucratic structures. During the pre-revolutionary period, agricultural producers, for example, had been used to dealing with a limited number of agents who performed a variety of economic functions: selling inputs and consumer goods; buying produce; lending money; and so on. The revolutionary state attempted to substitute many of these functions, by setting up a host of separate institutions and service enterprises. As explained by the Vice Minister of MIDINRA with responsibility for the Agrarian Reform:

> We substituted the logic of [the previous] system with another based on a combination of institutions and enterprises. . .for example, in Jalapa [a highly productive zone in the North of the country] there are 16 different organizations which provide goods and services for agricultural production, and the poor producer has to deal with all of these. (Porras, *Barricada*, 30 March 1987, p. 3)

Other, more technical, problems also impeded the planning. Particularly important here was the question of information. Little was known about how the economy was structured, the complexity of production systems, the logic of different economic agents, and how the different economic sectors and activities (as well as institutional forms) were articulated. Very often the necessary information and studies on which decisions, policies and plans should have been based, simply was not available. Moreover, as has been pointed out by Baumeister, it emerged that when such information was forthcoming, it was often 'overpoliticized', inflating the importance in the economy of the 'classic' antagonists: the state sector and the bourgeoisie. It is claimed, for example, that work on the first annual economic plan proceeded on the assumption that the state controlled half the land, whereas in reality it controlled approximately a fifth (Baumeister, 1988a, p. 230).

Planning and policy design had proceeded on the basis of a dualistic vision of the rural economy, where the dynamic sectors consisted of state enterprise sector and private (capitalist) producers. Relatively little was known about the large mass of small producers who tended to be bypassed by the state in certain areas of economic policy (Ibid., p. 231). According to Kaimowitz, the vision of the Nicaraguan economy that informed decisions on policy and strategy during the early years of the post-revolutionary period was that related to the 'agro-export model' which emphasized the dependent character of the economy, the scale of capitalist production and the considerable extent of semi-proletarianization of the rural population (Kaimowitz, 1986a, p. 100). This conception derived from analyses carried out during the pre-revolutionary period (Nuñez, O. 1980; Wheelock, 1975), which were reinforced by a large survey of the rural population carried out by CIERA in 1980.[3] Results from this study contributed to a vision of a rural society where 65 per cent of the population was composed either of permanent or seasonal labourers, as well as poor peasants (or 'semi-proletarians') (CIERA, 1980).

A more accurate description of Nicaraguan reality was the 'peasant capitalism' model which was to gain currency in later years. It stressed to a greater degree the role of small and medium-sized independent agricultural producers integrated in the market, and fully proletarianized labourers. As Kaimowitz points out:

> The two models differ widely in their implications regarding agricultural policy. The capitalist agro-export model provides a rationale for emphasising the role of the state farms and the large agricultural bourgeoisie, opposing both widespread land redistribution and strong support for small basic grain producers, and aggregating all of Nicaragua's rural poor into one organisation. The peasant capitalist model, by contrast, implies the need to support strongly small and medium-sized individual producers and

to redistribute land. Its proponents also favour the idea of separate organisations for independent agricultural producers and agricultural wage workers. (Kaimowitz, 1986a, p. 101)

The difficulty of gauging accurately the nature of rural social structure is evidenced by the fact that even proponents of the 'peasant capitalism' model presented different interpretations. An alternative interpretation of the data contained in the original 1980 CIERA survey revealed not only the importance of a sector of rich peasant producers but also of a category of middle peasants, who neither sold nor purchased labour power to any significant degree (Zalkin, 1988a). A simplified presentation of these three interpretations appears in Table 7.11.[4]

This discussion of differing interpretations of rural social structure raises two important points in relation to the question of planning and economic policy formulation. Firstly, as already indicated, lack of knowledge and inaccurate perceptions contributed towards certain imbalances and biases in the allocation of resources among different social groups. Secondly, what emerges from the more accurate models is the extremely heterogeneous character of rural society. Moreover, to these groups of rich, middle and poor peasants, capitalist producers, and agricultural workers, were added during the post-revolutionary period a sizeable state farm and co-operative sector. The logic which orientates the reproduction of these forms of production is very different. For policies to be effective as regulatory mechanisms or as incentives, the process of policy design should take into account these differences (Schejtman, 1983). Such an approach, though, requires a level of sophistication in planning and policy design which is extremely difficult to achieve in the best of circumstances, and was certainly not practised during the early years of the post-revolutionary period.

Lack of information and analyses regarding socioeconomic structures and relations, as well as the over-politicization of certain analyses, also affected another important area associated with food policy, namely marketing. The mass of the rural population had, it was believed, been exploited not only by the agrarian bourgeoisie but also by commercial capital. Food price and subsidy policy, plus a number of regulations governing wholesale and retail trade, aimed to expand the role of state marketing agencies in procurement and wholesaling trade, and displace private merchants from these activities. This approach, however, failed to conceptualize the complex

TABLE 7.11   *Alternative interpretations of rural social structure, 1978–80*

	Agro-export model 1 %	Peasant capitalism model 2 %	Middle peasant model 3 %
Rich peasants/ Peasant capitalists	4.7	32.5	17.8
Small independent Producers/Middle peasants	13.4	–	32.1
Poor peasants/ Semi-proletarians	57.1	36.8	33.3
Proletariat	24.8	30.7	16.8
Total	100	100	100

SOURCES   Based on data contained in IFAD, 1980 (Model 1); IHCA, 1985 (Model 2); and Zalkin, 1988a (Model 3). Model 2 is presented in Kaimowitz, 1986a: 105.

relations which articulated commercial capital and peasant pro-ducers. A relatively small group of large merchants constituted the nucleus of a commercial system which, while highly exploitative from the point of view of the small producer, was able to move agricultural produce to the towns and cities, and essential inputs and consumer items to the countryside: articulating in the process not only rural and urban markets but also national and international markets. The complexity of merchant–peasant relations (as well as the nature of distortions and dislocating effects of attempts by the state to regulate commercial activities and directly control a portion of rural–urban trade) are described in the following terms by CIERA:

[following the revolution] a series of commercial relations which gave fluidity to the system began to disappear affecting, in particu-lar, rural areas. The wholesale merchant, or the 'mobile' inter-mediary who sometimes acted as an agent of the former, supplied producers in the countryside with the products they needed. . .on time and on credit. The merchants would be paid with the basic grains harvest or he would make futures purchases. Although the peasant producer was exploited by the merchant through the price system, and remained permanently in debt, the producer benefited from the fact that both imported and national goods were delivered to his house, that such goods arrived when they were needed and could be obtained without the producer having to provide cash or transport. The merchant had a profound knowledge of rural needs, had developed a network of relations in the city and in the Central American region, and had the necessary transport and capital. As such the system worked efficiently. . . .

When these agents disappeared, the producer began to require transport to take his grains to ENABAS, was obliged to look for goods in the towns, and had to enter into a series of impersonal relations with the bank, MICOIN, PROAGRO, etc. . . .Such a process of change and reaccommodation takes time and the first effects are those of distortions, disequilibria and discontent. The merchant, while labelled as exploiter, was not always perceived as such. In practice he entered into paternalistic relations with his clients. Such relations had existed for generations and did not only facilitate the supply of basic goods, but served other functions, including the provision of medical services, general adviser, and even the role of godfather. (CIERA, 1987c)

In brief, it can be said that these types of pre-revolution commercial relations maintained low levels of living for the mass of peasant producers, but they also ensured that basic grains and certain other crops would be produced and delivered to urban areas. In contrast, revolutionary policies served to increase the levels of living of a sizeable sector of the rural population, but had the effect of disarticulating production and marketing circuits.

State control of marketing, then, dislocated marketing circuits in two important respects. Firstly, it ruptured the traditional networks linking rural and urban markets, thereby affecting the flow of grains and other food products to the towns as well as the availability of manufactured goods or processed food products in rural areas. Secondly, the state failed to recognize the extent to which the reproduction of the peasant economy depended on imported goods. As a number of studies have shown, many of the production inputs and implements, as well as consumer items required by the peasant household, are not produced nationally (DGFCDC, 1988a). Decisions regarding the use of foreign exchange tended to prioritize 'heavy' producer goods, mass or urban consumption goods (food, medicines, and so on), and general agricultural inputs such as fertilizer, pesticides and seed. For several years, not much importance was attached to so-called 'peasant goods' such as machetes, maize grinders and rubber boots in decisions regarding the allocation of foreign exchange. Since many of these goods were obtained from other countries in the region, their acquisition was also affected by the collapse of the Central American Common Market during the first half of the 1980s.

State-centred Accumulation Bias

Resource allocation determined by the plan clearly favoured the state sector. With regard to consumption, this imbalance is reflected in data showing the evolution of public and private sector consumption. As indicated in Table 7.12, public sector consumption measured in constant prices increased from less than three billion córdobas during the late 1970s to more than nine billion in 1985, or from approximately 12 to 36 per cent of GDP. Over the same period private consumption fell by half.

Planning imbalances favouring the state sector were particularly obvious in the area of investment. It has been estimated that during the 1970–78 period private sector investment accounted for more than 60 per cent of the total. The state sector invested primarily in infrastructure to support private production (Kleiterp, 1988, p. 16). Towards the middle of the 1980s (1983–85) the state realized an estimated 81 per cent of total investment and 73 per cent of investment in agriculture and agro-industry (see Table 7.13).

Production inputs and investment resources were concentrated largely in state agricultural and agro-industrial enterprises, which were considered the 'engine of growth' for the economy. The scale of this imbalance was alluded to by the Minister of Agricultural Development and Agrarian Reform when he addressed delegates at the First National Congress of the Peasantry held in April 1986:

> We began to execute many projects, and given our desire to increase production rapidly and because we were involved in a process of land redistribution, we could not articulate the investment programme with the peasant movement or the sector of small- and medium-sized ranchers who are still waiting for the Revolutionary Government and the Ministry of Agricultural Development to design a comprehensive investment programme for their benefit. Considerable resources were channelled towards high technology and irrigation projects while the peasantry did not receive the same benefit. (Wheelock, 1986, p. 22)

TABLE 7.12 *Evolution of Public and Private sector consumption, 1978–85 (in millions of córdobas at 1980 prices, and percentages)*

	1978	1980	1981	1982	1983	1984	1985
Consumption	22 837	21 269	19 392	18 284	19 579	20 256	19 941
Public	2 843	4 103	4 654	5 441	7 458	8 748	9 361
% GDP[1]	12.4	19.7	21.9	23.4	31.4	35.3	35.9
Private	19 994	17 166	14 738	12 843	12 122	11 508	10 581
% GDP[1]	71.0	82.6	73.9	67.8	56.7	55.5	57.9

SOURCE Planning and Budget Office (SPP).
[1] Percentage of GDP at current prices.

TABLE 7.13 *Evolution of state and private investment, 1980–82, 1983–85*

	1980–82 %	1983–85 %
Accumulation (total)	100	100
State	75	81
Private	25	19
Agric./Agro-industry	100	100
State	58	73
Private	42	27

SOURCE Arguello, Croes and Kleiterp, 1987.

An additional problem existed in that state enterprises assumed something of an enclave character, with limited interaction with other forms of property and farming systems. This relation (or lack of it) contrasted sharply with the pre-revolutionary model, where large landowners performed a series of functions that, while involving exploitative relations, provided informal credit, certain inputs, transport, consumption goods, and so on which were necessary for the reproduction of the peasant household. The transformation of social relations associated with the process of revolutionary change dislocated this system. The failure of state enterprises to substitute these functions made the access of some peasant producers to essential goods and services even more difficult.

While the production performance (in volume terms) of state agricultural enterprises compared favourably with that of other forms of production (see Table 7.14), they incurred significant financial

TABLE 7.14   *Evolution of state-sector agricultural production, 1982–87*
(production levels in 000s)

Product	Concept	1982/83	1983/84	1984/85	1985/86	1986/87
Coffee	Volume (QQ)	336.9	218.0	310.5	261.0	183.3
	Index	100	65	92	77	54
	%*	21.5	20.4	27.8	24.4	18.4
Cotton	Volume (QQ)	433.5	442.0	394.5	290.3	192.2
	Index	100	102	91	66	44
	%*	24.7	23.5	26.2	26.3	28.3
Sugar-cane	Volume (ST)	884.4	1 015.0	1 245.5	972.6	942.6
	Index	100	115	141	110	107
	%*	29.6	32.4	47.2	36.9	40.7
Rice	Volume (QQ)	758.0	890.7	690.7	779.5	841.4
	Index	100	118	91	103	111
	%*	34.4	39.5	34.7	40.9	45.8
Sorghum	Volume (QQ)	116.1	265.3	335.0	616.6	676.3
	Index	100	228	288	531	582
	%*	9.3	12.3	13.7	19.4	22.2
Maize	Volume (QQ)	312.2	503.5	532.2	755.1	293.8
	Index	100	161	170	242	94
	%*	8.8	10.5	12.2	18.6	6.4

		1982	1983	1984	1985	1986
Beef	Vol. (lbs)	19 542	22 218	19 254	13 851	9 782
	Index	100	114	99	71	50
	%*	30.9	32.6	32.7	31.7	28.6
Milk	Vol. (gls)	3 507	3 390	3 210	3 275	3 682
	Index	100	97	92	93	105
	%*	25.6	35.2	37.4	37.8	50.7
Chicken	Vol. (lbs)	5 194	5 958	5 764	5 826	5 847
	Index	100	115	111	112	113
	%*	23.3	25.2	27.6	25.8	25.9
Eggs	Vol. (doz)	4 796	3 891	4 018	5 454	6 063
	Index	100	81	84	114	126
	%*	26.5	20.8	23.0	25.6	27.3
Pork	Vol. (lbs)	7 647	8 318	8 258	8 337	8 540
	Index	100	109	108	109	112
	%*	74.2	57.4	53.3	37.1	41.1

SOURCE   MIDINRA.
QQ: Quintals; ST: Short tons.
* Percentage of national production.

losses. According to one analyst, the explanation for such losses
'could be not be found in the relatively more familiar territory of the
firm's institutional design and inner operation. Instead, their main
difficulties seemed to stem from. . .the macro components of the
food policy itself', notably those aspects related to exchange rate,
domestic price, interest rate and wages policy (Biondi-Morra, 1988,
p. 2).

In 1983, the government agreed to wipe off the losses of state
enterprises. Within two years, however, this sector had again accumulated major debts and a second bail-out was approved (Ibid,
p. 376). As Biondi-Morra points out: 'This turn of events was
particularly disturbing to policy makers since it called into question
the feasibility of the so-called new model of state accumulation. . .'
(Ibid).

A planning imbalance favouring accumulation over consumption
emerged clearly in 1982, when resources were increasingly concentrated in relatively large and often slow-yielding development projects. In that year investment accounted for 21 per cent of GDP. As
more and more resources were channelled towards large-scale projects, the tension between accumulation and consumption increased.

Between 1980 and 1984 the composition of imports altered considerably as capital goods destined for industry and agro-industry
increased their share from 7 per cent to 18 per cent of total imports,
while the proportion of non-durable consumer goods was reduced
from 24 to 13 per cent. This tension contributed to the problems of
shortages of basic consumer goods that became increasingly apparent
from 1982 onwards.

Financing such projects also added to inflationary pressures. The
public investment programme, while initially overly ambitious, became unsustainable while the country was at war and subject to the
types of economic boycott measures outlined above. As explained by
President Ortega:

> We began with great expectations, attempting to resolve problems
> which had been with us since colonial times. . .In the midst of a
> war, we have had to shoulder the burden of multiple investment
> projects that imply an extraordinary effort for the country. We are
> now trying to. . .explain to functionaries of the Revolutionary
> State that we should be strong enough and sincere enough to speak
> to the people to tell them what exactly is possible and not under-

take to resolve things we are unable to resolve. (*Barricada*, 20 July 1987)

The source of this imbalance was to be found not only in the climate of urgency alluded to by Ortega, which was perhaps an inevitable feature of the immediate post-revolutionary phase, but also in the strength of certain fractions of the technocracy that adhered to an ideology of modernization which saw in the large-scale capital intensive development project the quick and easy way out of underdevelopment. There was not only the will to invest in projects of this nature, but also the resources, as foreign governments, notably of OECD and socialist bloc countries, provided considerable aid geared precisely towards projects of this nature (Barraclough *et al.*, 1988). Once the investment dynamic was set in motion, it attained a momentum which proved extremely difficult to constrain.

Notes

1. The 1982/83 agricultural cycle is the first year for which MIDINRA provides a breakdown of production by forms of property (state farms, large-scale private producers, and small and medium producers (including co-operatives).
2. The term 'urban bias' is used here in a fairly restrictive sense. Several important policies and programmes attached a high priority to the rural and agricultural sectors, notably those associated with credit, health and education.
3. The *Encuesta de los Trabajadores del Campo* gathered data from more than 50 000 heads of rural families.
4. The table is intended to give a rough approximation of how different analysts perceived rural social structure. Since Zalkin's model (# 3) does not include the agrarian bourgeoisie, this category has been eliminated from the other two models and the figures adjusted accordingly.

8 The Changing Balance of Social Forces, Participation and the Policy Process

INTRODUCTION

The types of constraint and contradiction reviewed above provide a necessary backdrop for understanding the policy changes which emerged during the mid-1980s. Throughout this study, however, I have stressed the need to refer to another set of conditions associated with state–society relations and changes in the correlation of social forces in order to understand the shift from orthodoxy to reform: the reduced emphasis on direct state control of the means of production; changes in the domestic terms of trade favouring agriculture and the peasantry; a greater degree of free trade in agricultural products; and the increased availability of goods used or consumed by the peasant household.

In this chapter I undertake a more detailed examination of how specific developments at the level of civil society, transformations in social structure and changes affecting institutionalized forms of 'popular participation' affected state–society relations and the capacity of different groups to influence the policy process. Particular attention is focused here on the peasantry, the organized working class and the urban informal sector, and the mass organizations which represented their interests. I also consider, more briefly, a number of developments affecting the bureaucracy.

STATE–SOCIETY RELATIONS

To explain what one writer has called the 'shift from state-centred accumulation to the strategic alliance with the peasantry' (Kaimowitz, 1988), it is necessary to examine developments at the level of civil society that served to restrict the autonomy of the state and which saw the correlation of social forces move in favour of certain sectors

226

of the peasantry. Through this type of analysis we avoid the limitations inherent in explanations which see policy reforms solely in terms of attempts to correct policy errors, or simply as pragmatic adjustments to changing economic, political, military and international circumstances or crisis conditions.

Before turning to the reform process itself, however, it is important to address the question of why the state assumed such a dominant role in rural society following the revolution and why resources for production and investment were concentrated to such a degree in the APP sector. It is tempting to seek an easy answer to these questions by focusing on the issue of Sandinista ideology.

Orthodox ideological positions claiming the superiority of state enterprises and the need for forced modernization/agro-industrialization clearly found expression amongst political leaders and the technocracy. A technical/professional stratum which had associated itself with the revolutionary movement of the later 1970s was particularly influential in shaping development policies and programmes during the early post-revolutionary period which stressed the need for large-scale capital intensive development (Baumeister, 1988b, p. 5). And it was within the state sector that engineers, agronomists and others were given free rein to implement their plans and projects. The APP was, in effect, the terrain where technocratic dreams would come true. As the Minister of Agriculture explained:

> These people have identified with the revolution because. . .the Nicaraguan private enterprise sector never allowed them to apply their expertise on the scale which is now possible. Working within the state sector they are not constrained. They can build their sugar refineries, dairy and other projects. They see that they have within their hands the capacity to transform [the economy]. (author's translation – Wheelock interviewed in Invernizzi *et al.*, 1986, p. 204)

To better understand 'state-centredness', however, we must consider not only the question of ideology and the influence of a specific technical/professional stratum within the central state apparatus, but also refer to three structural conditions existing both before and immediately after the seizure of state power by the Sandinistas. Firstly, the pre-revolutionary state already exercised a prominent role in the Nicaraguan economy, acting as intermediary between the world market and national producers (Nuñez O., 1987, p. 43), by

creating favourable infrastructural conditions for agro-export producers, as well as supporting more directly economic activities controlled by the Somoza group (Weeks, 1988).

Secondly, the insurrectionary process 'decapitated' to some extent
rural society, removing from power certain elements of the local
elite, composed of large landowners and merchants among others.
This created, in effect, a vacuum which would not be filled by the
rural masses, given a third structural condition which characterized
pre-revolutionary Nicaragua, namely the fact that the mass of the
rural population did not constitute a cohesive social force. The
Nicaraguan peasantry was dispersed and unorganized and not integrated to any significant degree in the revolutionary movement.
Attempts to organize the rural population in the northern interior of
the country in the 1960s, as well as agricultural workers in the
northern Pacific region during the late 1970s, were repressed by
landowners and the National Guard (CIERA, 1984d, pp. 26–7). As
Chamorro explains:

> To safeguard the requirements of the agro-export sector for land
> and labour, domination in the countryside was secured primarily
> through the institutions of political society, thereby depriving the
> rural population of any real participation in the political life of the
> society. (Chamorro, 1983, p. 9)

While the FSLN had received support from peasants during the years
of guerrilla warfare in the mountains of the interior of the country,
active support tended to be fairly localized. When, by the late 1970s,
the revolutionary struggle assumed a national dimension, it was the
urban rather than the rural masses that actively engaged in the armed
struggle to overthrow the Somoza dictatorship.

While rich peasant producers constituted, in quantitative terms, an
important social group, their economic power had been restricted by
the nature of the agro-export model and Somocista domination,
which restricted the access of many rich peasants to resources necessary to sustain a process of extended reproduction. This group also
remained unorganized. While certain fractions of the agrarian bourgeoisie had formed producer associations during the 1970s these
remained elitist in character and did not attempt to incorporate, on
any scale, smaller producers (CIERA, 1989c). By the time the
Sandinistas seized power, the Union of Nicaraguan Agricultural

Producers (UPANIC), an umbrella organization representing commercial farming interests, was barely five months old.

As for the agrarian bourgeoisie that remained once the Somoza group had been eliminated, we saw earlier that certain producers gradually withdrew from production, withheld investment or decapitalized their enterprises. As more antagonistic relations developed between the state and the associations representing bourgeois interests, the capacity of the latter to influence the policy process was reduced, although (as indicated below) from 1984 onwards certain fractions of the agrarian bourgeoisie switched affiliation and joined the 'pro-revolution' agricultural producers organization, UNAG.

The highly limited development of civil society in rural areas, and changes in local power structure, created conditions in which the post-revolutionary state could exercise freely its 'relative autonomy'. Into the vacuum stepped party officials, the bureaucracy and managers of state enterprises: the central state bureaucracy doubled in size during the early post-revolutionary period.

This situation helps to explain both the 'state centredness' of the post-revolutionary development model and the urban bias which characterized certain government programmes. Not only did the urban masses make up the core of the insurrectionary movement, but in urban areas civil society was far more developed during the pre-revolutionary period. Relatively large sectors of the urban population were organized in trade unions, professional/political organizations, student associations, and so on. Nearly a year before the seizure of state power by the Sandinistas, urban neighbourhood residents had also begun to organize themselves in Civil Defence Committees (CIERA, 1984d). It was organizations such as these that were to exert a powerful influence on the policy process during the immediate post-revolutionary period. The fact that the bureaucracy was concentrated in Managua also contributed to urban bias. It was not until 1982, when the state administrative apparatus was decentralized, that regional interests began to carry more weight.

THE EMERGENCE OF THE PEASANTRY AS A DOMINANT SOCIAL FORCE

This correlation of urban–rural social forces, as well as state–rural society relations, was soon to change. One of the most significant

TABLE 8.1   *Growth in membership of UNAG, 1982–86*

	Members
1982	65 820
1984	75 228
1986	125 824

SOURCE   UNAG – see IHCA, 1989, p. 39.

political developments in the years leading up to the reforms concerned the growing strength of the organized peasantry.

Formed in 1981, by the next year the organization already claimed membership of nearly 66 000 producers. By the end of 1986, there were 125 000 members; approximately two-thirds of the total number of agricultural producers in the country (see Table 8.1).

Important changes also occurred in the social composition and demands of the organization. When the organization was established its membership consisted primarily of co-operative members who had previously been affiliated to the Association of Rural Workers (ATC). While many of the organization's leaders were drawn from the ranks of the rich peasantry, early demands and activities centred primarily on the development and consolidation of the co-operative movement and the recruitment of smaller producers. In 1984, however, following a change in leadership, the UNAG started to recruit many commercial farmers who included local community leaders and so-called 'patriotic producers' (Luciak, 1987, p. 43; A. Bucardo and D. Nuñez interviewed in IHCA, 1989a, p. 35; Nuñez, D., 1989).

While the general demands of the organization, centring on issues associated with the land problem and improved access to basic goods, continued to favour co-operatives, poor and middle peasants' demands, associated more directly with larger producers' interests, came increasingly to the fore. Two specific areas of tension between small and large producers related to the question of land redistribution and the allocation of goods. Referring to the former, Luciak writes:

Land pressure from displaced peasants in the war zones and from farmers with insufficient land resulted in land invasions in the region of Boaco and Chontales during 1985. The invasions were often supported by the local UNAG and FSLN representatives. . .

This resulted at times in UNAG members invading land of other UNAG members. The national board of directors of UNAG had to resolve these problems by exerting pressure on the FSLN to remove the invaders. The national office of the UNAG argued that invasions did not resolve the problem of land pressure and that the agrarian reform had to be carried out henceforth in an 'orderly fashion'. This position was essential if the fears of the medium and large producers were to be allayed, but it created antagonism on the part of the impoverished and displaced farmers. (Luciak, 1987, p. 43)

To avoid tensions such as these, the UNAG placed considerable emphasis on the need to redistribute state lands and to compensate landowners whose lands were affected by the law. The organization also encouraged a more flexible approach to co-operativization and the redistribution of land to individual producers.

Concerning the allocation of goods, the same author writes:

Limited resources force the organization at times to choose whether it should satisfy the demands of key big producers or solve problems of the small and medium farmers. In interviews, conducted in Juigalpa on the occasion of the celebration of UNAG's fourth anniversary, many small farmers complained about priority treatment given to big producers. Since the cooperation of the capitalist farmers is vital to the revolutionary project, they are allocated scarce resources, such as jeeps and tires. The peasants watch the capitalist producers driving round in their jeeps, while many times they are not able to secure transport facilities to get their own crops to market. (Ibid., pp. 53–4)

The drive to recruit medium- and large-scale producers also forced the members of collectives into a minority position within the organization. As indicated in Table 8.2 below, only 22 per cent of the organization's card-holding members belonged to collectives in 1985. Moreover, a series of problems affecting the development of the co-operative movement meant that many of these 'collectives' did not, in fact, operate as such. A CIERA study of 71 production co-operatives (CAS), carried out in 1985, found that approximately half could be categorized as collectives. Another 30 per cent were found to operate more as capitalist enterprises, while another 23 per cent had no coherent organizational structure (CIERA, 1985c).

TABLE 8.2 *Membership statistics of UNAG, 1985*

Collectives (CAS & CT)	Credit and service[1]	Private or associated Members[2]	Total
23 025	45 027	37 947	106 134[3]

SOURCE Based on UNAG (see CIERA, 1987, p. 24)
CAS Sandinista production co-operative.
CT Work collective.
[1] Members of these co-operatives are generally loosely associated private farmers. Includes also members of so-called 'fallow row' (*surco muerto*) co-ops.
[2] Private producers who may or may not belong to the organization's base structures.
[3] Does not include members participating in certain producer commissions (*comisiones por rubro*).

These developments affected the types of demands put forward by the organization's members.

What is referred to in Nicaragua as the sector of 'medium-sized' producers (rich peasants/'peasant capitalists') constituted historically an important sector in the agrarian structure. As mentioned earlier, under the previous regime this group had been deprived of essential resources (apart from land on the agrarian frontier) and forms of organization conducive to economic growth, social development and power (Nuñez D., 1987, pp. 42–3). That the interests of this sector should come increasingly to the fore reflected not only the extent to which these producers had been able to organize and increase their collective bargaining strength but also the major structural changes which had transformed thousands of landless labourers and poor peasants into middle or rich peasants or members of collectives integrated in commodity markets.

There is no accurate data which enable us to quantify changes in rural social structure during the post-revolutionary period. Certain observations can be made, however, which point to a considerable reduction in the size of the poor peasantry and the expansion, in areas of the country outside the war zones, of what constituted a small commercial farming sector, integrated by co-operatives as well as middle and rich peasants. Three policies or programmes in particular were instrumental in producing these changes. Firstly, as a result of the agrarian reform, nearly 63 000 workers and peasants had received land by the end of 1986. Secondly, an estimated 76 000 producers (approximately 40 per cent of all peasant families) had joined co-operatives, mainly credit and service co-operatives. Thirdly, an estimated 80 000 families participated in the National Development Bank's (BND) rural credit programme. Improved access to credit had the effect of stimulating integration in product markets.

As the UNAG grew in strength it adopted a higher profile in the participatory processes associated with legislative and executive functions. Throughout 1984, successive UNAG leaders (Wilberto Lara and Daniel Nuñez) demanded a far greater say in planning and economic policy decision-making (Torres and Coraggio, 1987, pp. 200, 204).

When the National Assembly came into being in 1985, nine out of the ninety-six full-time representatives from seven political parties were UNAG members, while another seventeen were 'substitutes', entitled to sit-in for representatives who could not appear for one reason or another. The fact that they were drawn from different parties (FSLN, Conservative and Liberal) meant, however, that they did not always vote as a bloc. They nevertheless participated actively in the legislature's agricultural commission, which was influential in determining agricultural policy and was presided over by the UNAG's President (Luciak, 1987, p. 49).

Even more important from the point of view of UNAG's capacity to influence the policy process was the organization's direct representation on a variety of executive councils and commissions which operated at both central and regional levels. At the national level, the President of the UNAG participated in the National Planning Council where the major policy decisions were approved. UNAG representatives also participated in executive commissions concerned with the design, review and implementation of policies and plans associated with the Agrarian Reform programme, credit, producer prices, taxes, the supply of basic inputs and consumer goods, production levels for coffee, cotton, beef, sugar and basic grains, and so on, as well as the provision of health and adult education services in rural areas (Ibid., pp. 49, 54; Wilson, 1987; Nuñez D., interviewed in IHCA, 1989, p. 38).

The UNAG also participated actively in the municipal councils, which played an important part in determining resource allocation and in proposing projects at the community level (Wilson, 1987, p. 248). The process of regionalization of the state planning and administrative apparatus, which began in 1982, provided an institutional framework through which the UNAG and other mass organizations with a strong regional base of support (notably the rural workers' organization) could exert greater influence on the policy and planning process.

While the UNAG was closely linked to the FSLN and generally supportive of the government it nevertheless gained a reputation as an effective pressure group, channelling the demands of its membership upwards and getting results (Vilas, 1986b, p. 29). As pointed out by Luciak:

> UNAG is an organization with a 'bottom-up' approach to policy formation, a fact amply demonstrated by the functioning of base assemblies, whose meetings provide impressive examples of popular democracy at work. UNAG holds base meetings at the regional level. In a given region, hundreds of local assemblies are held, which serve to collect opinions and survey problems of the producers. Whenever possible, problems are dealt with on the spot. The consultation process goes on at the local level for a period of several weeks at a time and culminates in a regional assembly. The questions which have to be dealt with at the regional or national level are taken up in this regional assembly with representatives of UNAG, the government, and the party. (Luciak, 1987, p. 46)

This process played an important part in decisions to increase the supply of work implements and basic consumer goods to rural areas. In 1984, assemblies were held throughout the country. Through such meetings leaders realized the levels of discontent which existed, associated with problems of shortages of essential inputs, implements and other goods. One producer was reported as saying: 'It is no use them coming to tell us to increase production if they don't bring us the things we need to produce' (see Serra, 1988, p. 32).

During early 1986, base assemblies were again held throughout the country, culminating in April in the First National Peasant Congress, attended by some 500 peasant delegates and several top government leaders. The demands which emanated from the meeting reinforced the reform dynamic initiated earlier. Particular stress was placed on the need for a more flexible approach on the part of the state regarding 'appropriate' co-operative models; greater respect for individual producers and the need to give confidence to larger producers; improved rural–urban terms of trade and rural supply systems; and a greater role for women in the peasant movement (Bucardo, interviewed in IHCA, 1989, p. 37). What was noteworthy about the meeting was not only the extent to which government leaders endorsed the reform proposals but also the self-critical tone of several of the speeches by government leaders when evaluating state–peasant relations (Wheelock, 1986).

THE WORKING CLASS: A NEW ALLIANCE AND A SPECIFIC TRADE-OFF

The abandonment of the 'cheap food' policy, which had guaranteed urban workers access to food at subsidized prices, would clearly have an immediate impact on the levels of living of the working class. Curiously, however, the two major organizations representing industrial and agricultural workers, the CST and ATC respectively, accepted the policy changes with little opposition. Why was this so?

In terms of numerical strength, the trade union movement had grown considerably, from an estimated 27 000 workers before 1979, to 145 000 in 1983, reaching some 260 000 by mid-1986, 56 per cent of the total number of wage-earners. In 1985, 82 per cent of all unionized wage-earners belonged to two Sandinista mass organizations – the CST with 65 per cent of the total, and the ATC with 17 per cent (Vilas, 1986a, p. 12; 1986b, p. 28; Stahler-Sholk, 1986). The total number of unions increased from 165 during the late 1970s to some 3000 by the late 1984 (Tirado, *Barricada*, 5 September 1984, p. 5).

While the trade union movement grew in numbers, the organizational strength of the main trade union federation declined. The CST tended to prioritize the Sandinista party line which stressed the need for national unity, increased labour productivity, austerity and self-sacrifice in order to win the war and create a 'survival economy'. This meant, in practice, subordinating more economistic class demands which, in turn, weakened the organization's base of support and produced tensions between the leadership and the rank and file (Florez-Estrada and Lobo, 1986, pp. 28–9).

The ATC, however, with a virtual monopoly in the organization of agricultural workers, proved more successful in combining or harmonizing class and party demands. It was estimated that in approximately 20 per cent of state agricultural enterprises, as well as in some private enterprises, the participation of workers had been institutionalized in the decision-making process at the enterprise level, while considerable social benefits had been achieved. The latter included,

for example, channelling of 25 per cent enterprise profits into a social
fund (Ibid., p. 29). Developments such as these were also facilitated
by the priority accorded via the state's development strategy to the
agricultural sector (Vilas, 1986b, p. 27).

In addition to adhering closely to the party line, the main trade
union organizations were also subject to specific government controls
which restricted certain forms of pressure. Most important in this
respect was the State of Economic Emergency imposed in 1981,
prohibiting strike action (Vilas, 1986a, p. 13) and demonstrations.

The fact that the main trade union organizations were prepared to
accept the abandonment of cheap food policy also related to a
reconceptualization of the nature of the class struggle. As Vilas
points out:

> During the early 1980s. . .the politico-ideological conflict with the
> bourgeoisie was relegated to a secondary level. The class contra-
> diction that had been at the front of [workers'] mobilizations in
> 1981, gave ground to the anti-imperialist contradiction, the urgent
> requirements of production and defense and the primacy of national
> unity. (Vilas, 1986a, p. 14)

It has been estimated that approximately 53 000 workers (46 per cent
of unionized labour) participated in some form of defence activity
(Florez-Estrada and Lobo, 1986, p. 28).

Towards the end of 1984, however, attention focused not only on
the external enemy but also on a new internal enemy. This was not
the industrial or agrarian bourgeoisie, but private commercial capital
and certain small-scale informal sector traders who were seen as
benefiting from, and indeed contributing to, the inflationary spiral
and bleeding the 'productive sectors' of the economy of vital resources (Vilas, 1986a).

The identification of new class enemies coincided with a new
definition of the 'historical subject' of the revolution. In official
Sandinista discourse, less emphasis was placed on the 'people' or the
'popular sectors' in general and more stress on the notion of a
worker–peasant alliance of 'productive' sector workers in general.
Within this framework, the CST recognized the need to give incentives to the peasantry to increase food production and tackle problems of inflation and shortages. It was considered important, though,
that the benefits did not accrue to merchants and speculators. Hence
the state would continue to procure a portion of the harvests to

supply both the working class and the army, and in conjunction with the mass organizations attempt to clamp down on illegal commercial activities.

Explaining the response of the main union organizations to the change in policy should not, however, be limited to the question of state–union relations and the effectivity of Sandinista ideology, but also to a series of 'compensatory' measures, which were themselves a product of working-class demands. These were expressed in the resolutions of the Fourth National Assembly of Trade Unions, held in January 1985, which not only supported government appeals to increase production and productivity but also called on the government to improve workers' access to basic consumer goods, and for stricter controls on traders and speculators.

These demands were translated into concrete actions the following month when an agreement was signed by the CST and MICOIN, under which workers and public-sector employees would be given privileged access to sixteen consumer goods. This, it was hoped, would begin to curb the decline of real wages of workers and state-sector employees which had declined by 38 per cent between 1981 and 1985 (in relation to the general retail price index – see Vilas, 1986a, p. 19). The products involved were primarily basic manufactures such as personal hygiene products, clothes, footwear, kitchen utensils and batteries. A limited number of processed food products, including powdered milk and cereal mixes used for drinks, were also distributed to workers.

As we saw earlier, an increasing number of Managua's state-run supermarkets were converted into commissaries (*Centros de Abastecimiento de los Trabajadores – CATs*) where only workers (and family members) with union cards could shop. Such centres gradually extended to other cities, while in smaller towns and the countryside an increased supply of goods was delivered to commissaries located in work-places.

The MICOIN–CST agreement prioritized certain categories of workers, principally agricultural and industrial labourers. In practice, however, other groups also benefited, notably the bureaucracy which, via the National Union of State Employees (UNE), was also represented by the CST. According to Phipps: 'Sandinista union leaderships, in securing the extension of the CATs system to non-productive workers, acted to promote the short-term interests of their members, but against the overall objective of government policy.' (Phipps, 1988). Sandinista cadres and militants operating within the party structures were also influential in this respect. As *Envio* points out:

> The revolution could have realized a transference of real purchasing power if it had limited this transference to the productive workers, but it could not resist the political pressure exercised by its own militants who represented non-productive sectors and who, given the rise in prices, defended their demand for increases in their social salary. . .The history of the CATs. . .exemplifies how political pressure subverted the state measure. At the beginning, 100,000 CAT cards were given out. By August 10, 1986, the moment in which an effort was initiated to reduce the number of CAT cards in circulation, there were 350,000 CAT card holders. Even retired national lottery sellers had gotten cards. (IHCA, 1986a)

Towards the end of 1985, assemblies were held in over a thousand work centres in which more than 90 000 workers participated. These assemblies culminated in a three-day national conference attended by 1300 delegates and several members of the Sandinista National Directorate, which placed issues associated with the supply of basic goods and price control next to defence as the top priority. In its closing statement, the conference agreed to:

> take actions to recuperate the real salary by forming a national commission which will proceed to look at ways of:
>
> a) reducing and controlling the prices of basic products, on the basis of a strict revision of costs of production, transport and a substantial reduction of the profits of marketing and import enterprises.
>
> b) implementing on a more satisfactory basis the CST–MICOIN agreement, with the purpose of guaranteeing distribution through official channels – CAT, rural and workplace commissaries, and the territorial network. This would involve directing efforts towards eliminating sources of supply of products to the speculative market, as well as demands that MICOIN and MIDINRA exercise a strict control over distribution, eliminating where possible unnecessary links in the distribution chain.
>
> c) promoting self-provisioning in the countryside, obliging state

and private enterprises to support these activities. (*Barricada*, 9 September 1985, p. 3)

From these assemblies emerged a series of economic demands that placed less emphasis on salary increases (which in a context of shortages and rapid inflation were considered of limited benefit in any case) and stressed the need for stricter controls over the distribution of basic goods and prices, as well as more direct links between producers and consumers. As Florez-Estrada and Lobo write:

> The CST now directs its efforts towards guaranteeing an agreement signed with the State, whereby enterprises distribute their goods directly to the workers' commissaries in order to restrict flows to intermediaries that speculate with prices. The CST also participates in a commission established to analyse costs of production in order to reduce the prices of basic goods and to reduce the profit margins of commercial state enterprises. (Florez-Estrada and Lobo, 1986, p. 28)

In October, the CST demands for price reductions on basic manufactures were met when the prices of numerous products sold in the commissaries were reduced by between 15 and 25 per cent.

These demands were strongly supported by the FSLN, several of whose leaders attended the three days of discussion and debates which took place during the September conference. As pointed out by Vilas, while both the FSLN and the state attempted to alleviate the impact of the crisis on the working class, the party was probably more supportive of working-class demands than was the state:

> The tendency has been for state institutions to support the administrators of state enterprises whenever a conflict arises between the latter and the union. . .This concern on the part of the state would appear to reflect a reaffirmation of the principle of authority over what is perceived as labour indiscipline. The response to union demands is slow. . .until such time as the union, or the ATC or CST appeal directly to the National Directorate of the FSLN and the situation begins to resolve itself. (Vilas, 1986a, p. 29)

During 1986 the network of CATs was expanded, increasing from three to seven in the capital alone, and the number of products sold in these retail outlets increased to forty. Certain food products, not contemplated in the original agreement, were also distributed through the CAT network (MICOIN, 1987). Nevertheless, agreed quotas were often not met and real wages continued to decline as workers still had to rely heavily on the open market, notably for food products.

An evaluation of the impact of the economic crisis and government policies on the levels of living of different socioeconomic groups, carried out by the Centre for Research and Studies of the Agrarian Reform,[1] noted that the prioritization established in relation to the working class was relatively ineffective:

> The prioritization of the working class is expressed primarily in the application of the CST/MICOIN agreement. While this agreement attempts to improve the access of the workers to a variety of basic manufactured goods, the supply of goods experienced serious limitations in terms of the quota offered and the inconvenience of having to go to the CAT [read distance from workplace or home and long queues]. . .One can say that the sector most affected by the economic crisis in 1986 was that comprised of urban formal sector wage earners, that is industrial workers and public employees. (CIERA, 1987a, p. 3)

Working-class pressure and demands associated with the defence of real wages had resulted also in significant increases in payments in kind. From 1983 until mid-1985 a large component of workers' income derived from this source. In 1984, some branches of industry had calculated that more than 45 per cent of workers' real income derived from payments in kind. This method of payment was eventually prohibited by the government when it became apparent that extremely large quantities of products were being sold by workers to merchants at prices far in excess of official prices. A report of the Ministry of Industry claimed that in 1984 five state-owned footware enterprises had sold (at very low prices) an average of seventy-three shoes per worker, while two state-owned textile enterprises distributed to their 2750 workers an average of 173 yards of cloth per worker (Vilas, 1986a, p. 32). Moreover, levels of absenteeism increased as workers dedicated less time to factory work and more time to selling on the open market.

By 1987 the government was coming under increasing pressure from the unions to change both its wages and basic-goods supply policies. The policy of linking wages and salaries to inflation, which had operated for a short period between October 1984 and May 1985, was taken up again in 1987 but under a new modality. This time the decision was taken to link wages and salaries of formal sector workers to the increase in the cost of a basket of fifty-four products, the distribution of which was largely controlled by the state. Five of these products would be channelled through the territorial network of 'people's stores', forty via the workers' supply centres (CATs), and nine through the rural supply centres (Ortega, *Barricada*, 7 June 1987, p. 3). During the first half of 1987 alone, two wage increases were announced (April and June), averaging 56 per cent and 30 per cent respectively. Wage rises for lower-paid workers were considerably larger than the average (Wheelock, *Barricada*, 27 April 1987, p. 4; Ortega, *Barricada*, 7 June 1987, p. 3).

The trade unions also pressured the government to reprioritize certain work-place commissaries in the allocation of basic goods. In April 1987, the leaders of both the CST and the ATC called on the government to resupply certain strategic enterprises (*Barricada*, 3 April 1987, p. 1). The enterprises to be given priority status were to be determined in consultation with the unions. Some sixty enterprises were selected, involving approximately 60 000 of the 160 000 workers in the capital region which were entitled to use the CATs (*Barricada*, 4 August 1987). The availability of certain food products such as chicken and eggs also increased. A report in the party newspaper, *Barricada*, noted that the supply of these two products had increased by some 200 per cent and that in order to benefit the working class the quota of these products assigned to the territorial network of official outlets selling to the general public was reduced (*Barricada*, 14 June 1987, p. 4). The network of state-controlled supermarkets was also increased in and around the capital, with nine extra outlets planned for 1987.

THE URBAN INFORMAL SECTOR AND THE CDS: DECLINING PARTICIPATION IN THE POLICY PROCESS

As indicated earlier, of all the mass organizations, it was the CDS, representing urban neighbourhood dwellers, that participated most actively in the process of food policy design and implementation during the early 1980s. The rank-and-file membership of this organization which, according to some estimates, had reached nearly 600 000 (CIERA, 1984d, p. 56), was composed to a large extent of urban residents whose sources of income derived from activities associated with the informal sector. Such activities involved primarily petty-trading, family-based food processing and handicrafts, and non-professional services (carpenters, plumbers, and so on).

From mid-1984, important changes took place in the form and extent of participation of the CDS in the process of food policy design and review. Prior to this period, the organization had taken an active role in the policy process, influencing the definition of policies relating to food distribution, and directly overseeing policy implementation, particularly in urban areas. The CDS played a major role in establishing, in 1982, the guarantee card system, which was gradually expanded to provide family quotas for a number of essential food and non-food products. It was also influential in defining which types of retail outlet would constitute the basis of the official retail system. Pressure from the CDS influenced policy decisions that resulted in the expansion of the territorial network of 'people's stores' and the prioritization of this distribution network as opposed to retail outlets located in ('formal' sector) enterprises and state institutions. The CDS selected which of the local retailers would distribute the basic goods sold on the guarantee card system (Utting, 1983).

With the setting up, in 1983, of a high level food policy review board – The National Supply Commission – the CDS were able to influence the nature of the measures incorporated into the Law of Consumer Protection, which was passed in July 1984 and subsequently reinforced in August 1985. The law increased the number of basic products to be included on the guarantee card system and introduced a series of controls on marketing activities. These included the nationalization of the wholesale distribution of eighteen food and manufactured products, restrictions on the territorial movement of basic goods, and stricter controls on retail prices of certain products sold on the parallel market. Once these measures were taken, however, the commission became less active and was eventually disbanded. While the rural and industrial workers' organizations continued to participate in the policy process via the more informal relations outlined above, the participation of the CDS declined markedly.[2]

In September 1984, measures opposed by the CDS were introduced to channel a proportion of the total supply of the 'guaranteed' products to the state supermarket chain where they would be sold at prices just below the open market price. Although the CDS, supported by the newspapers, opposed these measures, the economic logic of the planners held sway. By setting up this official parallel market, the government was accepting the existence of the parallel or black market as a fact of life. It was considered necessary to compete with this market both as a means of appropriating surplus for the state and in order to extract liquidity from the economy. The total quantity of goods channelled to the new official parallel market would, it was argued, represent a very small percentage of total supply and would not have any significant affect on supplies to the guaranteed-price stores. The CDS, however, did not agree, but lost the argument (Utting, 1985).

Part of the problem stemmed from the fact that direct channels of communication between the CDS and MICOIN were broken when a government reshuffle brought about a change in the top ministry personnel. Previously, informal channels of communication between CDS leaders and top MICOIN officials had been relatively effective in harmonizing relations between these two institutions. As one of the national leaders explained in a personal interview: 'Before I could just pick up the phone and talk to a particular vice-minister about such and such a problem – now it's not so easy.'[2]

The CDS was also angered by the fact that it had not been consulted about a policy change of such importance which introduced a qualitatively new set of principles into food policy. In response to the furore the measures provoked, the newly-appointed Vice Minister of MICOIN was obliged to appear in front of 1000 CDS representatives in Managua to explain the new measures. As one delegate explained at the meeting: 'They should have proceeded in the same way they did with the Law of Consumer Protection when we were consulted beforehand.' (*Barricada*, 27 September 1984, p. 1)

The problem, however, was to persist. Evaluating the situation in 1986, a CDS leader expressed the following view:

> The state has to improve its communication with the people. No longer are they [the government] explaining the problems or measures. Why, for example, have eggs recently disappeared from the official retail outlets? Neither have they explained adequately why prices and salaries were recently increased.[3]

At the beginning of 1985 the National Planning Council was established as the highest planning authority. The CST and ATC were invited to participate in an important commission of the council overseeing production, prices, basic-goods supply, salaries and employment. The CDS, however, were conspicuously absent from this commission.

The declining participation of the CDS in the policy process was to a certain extent symptomatic of an overall crisis affecting the organization. Throughout 1984 and 1985, the active participation of community members in CDS activities, including those associated with overseeing the implementation of food pricing and distribution policy, declined sharply. Much of the urban population became critical of the organization, which was seen to have divorced itself from real community interests and concerns. As the CDS leader remarked in 1989, when analyzing the problems of the past:

> In those days, the CDS were a parastatal and para-party organization. Why do we say that? Because what the people of the local communities did was what they were told to do. When MICOIN needed the CDS [that ministry] drew up a plan and the CDS complied. In other words, the CDS worked for MICOIN. . .and in effect were activists of the State, the Government and the Party. [They] rarely had time to work to resolve the specific problems of the *barrios*. (Cabezas, 1989)

In September 1985, the general assembly of the CDS met for several days to evaluate the crisis affecting their organization. Many delegates recognized that the organization's leaders had lost touch with the rank-and-file membership. The assembly proposed a new programme which was thought to be more in tune with community interests.

The informal sector, then, was squeezed not only economically through the imposition of controls on commercial activities and cuts in certain social programmes, but also in terms of participation in the policy process itself, as exercised through the CDS. It was also 'squeezed' ideologically, with government rhetoric becoming increasing hostile towards petty-traders, particularly unlicensed merchants and street vendors. At times the 'anti-speculator' rhetoric was employed to refer to a whole range of 'informal' activities. Commenting on the opinions of certain CDS leaders, one government report agreed that it was wrong:

> to lump together under the category of 'speculator' the numerous occupational groups which make up the urban informal sector, particularly when many of these perform useful social functions. . .

These differences are not reflected either at the level of ideological discourse or in specific policies, particularly those relating to the supply of basic goods. (CIERA, 1987a, pp. 24–5)

This hostility derived not so much from the political positions that this sector had assumed, which from the time of the insurrectionary period had been fairly supportive of the Sandinistas. Indeed, a remarkable feature of the 1983–85 period was the failure of the Contras, despite the gravity of the economic crisis, to open up an internal urban front and draw on the support of traders and petty-commodity producers. State hostility derived more from the perceived economic threat posed by the rapid expansion of this sector which, as we saw earlier, had increased from 27 to 38 per cent of the economically-active population between 1980 and 1985. While this expansion may be partly explained in terms of a mass 'survival strategy' to defend levels of living in the midst of a severe economic crisis (Escuela de Sociologia, UCA, 1986) it nevertheless undermined the 'survival strategy' designed by the state, which stressed the need to stimulate production of basic goods in 'formal' sector enterprises and the peasant sector, as well as to regulate the distribution of those goods.

THE BUREAUCRACY: INTER- AND INTRA-INSTITUTIONAL TENSIONS

To explain the changes in food pricing and marketing policy and state–peasant relations it is also important to refer to a number of developments at the level of the state administrative and planning apparatus.

Within the Ministry of Agricultural Development and Agrarian Reform there were a number of divisions and top ministry personnel supportive of the types of demand put forward by the UNAG. From early in the post-revolutionary period, a clear ideological tension existed within the ministry between a technocratic fraction which favoured concentrating resources in large-scale state enterprises and development projects and a rather pro-peasant fraction. During the mid-1980s, the position of the latter was reinforced, not least because of the way in which the state-centred accumulation model had performed in practice. In a reshuffle of top ministry personnel, in 1986, extra weight was given to the office of Vice Minister for Agrarian Reform when a *comandante* was appointed to the post.

Other tensions existed between the regional and central levels of the state apparatus. The decentralization of the state administrative apparatus, which took effect from 1982 with the implementation of the 'regionalization' process, increased the power of regional party and ministry delegates. In general, they tended to be far more in tune with peasant demands than were central-level officials.

A third area of tension which became particularly apparent during the latter half of the 1980s was that between the 'production' or 'spending' ministries (notably Agriculture) and state finance/external trade institutions (Fitzgerald, 1989). Concerned with growing macro-economic disequilibria, wastage of imported goods and the negative effects of distortions in the price system, the latter pushed for an adjustment/stabilization package (fully implemented during 1988 and 1989) that involved a considerable freeing of prices, massive devaluations of the national currency, restrictions of state expenditures and changes in the sectoral allocation of resources. A technocratic fraction comprising economists gained in influence and power, occupying during the latter half of the 1980s key positions within the Ministry of Finance, the Central Bank and the Planning and Budget Office.

Moreover, weaknesses emerged not only in the position of a specific fraction of the technocracy but, more generally, at the level of the bureaucracy as a whole. In an attempt to compensate for the decline in real incomes, an increasing number of public functionaries sought alternative employment, took on two jobs at once, moved from one state agency to another in search of slightly higher wages, and engaged in quasi-legal or corrupt practices. Developments such as these clearly affected the capacity of the state to intervene effectively in the economy and increasingly called into question the feasibility of the state-centred accumulation model.

CONCLUSION

In this case study I have attempted a more comprehensive analysis of both the nature of the crisis which prompted a new policy approach during the mid-1980s and the way in which different interest groups were able to shape the content of the reform package. We have seen how the post-revolutionary development model which unfolded during the early 1980s was characterized by a heavy emphasis on state-centred accumulation and urban-centred consumption. This model encountered definite limits during the 1983/84 period. Diverse forms of external aggression and the expansion of the military budget had serious effects on the economy. Practices engaged in by different class fractions and social groups in response to a situation of shortages, planning imbalances and structural change undermined the capacity of the state to mobilize and appropriate surplus and to plan the economy.

The extent to which the state could regulate and control patterns of production, distribution and accumulation was also undermined by conditions relating to the low level of development of the productive forces, including, for example, the scale of petty-commodity production and limited information regarding the complexity of social structure and the forms of articulation of different groups and property sectors. Government policies favouring high rates of accumulation, the elimination of highly exploitative social relations, and the expansion of basic-needs programmes, had the effect of rapidly expanding the money supply, causing major distortions in relative prices, and increasing the external trade deficit. These, in turn, served to intensify problems associated with market shortages, inflation, the proliferation of informal-sector activities, wastage and inefficiency.

The hegemonic content of the Sandinista 'project' also suffered a number of setbacks during 1983 and 1984. Certain sectors of the peasantry in the interior of the country and the ethnic populations of the Atlantic Coast regions not only engaged in a variety of 'avoidance and non-cooperation' strategies (Fforde, 1984), but also turned against the Sandinistas politically. In this context, the possibility emerged that the US-backed contras would develop a large social base and seriously threaten the Sandinistas' hold on power.

To understand, though, the shift towards a more pro-peasant strategy and the emergence of policies which affected in a highly differentiated manner various urban groups, it is necessary to move beyond an analysis of the crisis of the state and look at a number of major changes which had occurred in the balance of social forces.

Between 1981 and the mid-1980s, the vast majority of peasant producers became organized in a national association. Through mass mobilizations and participatory structures, the UNAG was able to exert considerable influence over the policy process. The conversion of quantitative strength (membership) to qualitative strength (capacity to influence the policy process) was facilitated by the regionalization process, which provided a greater opportunity for 'popular participation' at the local level.

As the contradictions inherent in the state-centred accumulation and urban-centred consumption model became more apparent, so the influence of certain technocratic fractions within the central administrative and planning apparatus decreased, while that of others favouring peasant and regional interests, as well as economic liberalization, increased.

The new approach also reflected a number of weaknesses in the main organizations representing the working class and the bureaucracy. An important trade-off, however, had occurred, enabling these groups privileged access to a range of basic manufactured goods. That the working class was prepared to make certain economic–corporate sacrifices in areas associated with basic-food provisioning related not only to the fact that certain short-term gains had been achieved in other areas, but also to a set of longer-term interests associated with the perceived advantages of consolidating a worker–peasant alliance to restrict the power of a new 'class enemy', namely private commercial capital, which was seen to be reaping extraordinary profits in an economy characterized by shortages and inflation. In such a situation it was considered crucial to stimulate domestic production of basic food products through higher producer prices and the rearticulation of urban–rural marketing circuits in order to increase the flow of goods to and from rural areas. To achieve this, the activities of state marketing agencies were complemented by those of the UNAG and certain private merchants, whose activities were to some extent regulated by the state through a system of licences and permits.

Official Sandinista discourse actively supported the notion that the reforms formed part of a strategy to consolidate the worker–peasant alliance. However, the possibility of forging such an alliance in practice was problematic, given that the reforms had largely eliminated food subsidies – one of the principal instruments for reconciling the contradictory interests of workers and certain sectors of the peasantry. Nevertheless, a joint campaign by UNAG and MICOIN encouraged peasant producers to sell a portion of their produce to ENABAS at prices lower than those offered by private merchants in order to supply the workers and the army. State industrial enterprises were also encouraged to increase direct sales of manufactured goods to both urban and rural consumers. Meanwhile, ENABAS and other state trading agencies were instructed to reduce costs in an attempt to lower wholesale prices, while in urban areas mass organizations and MICOIN mobilized in a campaign to check retail prices and denounce or fine 'speculators'.

Constraints imposed on government economic strategy by the expansion of the urban informal sector, plus the crisis within the organization of the CDS, altered relations between the state and this sector of the population. The abandonment of 'cheap food' policy and the urban-centred consumption model must also be related to the declining organizational strength of the CDS and its exclusion from certain participatory processes and policy-making institutions.

Notes

1. The author acted as adviser to the research team that carried out the study.
2. Interview with Ronald Paredes, March 1985.
3. Interview with Ronald Paredes, February 1987.

Part IV

The Political Economy of Economic and Food Policy Reform in Dependent Transitional Economies

9 The Third World Experience in Comparative Perspective

INTRODUCTION

In the preceding case studies I have identified the major changes in economic and food policy which characterized the shift from orthodoxy to reform in four dependent transitional economies. In this concluding section, I summarize the principal similarities and differences in policy approach and outline briefly the component features of the crisis with which the reforms attempted to deal. I then examine the nature of the contradictions which accounted for the crisis. Finally, I outline the types of changes which occurred in social structure, at the level of civil society and in 'participation', which affected the capacity of different social groups to influence the policy process.

THE CONTENT OF THE REFORMS

The economic policy reforms introduced in Mozambique, Vietnam, Cuba and Nicaragua were generally associated with several or all of the following aspects:

1. New forms of property relations and/or organization of the labour process, intended to provide incentives to petty-commodity (and in some cases capitalist) producers and overcome problems associated with stagnant production and low labour productivity. In Mozambique, Vietnam and Nicaragua there was a definite trend toward decollectivization in agriculture when government policy on co-operative organization was relaxed; the size of the state-farm sector reduced and increasing amounts of land redistributed to individual peasant families (Mozambique/Nicaragua); or co-operative land sub-contracted to teams of workers or peasant households (Vietnam).

253

2. Changes in domestic pricing and marketing policy to increase marketed production of agricultural commodities and rearticulate urban/rural marketing circuits. A major feature of the reforms in all four countries was the attempt to shift the relative prices of agricultural and manufactured products in favour of the peasantry. The reforms involved measures to increase agricultural prices, often through deregulation, whilst continuing to regulate the prices of manufactured products. The character of food marketing systems generally experienced major modifications as state control at the level of procurement of certain products was relaxed and a greater space provided for producers and merchants alike to involve themselves in the marketing chain. While official policy became more tolerant of private trading of many agricultural products, controls on urban informal sector activities continued to be exercised or were even tightened.

3. Changes in the sectoral allocation of resources to correct imbalances which favoured heavy industry and large-scale, slow-yielding development projects (which siphoned-off resources at the expense of consumer goods supply and, in some cases, short-term export production). An important aspect of the reforms was the attempt by governments to increase the supply of agricultural inputs and implements to rural areas, as well as basic consumer goods to peasant and working-class groups. This generally implied significant changes in the accumulation/consumption balance and in the composition of imports.

4. Changes in monetary, fiscal and exchange-rate policy to reduce public-sector and trade deficits, correct distortions in relative prices, tackle inflation and restore the value of the local currency. Consumer subsidies were often reduced and cuts experienced in certain social programmes and public-sector employment. Austerity and stabilization programmes, however, often incorporated 'compensatory' measures to protect low-income or 'vulnerable' groups.

5. New systems of planning and/or economic management of state enterprises in order to improve enterprise efficiency through administrative decentralization, increased horizontal linkages and productivity bonus schemes.

Differences in Policy Approach

While many similarities characterized the reform experience in the four countries, clear differences in policies have also been noted. Particularly important among these is the contrast between the experiences of Vietnam, Mozambique and Nicaragua, on the one hand, and Cuba on the other, where the reforms did not bring about significant changes in property relations and in the size of, or degree of control exercised by, the state sector. The central issue to be resolved in Cuba, at least until the late 1980s, was not that of a major food crisis and related manifestations of chronic shortages of essential food products and stagnation in staples production, but rather problems associated with non-essential consumption. In this respect, the case of Cuba would seem to resemble more closely that of several of the more industrialized socialist countries.

Other differences distinguish the case of Mozambique from that of Vietnam and Nicaragua. In Mozambique it was the sector of commercial farmers that benefited most from the reforms. While rich peasant interests stood to gain from the reforms introduced in Vietnam and Nicaragua, it would appear that the policy changes benefited a far larger sector of the peasant population. Moreover, in the latter two countries the government continued to attach a high priority to the development of the co-operative sector at least during the early phase of the reform process.

The reform experience of Nicaragua contrasts with that of Vietnam and Mozambique in a number of respects. Firstly, the policy changes of the mid-1980s were perceived not just in terms of a pro-peasant strategy but as part of a strategy to strengthen the worker–peasant alliance. As such, an important element of the reform package consisted in measures geared towards improving the access of the urban working class and fractions of the middle classes (notably the bureaucracy) to certain consumer goods. In Nicaragua it also proved extremely difficult to achieve any significant reduction in the accumulation/consumption balance during this particular phase of the reform process.

How, then, do we account for these similarities and differences in approach? In order to answer this question it is necessary to specify (a) the nature of the crisis confronting the state; and (b) the correlation of social forces in each country.

THE CRISIS OF THE STATE

From the analysis contained in previous chapters it emerges that the reform process in dependent transitional economies occurred in the context of a crisis of the state, which expressed itself in the inability of the latter (a) to mobilize adequate resources for consumption and accumulation; and (b) to direct the process of development and change.

The Crisis of Surplus Appropriation

As we saw in Chapter 1, post-revolutionary states generally constitute themselves as the central agency with responsibility for 'guaranteeing' the resources required, both for basic needs provisioning and accumulation, in order to achieve what one writer refers to as three simultaneous transitions involving the elimination of exploitation and poverty, agricultural modernization and industrialization (Saith, 1985).

In small, underdeveloped, transitional economies agriculture generally plays a crucial role in the three transitions, providing not only food and raw materials for domestic consumption and industry, respectively, but also the agro-export products upon which much of the country's foreign exchange revenues depend. As Fitzgerald points out, it is the foreign trade sector, heavily dependent on the export of agricultural products, which comes to represent 'heavy industry' (or Department I of the economy), since it is essentially through imports that producer goods are acquired in societies such as these, which generally lack a large industrial base (Fitzgerald, 1985b, p. 6).

The establishment of a state-farm sector and a state-controlled procurement system for acquiring surplus from peasant, co-operative or capitalist farms; the nationalization of foreign trade; and the imposition of regulations governing the acquisition and use of aid, constitute key mechanisms through which food and agricultural products are appropriated by the state for basic-needs provisioning and accumulation. In all four countries, serious problems arose affecting levels of food and agricultural production, state procurement, export revenues and levels of aid.

In Mozambique, stagnation in the state-farm sector and declining levels of peasant production imposed severe constraints on the availability of food during the years leading up to the 1983 policy reforms. Procurement levels of rice, for example, fell from 70 000 to 19 000 tons between 1978 and 1984. While Mozambique was able to diversify its sources of external assistance during the early 1980s, pressure on imports was increased as visible trade earnings declined by nearly half during the early 1980s, from 9.9 billion meticals in 1981 to 5.2 billion in 1983. Imports, which had nearly trebled between 1975 and 1981, fell by more than a third between 1981 and 1985.

Vietnam experienced a 15 per cent decline in cereals production between 1974 and 1978, just prior to the introduction of the first reforms in 1979/80. Procurement levels of staples declined from around 20 per cent of national production in the early 1960s to 15 per cent in the mid-1970s. Access to external supplies of food and other resources was affected during the latter half of the 1970s by the reduction in aid following the war between North and South Vietnam and involvement in Kampuchea.

In the case of Cuba, it can be argued that the precise nature of the problems faced by the state in relation to resource mobilization and surplus appropriation varied according to different phases of a very gradual and piecemeal reform process. In general, however, it would seem that the reform process related less to a crisis of basic needs provisioning as to problems associated with accumulation and non-essential consumption. In analyzing the determinants of economic and food policy reform in Cuba, two periods are of particular interest. Firstly, the years prior to the early 1970s, when various economic policy reforms were introduced, and secondly, the period prior to the early 1980s when the free peasant markets were established and a significant shift occurred in the accumulation/consumption balance. In the late 1960s, problems of shortages of food and other consumer goods arose. Between 1958 and 1968 marketed production of important root crops such as cassava and malanga fell by 44 and 78 per cent respectively, while annual per capita consumption of rice fell from 42 kilos during the mid-1960s to 25 kilos in 1968. Export revenues fell during the late 1960s, affected by low world sugar prices. Throughout the 1970s there was a marked improvement in levels of basic-needs provisioning. Consumer expectations were affected by increasing contacts between Cuba and 'the world's foremost consumer society' (Benjamin *et al.*, 1984, p. 63). By the end of the decade, one of the primary issues of public concern related to the restricted variety and quality of food products and other consumer goods.

Problems associated with surplus appropriation were instrumental not only in prompting the reforms of the 1970s and early 1980s but also the 'counter-reforms' introduced in 1986 and 1987. The restrictions imposed on imports as a result of the impact on banana and sugar exports of drought and hurricane conditions, and the deterioration of the external terms of trade resulting from the fall in oil prices and the value of the dollar, contributed to the policy changes associated with the rectification process and the austerity programme which emphasized the need for increased self-reliance.

In Nicaragua, the reforms introduced in 1985/86 followed a critical two-year period in which shortages of basic food products had become a regular feature of the economy. This situation appeared all the more dramatic coming as it did after three years of improvements in general consumption levels following the revolution in 1979. Between the 1983/84 and 1985/86 agricultural cycles, production levels in virtually all the major product sectors either declined or remained static, falling by 20 per cent in the case of rice and 8 per cent for maize, both major staples. State procurement levels of grain, milk and certain agro-export products also fell from around 1983 onwards. Between 1983 and 1986, export revenues fell by half while the amount of foreign aid committed each year fluctuated considerably. Access to external resources from Western sources became more difficult following 1982 when certain international development and finance agencies (World Bank and the Inter-American Development Bank (IADB)) followed the example of the United States in halting assistance to Nicaragua. To compensate for this financial boycott and the subsequent suspension of petroleum 'aid' from Mexico, Nicaragua turned rapidly towards the socialist bloc countries for assistance but, by the mid-1980s, reached the upper limits of its capacity to handle and use the goods coming into the country, let alone repay loans and credits.

The Crisis of 'Direction':[1] Planning and Hegemony

The second feature of the crisis of the state referred to above relates to the increasing incapacity of the party/state to direct the process of social change and economic development. In analyzing this aspect it would seem useful to identify two specific sets of crisis conditions. These relate to the questions of planning and hegemony.

Planning

In all four countries, we have seen how the development strategy which characterized the pre-reform era was based on fairly orthodox socialist principles which stressed the need for centralized planning and state or collective control of the means of production, so that production, distribution and accumulation would conform to socially-determined priorities. In this way the party/state would direct the transition from dependent capitalism to socialism by closely regulating the development of the productive forces and the transformation of social relations. In all cases, the state encountered major limitations on the extent to which this level of 'direction' could be achieved. This was particularly evident in Vietnam, Mozambique and Nicaragua, where each state's capacity to regulate the price system and the production process was seriously weakened.

In Mozambique, shortages, price control and inflation led to the development of a parallel economy where prices were generally far in excess of those set by the state. Moreover, because of the high profits to be made in speculative and trading activities outside the control of the state, the flow of goods, capital and human resources to the private tertiary sector increased. The incapacity of the state to direct the evolution of the economy also related to the types of ideologically motivated planning methods that were adopted during the late 1970s and early 1980s, when ambitious goals were set – goals which bore little relation to means and led to a crisis of confidence in planning, particularly as far as the people responsible for meeting planned targets were concerned (Egero, 1987, pp. 99–101).

In Vietnam, inflation increased during the late 1970s and spiralled out of control throughout the 1980s, reaching several hundred per cent by mid-decade. By the end of the 1970s, prices in the so-called 'outside' economy were generally ten times official state prices, and activities associated with the 'outside' economy expanded rapidly. In this situation the state increasingly lost control over production and circulation (Fforde, 1984; Fforde and Paine, 1987).

In Cuba, planning problems became particularly acute during the late 1960s. The state's inability to substitute the activities of private agents expropriated during that period contributed to the proliferation of black-market activities. A combination of other problems (to be discussed below), characteristic of centralized planning models, led to considerable inefficiency and low labour productivity in state enterprises, thereby restricting the quantity and quality of goods produced. Such problems were to continue over the next decade and underpin the rationale behind the measures which established the free peasant markets.

In Nicaragua, inflation increased rapidly from 1982 onwards, reaching 747 per cent in 1986. The gap between official and parallel market prices widened, and price policy became largely ineffectual as an instrument for regulating production and exchange. State procurement agencies and processing enterprises were increasingly bypassed as marketing channels for both domestic food (for example, grains and milk) and agro-export products (for example, beef and coffee). This situation stemmed not only from the existence of a two-tier price system but also related to the serious problems encountered by state agencies in gaining access to production zones in the interior of the country, where the war situation and transport difficulties restricted commercial activities. Given the relatively high profit margins to be earned in informal-sector activities, labour shifted from rural areas, factories and the bureaucracy into urban-based petty-trading activities. The proliferation of the latter made the regulation of exchange almost impossible and also contributed to problems of labour shortages in agriculture, industry and large-scale development projects.

Hegemony

The state's capacity to direct the process of economic development and social change depends not only on its technical and administrative capacity to regulate the mobilization and flow of resources but also on the extent to which the revolutionary party can exercise leadership on the basis of a broad popular consensus. Hegemony, then, as defined in the Gramscian sense, is essential for the effective implementation of government policies and programmes. If the dominant group must resort to coercion, as opposed to consensus, to maintain its ruling position and if political cadres and public functionaries are seen to be associated with black-market activities, corruption, excessive privileges and inefficient bureaucratic practices, then the possibility of exercising the 'political, moral and intellectual leadership' to which Gramsci referred, will clearly be undermined. As a result of this situation, party/state directives regarding production and procurement are likely to be ignored and popular mobilization campaigns may be ineffectual. Moreover, counter-revolutionary forces are likely to operate to greater effect and develop a social base. Problems of this nature emerged in all four countries during the pre-reform era.

In Mozambique, widespread apathy and cynicism amongst the rural population led to a situation of peasant demobilization that blocked 'the processes of social, political and ideological transformation that the creation of the communal villages had set in motion' (Roesch, 1984, p. 309). Problems of worker apathy took root in factories and state farms, while popular support for the revolutionary government declined when bureaucratic corruption and inefficiency became more widespread. The party had lost the one resource it could count on during the immediate post-independence period: 'the ability. . .to mobilize and organize popular participation and popular forces in order to generate self-reliant solutions to problems' (Pinsky, 1985, p. 281).

Following the cessation of the war with the United States and the reunification of North and South Vietnam in 1975, the hegemony of the Vietnamese Communist Party declined. During the late 1970s and early 1980s a picture emerges of widespread cynicism and passive resistance in the South, coupled with sporadic guerilla activities in the Central Highlands and even occasional public demonstrations in certain cities in the North (Post, 1982). This was also a period when the credibility of the party was undermined through corruption and inefficiency of certain cadres and bureaucrats. The capacity of the party/state to direct the process of economic development and transformation of social relations declined considerably as peasants increasingly adopted so-called 'avoidance and non-cooperation strategies' and workers, peasants, bureaucrats and cadres alike engaged in illegal activities which caused the diversion of considerable resources away from sectors or activities prioritized in the plan towards the 'outside' economy (Fforde, 1984; Fforde and Paine, 1987).

In Cuba, discontent, associated with a fairly generalized 'dissatisfaction with the limits of consumption' (Benjamin *et al.*, 1984, p. 63), emerged during the late 1970s. This was manifested clearly during the 1980 boatlifts, when over 120 000 people left for the United States. The reforms of the early 1980s, however, generated new social tensions. Sectors of the working class and the co-operativized peasantry became increasingly critical of policies which led to rapid income and class differentiation, of the widespread abuses which characterized policy implementation, and of a party which had failed to take an active role in dealing with these and other problems associated with bureaucratic inefficiency and privilege. It was this situation which partly accounted for the subsequent policy shift from 'reform' to 'rectification'.

In Nicaragua, problems related to the question of hegemony during the first half of the 1980s tended to be more confined to specific social groups or fractions of these. Certain sectors of the peasantry (notably in the interior of the country) and ethnic groups of the Atlantic Coast region became disaffected during the early 1980s. This was expressed in the election results of 1984, where levels of support for the Sandinista Front were far lower in outlying rural areas in the interior of the country than elsewhere. More worrying from the government's point of view was the logistical and moral support given by some ethnic and peasant groups to the Contra forces. This support, along with tactics of forced recruitment, contributed to a threefold increase in the Contra forces between 1982 and 1984 and enabled them to extend the territorial conflict well beyond the areas bordering Honduras and Costa Rica.

SOCIAL CHANGE AND CONTRADICTIONS

Processes of post-revolutionary transformation of social relations and structures of income, wealth and power necessarily generate profound contradictions, which express themselves in various forms of conflict between different classes and interest groups as well as between such groups and the state. Given that transition also implies the transformation of dependency relations, conflict will also develop between the revolutionary state and certain foreign interests wishing to defend the economic and/or geopolitical domination formerly exercised by a world or regional power over the transitional society.

The contradictions which generate the type of crisis conditions outlined above, however, derive not only from the practices of groups or agents (both domestic and foreign) attempting to defend their interests or regain their dominant pre-revolutionary position. They also stem from certain actions taken by the state. These serve firstly to alienate classes or social groups allied in practice (through consensus and participation) and/or theory (according to party ideology) to the revolutionary project, or secondly, when the patterns of resource allocation determined by the state tend to undermine, rather than promote, the development of the productive forces.

These contradictions will be discussed briefly here in terms of three interrelated sets of practices involving (a) imperialist/'hegemonic' interests;[2] (b) domestic classes and social groups; and (c) the revolutionary state.

Imperialist/'Hegemonic' Practices

The fundamental contradiction which conditioned development prospects in Mozambique, Vietnam, Cuba and Nicaragua throughout most of their post-revolutionary history centred on the conflict between the revolutionary state and foreign powers with vested economic and/or geopolitical interests in the transitional society in question. The revolutionary project, involving the transformation of social relations and international realignments, encountered diverse forms of external aggression from world or regional powers. In the four countries considered here, pressures of this nature expressed themselves in a variety of forms: direct intervention of military forces, so-called 'low-intensity' wars involving the use of proxy guerilla forces, economic embargo/blockade measures, and diplomatic offensives to undermine the support from third parties (governments, international development agencies, banks, and so on) for a particular revolutionary government.

Pressures such as these had major implications for the problems of surplus appropriation, planning and hegemony outlined above. Yet while all four countries had to endure a variety of pressures of this nature, their impact varied considerably.

Attempts by the South African government to destabilize the Mozambican regime intensified during the early 1980s. In addition to providing direct support for the RENAMO forces, a variety of economic and military pressures were applied, including, for example, the reduction of transit trade via Maputo and engaging in threatening troop movements along the southern border (Egero, 1987, pp. 91–2). Meanwhile, RENAMO forces rapidly extended their military actions throughout most of the country. One estimate, cited by Littlejohn, calculates that the economic costs of destabilization between 1980 and 1986 exceeded the value of all the aid Mozambique received during that period (Littlejohn, 1988, p. 16). The overtly terrorist tactics employed by the MNR alienated much of the rural population and there was little evidence of their having developed a social base. Nevertheless, the capacity of the government to defeat the MNR and to organize local resistance was clearly undermined by its own lack of attention to peasant needs (Egero, 1987, p. 90).

The peasant economy was seriously disrupted due to the dislocation of trading circuits resulting from the destruction of means of transport and retail outlets (Mackintosh, 1986, 1987). Social services, co-operatives, communications and energy infrastructure were also major targets of attack (Egero, 1987, p. 90). The availability of food in many rural communities was affected as foodstocks and cattle were lost to the MNR. The negative impact of the war on agricultural production manifested itself not only in terms of production losses resulting from direct attacks on farms and infrastructure, and the displacement of the rural population, but also in terms of reinforcing the inherent state sector and urban biases underpinning government policies and programmes – biases which gave priority in resource allocation to the more defensible state farms, and encouraged production around the cities.

Unlike Mozambique and Nicaragua, the crisis of the state in Vietnam occurred not in the midst but in the aftermath of war. While the war with the United States clearly had a devastating social and economic impact, it would seem that problems of surplus appropriation, planning and hegemony were mitigated to some extent by substantial inflows of foreign aid, the effectiveness of decentralization and the role of ideology. Large quantities of aid, from the Soviet Union and China in particular, served to alleviate shortages of food, inputs and other essential products. The organization of the mass of the population into agricultural co-operatives enabled the government to implement a reasonably effective decentralized planning system conducive to local self-reliance. This same co-operative structure also facilitated mass mobilization and the propagation of an anti-imperialist ideology, which had a powerful cohesive influence.

It was conditions such as these, however, that were conducive to the development of the type of social relations of production which the reforms eventually recognized and legitimized. Particularly relevant here is the weakening of collective relations in the co-operatives. This resulted from a dual process which occurred from the mid-1960s onwards, whereby rich peasants joined and came to dominate many co-operatives, while party control at the local level was weakened as village cadres and activists diverted their attention away from the organization of the co-operative movement towards the war effort.

Moreover, easy access to external resources reduced the demands of the state on domestic sources of surplus. In these circumstances relations between the co-operatives and the 'outside' economy intensified. Other seeds of crisis and change were also sown during the war for reunification. Wartime inflationary finance had led to rapid price increases on the open market and, as Fforde points out, 'helped feed a steady erosion of the effectiveness of the State's pricing structure'

(Fforde, 1984, pp. 9–10), thereby contributing to the growth of parallel markets.

The crisis conditions with which we are concerned emerged more clearly during the post-war period, when each of the three elements mentioned above – aid, decentralization and anti-imperialist ideology – were rendered less effective as a means of facilitating the reproduction of the economy and the maintenance of hegemony. This was a period of worsening relations with China, which suspended its considerable quantity of aid to Vietnam. Following Vietnamese involvement in Kampuchea, several Western donors and international lending agencies also cut off aid. Restricted access to external resources greatly increased the demands of the state on domestic sources of surplus (Fforde and Paine, 1987). These demands were not compatible with the relatively 'autarchic', decentralized co-operative model that had developed, and tensions inevitably arose between central and local levels of the party/state bureaucracy. Such demands also reinforced the need to rapidly collectivize agriculture in the South – a process which alienated much of the peasant population. Following the cessation of conflict with the United States, anti-imperialist ideology lost its effectiveness as a cohesive force, and the war could be used less effectively as a justification for appealing for material sacrifice and hard work.

Unlike the other countries considered here, Cuba did not have to endure a prolonged war on national territory. Soon after the revolution, however, the United States administration imposed a trade embargo which during the 'Cuban missile crisis' of October 1962 temporarily became a total blockade. The so-called 'goods famine' of the early 1960s was to a large extent a product of these measures. Agriculture and the food industry in Cuba had become highly dependent on machinery, inputs and raw materials produced in the United States. Moreover, some 70 per cent of all food imports also came from the United States (Benjamin *et al.*, 1984, pp. 19–20). While the trade embargo was relaxed somewhat during the early 1970s, CIA support for US-based right-wing Cuban groups intent on invasion, sabotage or assassination continued throughout two decades and into the 1980s. The Reagan administration not only continued to support these groups, as well as the trade embargo, but even banned United States' tourists from travelling to Cuba. It also attempted to block Cuba's attempts to renegotiate its debt with international banks. Considerable pressures were placed on other countries to isolate Cuba. During the 1960s, several Latin American and West European countries also severed links with Cuba and the country was expelled from the Organization of American States. Until 1977, foreign ships which had docked at Cuban ports were refused entry to the United States. Not only the United States and its allies applied pressures. In 1966 there were chronic shortages of rice when China failed to deliver promised supplies, apparently in an attempt to force a change in Cuban/Soviet relations (Brundenius, 1984, p. 54).

In assessing the impact of imperialist practices on the Cuban economy and society it is clear that the destabilizing effects of the former were far more dramatic during the 1960s than in subsequent decades. While the effects continued on into the 1980s, they were not directly responsible, in the ways we have seen, for example, in Mozambique and Nicaragua, for accounting for the crisis conditions which prompted the reforms. What is important in the case of Cuba is rather the way in which pressures such as these reinforced orthodox approaches in terms of development strategy based on extensive nationalization of the means of production and central control. The strengthening of relations with the Soviet Union further reinforced these aspects, as imported technology and administrative and planning methods contributed towards the reproduction of certain features of the 'Soviet model' in Cuba. Moreover, as Benjamin *et al.* point out, the actions of the United States 'created a permanent siege mentality in Cuba' (Benjamin *et al.*, 1984, p. 184). The policies favouring rapid industrialization, as well as the 'tightening of the belts' ideology which emphasized the need for austerity, were consistent with this mentality. United States' policy towards Cuba had also forced the Cuban government to divert considerable resources towards maintaining a relatively large army. There was, then, a clear connection between imperialist practices and the problems of shortages of non-essential goods which affected levels of labour productivity and support for the regime.

In Nicaragua, increasing United States' support for the Contras from 1982 onwards, had negative effects on all three elements of the crisis. Surplus appropriation was seriously affected by the impact of the war, as maize, beans, coffee and livestock production were concentrated to a significant degree in or near the major war zones in the interior of the country. Export revenues were also affected as fishing, forestry and mining production declined. In 1984 and 1985 production losses caused by the war represented approximately 50 per cent of total annual export earnings. The war also served to disarticulate domestic trade circuits linking rural and urban areas and contributed to the class practice (examined below) of reverting to subsistence production.

As a part of a strategy to destabilize the Sandinista regime the United States also imposed an economic boycott which involved not only the US government but also major US-dominated international lending agencies such as the World Bank and the IADB. Pressures such as these restricted Nicaragua's access to development assistance and markets. While many countries stepped in to provide what was generally highly concessionary assistance, the aid relations developed with Western and socialist bloc countries often lacked the flexibility (in terms of choice of products, speed of acquisition, and so on) which a government needs to manage a crisis situation. Constraints such as these, linked to the question of access to foreign goods and markets, influenced policy decisions encouraging greater self-reliance.

The problems of inflation, shortages and the growth of informal-sector activities, which undermined attempts to plan the Nicaraguan economy, were all closely related to the impact of war and, indeed, formed a crucial part of the United States' strategy to destabilize the Sandinista regime. Increasing defence expenditures, which trebled in real terms between 1980 and 1985, were one of the major factors underlying the growing fiscal deficit, which increased from 9 per cent of GDP in 1980 to 25 per cent in 1984. Defence expenditures not only contributed to inflationary pressures but also to shortages of many basic goods and services as the army's share of basic supplies, including food, clothing and footware, as well as vehicles, increased.

As indicated above, the growth of the urban informal sector in Nicaragua was closely related to the income opportunities available in that sector relative to wage and income levels in other sectors. It was also related, however, to the displacement of large sectors of the rural population from the war zones to the towns and cities. Other effects of the war stimulated the development of petty commodity production in urban centres. It has been argued, for example, that the urgency associated with the army's demand for many goods and services forced this institution not only to assume direct control of economic activities but to rely increasingly on the informal sector (Marchetti and Jerez, 1988, p. 10). Planning, too, was undermined by the impact of the war on production, procurement and distribution in the war zones.

An important aspect of the United States' strategy to destabilize the Sandinista regime was the attempt to develop an internal front.

As mentioned earlier, these attempts began to yield partial results in 1983 and 1984, when sectors of the peasantry in more isolated areas in the interior of the country and the ethnic populations of the Atlantic Coast allied themselves more closely to the counter-revolutionary project. This strategy, however, had relatively little effect *vis-à-vis* the mass of the population concentrated in urban areas and in the Pacific coastal region, who remained somewhat more supportive of the Sandinistas, at least until the mid-1980s.

Contradictory Class Practices

From the analysis contained in previous chapters we can identify two principal class practices which contributed significantly towards the major problems of surplus appropriation and planning encountered in all four countries. The first relates to what may be called a process of 'mercantilization' (Nuñez O., 1987); the second, to the reduction of levels of marketed surplus or the diversion of this away from official procurement channels.

Mercantilization refers to a process whereby an increasing number of wage labourers, peasants and bureaucrats leave the enterprise, the land and the office, respectively, to engage in petty-trading activities, usually located in urban areas. The proliferation of these activities undermined the possibility of planning in two important respects: firstly, this process involved the expansion of specific types of marketing activities and agents which resisted state regulations; secondly, it impeded the growth of the state sector by draining the latter of both products and labour. To the extent that tensions developed between the state and this sector of the population (often drawn from classes and groups previously allied to the revolutionary project), mercantilization not only undermined planning but also hegemony. Problems concerning planning and hegemony were reinforced when, as occurred to varying degrees in all four countries, the role of the bureaucracy was compromised and the moral authority of the revolutionary party undermined as a result of the increasing involvement of public functionaries and cadres in black-market activities.

The extent of the phenomenon of mercantilization was noted above. Here I will focus on a second class practice associated with the reduction and/or diversion of surplus. This practice has three central aspects: firstly, the tendency of certain sectors of the peasantry in a shortage or war economy to revert to subsistence production and reduce levels of marketed surplus; secondly, the tendency of different types of agricultural producers to divert marketed produce from official state channels to the 'open' or 'black' market; and thirdly, the tendency of the working class (including poor peasants employed as temporary or part-time labourers) to reduce levels of surplus labour through a reduction in the intensity of labour or the period of time worked.

The tendency of peasant producers in Mozambique to reduce levels of marketed production has been noted by several writers (Mackintosh, 1986; Benjamin and Danaher, 1988). Faced with low food prices, shortages of essential goods and restricted access to marketing channels, many peasants reverted to subsistence production. This affected not only production of basic food crops but also of several important cash crops such as cashew nuts and cotton. Moreover, the insecurity which resulted from war and drought conditions during the early 1980s forced many households to withhold grain from the market for self-provisioning.

Confronted with the problem of low official prices, co-operatives and private producers increased their sales outside the state-regulated channels, usually selling to traders supplying the local parallel market or the major cities, where prices for products like maize, groundnuts and sugar were between 20 to 40 times official prices in 1985 (Mackintosh, 1986, p. 564). Not only private producers but also co-operatives engaged in such practices. In 1982 the General Union, representing all the co-operatives in the Green Zones around Maputo, broke with government regulations and began buying up the produce of the co-operatives to sell to hotels, restaurants and other outlets, at prices exceeding those set by the government (Benjamin and Danaher, 1988, p. 13). Producers resorted increasingly to barter as a means of acquiring the goods they needed, and many producers were prepared to deliver to state procurement channels only if they received goods in return. But the state's capacity to meet this demand was limited, and producers sold increasingly to traders and consumers with goods to barter (Mackintosh, 1986, p. 562). Moreover, as Hanlon points out, sources of produce destined for the black market also expanded as 'traders themselves began to invest their speculative profits in farming and fishing, both to provide a cover, and as a route to further illegal trading' (Hanlon, 1984, p. 196).

In Vietnam, many peasant families in the South responded to a situation of shortages in rural areas and the collectivization programme by migrating to the cities. This not only affected agricultural production but also led to a rapid expansion of the 'outside' economy, as many migrants became small traders. By the mid-1980s the number of small traders operating in Ho Chi Minh City was esti- mated to have exceeded by a third the already large numbers oper- ating at the end of the war.

Shortages of inputs and consumer goods in rural areas also acted as a disincentive to agricultural producers, many of whom responded by curtailing deliveries to state procurement agencies. In response to worsening material conditions and the declining efficacy of revol- utionary ideology and moral incentives, many rural families engaged in a variety of other strategies 'to cope with unwanted demands from the State' (Fforde, 1984). These included diverting labour-time away from collective practices towards private activities, and ignoring state/party directives regarding deliveries of grain and other products to state agencies, cropping patterns, and the use of new technologies and production methods. Faced with stagnant real incomes between 1965 and 1975, workers in industry turned increasingly to activities associated with the 'outside' economy to supplement state-sector wages (Fforde and Paine, 1987, pp. 94–5). As links with the 'outside' economy developed, problems of absenteeism and pilfering in state industrial enterprises increased.

In Cuba, one of the principal class practices that undermined planning and the mobilization of surplus within the state sector related to the diversion of products towards the black market. While the scale of these activities is difficult to assess, it apparently involved much of the population. The diversion of products occurred in numerous ways involving, for example, workers and administrators pilfering raw materials and products from state enterprises, agricul- tural producers failing to comply with government regulations re- garding the sale of produce through official channels, official retailers selling underweight goods to their customers, or consumers choosing not to consume but rather to sell a portion of the considerable quantities that were supplied on the ration card (Benjamin *et al.*, 1984). Serious problems of absenteeism, often on the part of workers wishing to devote more time to private sector activities, also arose.

The case of Cuba also illustrates how practices associated with black-market activities can undermine hegemony. The scale and rigidity of the rationing system in a context of excess demand necess- arily led much of the population to become involved with 'grey'- or 'black'-market activities. As Benjamin *et al.* point out, 'the black market forces Cubans to live by a double standard, and this is probably its most pernicious effect' (Ibid., 1984, p. 48). Under these conditions, not only does the dividing line between what is legal and illegal become blurred in certain spheres, but this lifestyle is also practised by party members and government functionaries.

Referring to Vietnam, Fforde and Paine also point out the extent to which illegal economic activity was considered normal. The system, they write, was 'run by people who were accustomed to diverting resources acquired on behalf of the state into activities more consistent with their own "local" interests' (Fforde and Paine, 1987, p. 130). The link, then, between practices such as these and the crisis of hegemony lies in the way in which the involvement of cadres and functionaries undermines the moral authority of the party and the state.

In Nicaragua, many peasant families restricted marketed output in response to both the deterioration in the domestic terms of trade between 1982 and 1985, and serious shortages of transport and basic manufactured goods required by the rural household. Moreover, the elimination of pre-revolutionary tenancy, exchange and informal credit relations meant that peasant producers were no longer obliged to dispose of the same quantities of grain in order to meet their obligations to landlords, merchants or moneylenders (Utting, 1987, p. 133). In response to these conditions and the disruptive impact of the war on production systems and marketing circuits, the peasantry restricted sales of grain to the state marketing agency, ENABAS.

The diversion of produce away from official marketing channels was practised to a considerable degree by rich peasants and larger capitalist producers. Despite strict regulations on wholesale and retail prices, and controls on the interregional movement of grain and certain other products, significant quantities ended up on the open or black market. In response to the decline in the relative price of milk, producers reduced sales to the state-owned or regulated processing plants and diverted milk to less controlled product sectors such as traditional cheese production and calf fattening, or simply sold raw milk on the local market. Smuggling of coffee and cattle into neighbouring countries, notably Honduras, also reached significant proportions.

The main contradictory class practices engaged in by the working class related to problems of absenteeism, 'foot-dragging' and the high levels of rotation of labour which moved from one enterprise to another in search of higher wages. Such problems derived from the sharp decline in real wages and the relaxation of coercive methods for retaining labour and increasing its intensity.

Contradictory State Practices

Above, I referred to two ways in which actions taken by the state may be said to be contradictory. The first related to policies, programmes or measures which serve to alienate classes or social groups allied to the revolutionary project; the second, to actions which undermine rather than promote the development of the productive forces. In analyzing the former, I will refer to the concept of 'crowding out' which has been used to describe state–peasant relations and the tendency of the state to marginalize the peasantry in the structure of resource allocation (Fitzgerald, 1988a, p. 18). Both for ideological reasons (the perceived superiority of state/collective forms of production) and institutional reasons (the operation of the 'soft-budget constraint'), state enterprises have both the approval and purchasing power necessary to obtain the goods they require at the expense of other sectors. The crowding-out of the peasantry, however, can also be the effect of a certain 'urban bias' which characterizes the pattern of resource allocation.

It would seem useful, however, to broaden the concept somewhat to refer to two other spheres where 'crowding-out' may be said to operate. The first relates to the accumulation–consumption balance and the crowding-out of consumption that usually occurs as a result of the phenomenon, described in Part I, of 'accumulation bias', which generally characterizes orthodox socialist development strategy. This aspect, however, affects not only the peasantry but also the working class and other social groups. The second relates to the question of power and control over the decision-making process – more specifically, the extent to which popular participation or 'people's power' is crowded out by bureaucratic/technocratic control. All three forms have important implications for surplus appropriation, planning and hegemony.

In considering the second set of contradictory state practices I will refer primarily to the problems of low productivity, inefficiency and waste in the state/collective sector which, as indicated in Part I, are linked to the soft-budget constraint and the 'crowding-out' of consumption which restricts the availability of 'incentive' goods (Fitzgerald, 1988a, p. 21).

The negative impact on the peasantry of 'crowding-out' was most apparent in Mozambique. The high priority attached to the development of the state-farm sector and capital intensive development deprived the rural population of essential resources. State farms received an estimated 90 per cent of agricultural investments between 1977 and 1982. During the early 1980s, shortages of agricultural implements, inputs and consumer goods intensified as the composition of imports altered, favouring goods required for an ambitious ten-year development plan. While the country still relied heavily on imports of consumer goods, only a small percentage of these ended up in rural areas, where over 80 per cent of the population lived. The priority attached to the urban population not only influenced the pattern of distribution of consumer imports, but also price policy, reflected in a worsening of the domestic terms of trade from the point of view of the rural producer. It also reinforced the priority attached to the state-farm sector, which constituted a production nucleus that could produce significant quantities of food for both the army and the urban population and which could be planned and defended with relative ease (Mackintosh, 1986, p. 576). This state-sector bias was reinforced by what Littlejohn refers to as 'a misguided conception of the mass of the peasantry as "subsistence farmers" not involved in marketing' (Littlejohn, 1988, p. 17). While contrasting ideological influences operated within FRELIMO, it was the urban-orientated 'Maputo ideology' which held sway over the 'ideology of the liberated areas', throughout much of the post-revolutionary period (Egero, 1987, pp. 93, 98).

State practices undermined production and planning in other respects as well. As Mackintosh points out, 'even before inflationary pressure became so serious and widespread, there was evidence that the planning system for agricultural marketing was itself a factor in the creation of the parallel market in rural areas' (Mackintosh, 1986, p. 568). This was due not only to the problems of consumer goods supply referred to above, or to pricing policy which established low and nationally uniform prices, but also to the failure to co-ordinate the purchasing activities of different state agencies. 'As a result,' writes Mackintosh, 'major state purchasers were competing, allowing private traders to play off one state institution against another to their own benefit' (Ibid., p. 568).

Serious problems of inefficiency and waste in Vietnamese industry associated with the second contradictory state practice referred to above were highlighted by several writers (Fforde and Paine, 1987; Spoor, 1988). Problems of low labour productivity also characterized collective agriculture, where the number of days worked by co-operative workers was often well below the number stipulated by the government (Werner, 1984, p. 51).

The 'crowding-out' effect appears to have assumed very specific forms in Vietnam. Compared to Mozambique, Cuba and Nicaragua, urban bias appears to have been relatively unimportant. Indeed, several writers note that the material situation of much of the urban population in cities such as Hanoi is generally worse than that of the surrounding rural population. Nevertheless, the quantity of resources allocated to state industrial enterprises and large-scale development projects tended to deprive the agricultural co-operative sector of essential consumption goods. While a number of industries were producing agricultural inputs, production levels of crucial farm implements and machines remained very low.

In relation to the question of popular participation and control of decision-making processes, the Vietnamese case also presents a number of variants. In general, the level of effective participation of co-operatives and mass organizations in decision-making processes was fairly restricted. Nevertheless, a certain community of interests often characterized relations between the peasantry and local party and state cadres, particularly during times of adversity (Post, 1982, p. 34; Gordon, 1982). This situation impeded policy implementation, as it led to rifts between the central and local levels of the party and the bureaucracy, and to the 'autarky' of the co-operatives (Fforde, 1985).

Use of the term 'crowding out' to describe state-peasant relations in Cuba would not seem to be entirely appropriate. What was apparent in this case was the relatively favourable situation experienced by private farmers during three decades. Relevant, though, was the impact of accumulation bias in crowding out consumption of non-essential goods and the negative effect this had on labour productivity. Considerable problems of inefficiency and waste were also prominent in Cuban industry.

What is less clear is the situation regarding people's power and participation. While the scope for participation had clearly broadened during the 1970s, particularly through the institutions of *Poder Popular*, it would seem that the planning process came to be dominated to a large extent by bureaucratic/technocratic methods, or what Castro refers to as 'the petty-bourgeois spirit of the capital', which stifled popular participation. Moreover, it appears that the party itself assumed, until the mid-1980s, more of a back-seat role in directing the economy, and, according to Castro, began to lose touch with the people (Castro, 1987b, 1987c).

In the case of Nicaragua, the 'crowding out' of the peasantry manifested itself mainly in terms of restricted access to production and consumption goods and means of transport, as well as declining real incomes. This form of 'crowding out' was an effect both of the priority accorded to the state sector, particularly in relation to the allocation of inputs and capital goods, and urban bias, which affected the allocation of consumption goods. 'Crowding out', however, assumed very uneven forms and was associated primarily with the non-collectivized peasantry located in the interior of the country. Certain sectors of the peasantry, notably those integrated in production co-operatives, generally experienced an improvement in their levels of living. Much of the peasantry gained improved access to inputs and services such as credit, health and education, the provision of which expanded rapidly following the revolution. Yet while the access of the peasantry to credit improved dramatically, credit policy failed to produce its conventional knock-on effect of stimulating marketed output, partly due to the highly subsidized rates offered by the state banks and the flexible attitude towards debt repayment. Moreover, during the early years of the revolution, lack of controls on the use of credit meant that a significant proportion was used for consumption as opposed to production. The granting of credit on these terms also meant that the peasant population could bypass the traditional moneylender who had often demanded repayment in kind (Utting, 1987, p. 133). Even improved access to free health services could have the effect of reducing the level of marketed surplus, since the peasant family no longer had to sell grains in order to obtain the income necessary to cover medical expenses (Zalkin, 1985).

In Nicaragua, consumption was increasingly squeezed following 1982, not only because of the impact on production of both class practices and the war, but also because of the investment dynamic in the public sector. During the revolution's honeymoon period (July 1979–late 1981) when development prospects looked highly favourable, numerous large-scale, slow-yielding projects were initiated, which altered the composition of imports away from consumption goods to capital goods and contributed to government deficits and inflationary pressures.

Looking at Nicaragua in comparative and historical perspective there would seem to be little basis for applying the term 'crowding out' to the question of people's power and participation. One of the hallmarks of the revolution was clearly its hegemonic character and the increased scope for participation of previously marginalized groups. Nevertheless, it took some years before the peasantry, through its national association the UNAG, emerged as an effective pressure group and participant in the policy process. Moreover, within this organization it would seem to be the co-operatives, middle and rich peasantry that were well represented and not the poor peasantry (Kaimowitz, 1986a). Also, we saw that during the mid-1980s there was a decline in the extent to which the organization, claiming to represent the interests of low-income urban households, participated in decision-making processes. These two developments – the rise of the UNAG and the fall of the CDS – were to have an important influence in determining the direction of the policy reforms introduced during the mid-1980s.

As regards the extent to which state policies and actions undermined the development of the productive forces in Nicaragua, it is relevant to refer to the negative impact on labour productivity of an austere wages policy and the lack of incentive goods, as well as problems encountered in distributing and using external aid. Port congestion seriously affected the distribution of imported inputs, spare parts and consumption goods, while a lot of machinery and equipment soon fell into a state of disrepair due to lack of maintenance. Up to a third of the country's tractors were reported to be in such a state in 1986.

SOCIAL STRUCTURE, CIVIL SOCIETY AND PARTICIPATION

Throughout this study I have argued that our understanding of the process of policy reform in Third-World socialist countries must take into account not only the nature of the crisis confronting post-revolutionary states but also the nature of changes occurring in the balance of social forces and in the capacity of different social/interest groups to influence, both directly and indirectly, the policy process.

Our analysis of these aspects has focused on the types of contradictory class practices noted above, as well as the question of changes in social structure (the numerical strength of different social groups), the development of civil society (the forms of organization and mobilization of different groups), and the 'participation' of different groups in decision-making processes.

On the question of changes in social structure, we have seen how the years leading up to the reforms were characterized by the growth of specific social groups – rich peasantry in Vietnam and Nicaragua and to a lesser extent in Mozambique; a technical/managerial stratum in Vietnam and Cuba; urban middle-class groups in Cuba. Concerning developments at the level of civil society, the cases of Nicaragua and Cuba highlight the relationship between the reform process and the increased capacity of specific social groups to organize and articulate interests and constitute themselves as pressure groups.

Regarding 'participation', it is clear that the degree of involvement of mass organizations in decision-making processes varied considerably from country to country as well as at different times within a specific country. What was often important was not only the regular institutionalized relations between government and masses (bilateral meetings, participation in assemblies or committees, and so on) but also the conjuctural circumstance of a national congress of workers or peasant producers, as occurred in Nicaragua and Cuba respectively, or a national dialogue, as took place in Mozambique. What the case studies of Vietnam and Nicaragua also indicated, was the importance of formal relations characteristic of institutionalized forms of participation, and informal relations between state officials and party cadres on the one hand, and specific social groups on the other.

It is probably in relation to Mozambique where information on these aspects is most limited. From the analysis contained in the case study, however, it is important to refer to four key developments which occurred during the latter 1970s and early 1980s. Firstly, during the latter half of the 1970s, 'commandism' (or *verticalismo*) gained the upper hand, given the way in which the principle of democratic centralism was applied in practice and the ongoing influence of colonial attitudes and social relations. In this context, a technocratic group within the central state apparatus, concerned with rapid modernization centred on large-scale state enterprises and projects, became extremely influential in shaping development policy.

Secondly, the period leading up the reforms was one in which participatory institutions and practices were revitalized. This process culminated in the national dialogue of 1982. By holding meetings throughout the country, FRELIMO leaders became increasingly aware of the extent of discontent in rural areas.

Thirdly, it is probable that rich peasant interests were well-represented in this dialogue. The relative importance of this sector of the peasantry derived not only from the intensification of social differentiation among the peasantry during the post-revolution period and, more specifically, improved opportunities for commercial farming in specific areas (such as urban green zones), but also from the fact that in relation to other sectors of the rural male population which had to migrate in search of employment, rich peasants generally enjoyed a more stable residence and, as such, could secure greater influence at the local level (O'Laughlin, 1981).

Fourthly, the pre-reform period was marked by a FRELIMO offensive against the 'internal class enemy'. This put the technocratic group on the defensive, weakened the alliance between them and the 'commercial group', and forced commercial capital into productive-sector activities. One interpretation of the political economy of the reform process suggests that the technocratic group attempted to reconstitute the dominant alliance by allying with commercial farmers (Hanlon, 1984).

The crucial variable to analyze in the case of Vietnam is that of state – co-operative relations. Institutionalized forms of participation by social groups at the centre of the policy stage appear to be relatively weak, given the absence of a mass peasant association and the apparently limited role played by the Women's Union (composed primarily of women producers) in the process of policy design. What is important, rather, is an alternative network of relations involving the co-operatives and rich peasant interests, on the one hand, and local levels of the state bureaucracy and the party on the other.

The historical dichotomy between state and commune was reinforced during the war years, as the co-operatives became more autonomous. The case study of Vietnam pays particular attention to an interpretation of events which differentiates peasant interests. The increasing strength of rich peasant interests within co-operative structures not only led to a weakening of collective relations and the growth of petty-commodity production, but also to alliances between such sectors and the bureaucracy and party representatives at the local level (Gordon, 1982). As such, class interests associated with rich peasants/petty commodity producers found expression within the party/state apparatus.

Orthodox positions within the state apparatus also came up against alternative positions put forward by groups within the public sector which had grown in strength during the previous two decades. The number of cadres, bureaucrats and public enterprise managers with training in economics and economic management had grown rapidly and by the mid-1970s the number of scientific, technical and management cadres in North Vietnam outnumbered the industrial working class. Such groups pushed for reforms associated the increased use of material incentives, decentralized planning and management methods and a greater space for private initiative.

A similar phenomenon occurred in Cuba, where we see during the 1970s and early 1980s the growth of a technocratic group within the state apparatus interested in applying new economic management and planning methods to accelerate economic growth. Particularly important in the case of Cuba is the rise of urban middle-class interests concerned with improved access to non-essential consumer products. The rise of such groups was a feature of the rapid growth of the 'non-productive' service sector of the economy during the 1970s. By 1979, this sector accounted for nearly 30 per cent of the total labour force.

In the case of Cuba there is considerable debate over the degree of 'popular participation' in the policy process. While the political and planning process was clearly marked by a high degree of hierarchy and centralization, it is clear that processes of consultation, operating through the Committees in Defense of the Revolution, the union structure of the Confederation of Cuban Workers and the local organs of People's Power, were institutionalized at different levels and became somewhat more effective during the 1970s.

Pressures favouring liberalization of food marketing were also brought to bear by the National Association of Small Farmers (ANAP). While ANAP represented both private and co-operative producers, the organization was dominated by private interests at the time when the free peasant markets were introduced in 1980.

The case study of Nicaragua provides a more systematic treatment of the changes occuring in social structure, civil society and participation. What this study shows is that any analysis of the way in which social forces intervene in the policy process, and more specifically of how changes in the balance of social forces influence that process, must consider not only which groups have increased their capacity to articulate interests, operate as pressure groups and influence decision-making processes, but also which have become weaker.

The mid-1980 reforms in Nicaragua coincided with the emergence of the UNAG – the organization representing agricultural co-operative members, small peasant producers, and many larger commercial farmers – as one of the most powerful of the country's mass organizations. Following the formation of the UNAG in 1981, the organization's membership grew rapidly, reaching over 140 000 in 1986, or approximately two-thirds of the total number of agricultural producers. During these years the UNAG developed into an effective pressure group and, while it was closely linked to the Sandinista Party, it remained relatively autonomous from the state. The influence of this organization was instrumental in promoting the shift towards a more pro-peasant strategy.

Important changes, though, had occurred in the social composition of the UNAG. While initially composed primarily of co-operative members and smaller peasant producers, the organization began to recruit more of the larger, so-called 'patriotic producers'. Reflecting the influence of these producers, the demands of the UNAG became less exclusively concerned with such aspects as the land problem and co-operativization or access to basic inputs. The organization began to call for a more flexible approach to co-operativization, the redistribution of land to individuals, a halt to land invasions, improved access to consumer goods and non-basic inputs/machinery/transport, and improved prices for agricultural products.

To understand the shift towards a more pro-peasant strategy, however, it is also important to refer to developments affecting the working class and urban petty-commodity producers. The industrial working class, organized mainly in the pro-government Sandinista Workers' Federation (CST) which represented approximately the same number of people as the UNAG in 1986, went along with measures which meant the abandonment of cheap food policy and which, in the short term at least, would have a negative impact on the levels of living of workers.

Acceptance of these measures coincided with the identification on the part of certain Sandinista organizations of a new internal 'class enemy' which was not the industrial or agrarian bourgeoisie, but private commercial capital and elements of the urban informal sector, which were seen as benefiting from and contributing to the inflationary spiral, the black market and shortages. The CST recognized the need to build a strong worker–peasant alliance, both to increase food production and, eventually, to ensure direct transfers between industry and agriculture. The agreement of the main union organizations also came about as a result of a specific trade-off. While the unions accepted increased food prices, they demanded (during the Fourth National Assembly of Trade Unions, held in January 1985), and got, privileged access to basic manufactured goods distributed through state retail channels.

The shift in economic strategy in Nicaragua also coincided with a decline in the influence of what for many years was the largest mass organization, the Sandinista Defence Committees (CDS), whose natural constituency was the urban informal sector. The CDS had for many years assumed an active role in the process of food policy design, implementation and review. During the latter half of 1984 and throughout 1985 the CDS were increasingly excluded from the decision-making process as priorities shifted towards social groups associated with the 'productive' sectors of the economy. This exclusion of the CDS coincided with a crisis within the organization itself, reflected in the declining participation of community members in CDS activities. Much of the urban population had become highly critical of the organization, believing that the leadership had divorced itself from real community interests and concerns.

As the limitations inherent in the state-centred accumulation model became more apparent, a technocratic fraction, associated primarily with the Ministry of Agricultural Development and Agrarian Reform, which had stressed the need for rapid modernization and state-enterprise development, went on the defensive. Meanwhile, other fractions, calling for a more pro-peasant approach, the relaxation of administrative controls and increased liberalization, pushed for policy reforms.

External Pressures

In considering the question of the extent to which demands and pressures from different interest groups influence the policy process, it is important to consider not only the situation *vis-à-vis* internal social groups, but also that relating to the ideological influences brought to bear by world powers, be they foreign governments or international agencies.

Given the degree of dependency of countries like Vietnam, Cuba and Nicaragua on the more industrialized socialist countries, it is necessary to consider the extent to which such ties (involving not only trade and aid but also education, technical assistance and training) facilitate the dissemination of ideas associated with *perestroika*. A closer look at the reform process in all four countries, however, indicates that the role of such influences in the reform process should not be overstated. In the cases we have looked at, the introduction of policy reforms pre-dates *perestroika* and, in most cases, even the Andropov period, when certain reform initiatives were considered in the Soviet Union. Moreover, establishing some sort of necessary link between Soviet ideological influences or pressures and the reform process in dependent transitional economies is shown to be particularly problematic when analyzing the case of Cuba. While *perestroika* was taking off in the Soviet Union, Cuba – probably the Third-World country most tied to the Soviet Union – was launching its 'rectification' drive and moving away from liberalization.

It would seem to be only in the case of Vietnam that one of the socialist giants had any significant influence in determining the types of policy reform introduced during the early 1980s. In this case, however, the protagonist was not the Soviet Union but China. While the Vietnamese reforms were introduced during a period when relations between the two countries were ruptured, it can be argued that the debates leading up to the reforms were indeed influenced by those taking place during the early post-Maoist period in China (White C., 1983).

These types of external influence would seem to be more relevant in a situation where closer ties develop between the small Third-World socialist state and the West. This is particularly apparent in the case of Mozambique, where pressures from the IMF, the World Bank, USAID and other Western donor agencies clearly prompted a decisive shift in the reform process, favouring economic liberalization and privatization.

The Vietnamese stabilization and adjustment measures of the late 1980s also followed on the heels of various IMF missions. The question arises, though, as to whether the same policy changes might not have been introduced even in the absence of relations with such agencies. Nicaragua's stabilization and adjustment programme, for example, was introduced while relations with the IMF, World Bank and USAID were broken. What seems clear, though, is that relations with such agencies have influenced the timing and content of the reform package, particularly with regard to privatization and support for capitalist producers.

It would clearly be wrong, though, to correlate conditionality with Western aid in general. This is brought out in the case of Nicaragua, where strong relations were maintained with many Western European countries, Canada, and multilateral agencies such as the United Nations and the EEC. Aid from these sources was channelled towards diverse institutional forms, including state enterprises, co-operatives and private producers. While sources such as these expressed legitimate concerns regarding the inefficient use of aid, there is little evidence pointing to conditionality which contradicted fundamental government principles and policy objectives.

CONCLUSION

What emerges from this study is that the nature of the crisis which prompted economic reform in dependent transitional societies was different from that which led to 'adjustment' in other Third-World countries, or *perestroika*-type reforms in the more industrialized socialist countries.

In many African and Latin-American countries, crisis and adjustment generally occurred in the context of 'external shocks' and the so-called debt crisis (Cornia and Jespersen, 1989; Mkandawire, 1989, Sandbrook, 1989; Schvarzer, 1989). While the economies we have looked at were for the most part highly dependent on foreign markets and aid, the scale and nature of relations with socialist countries and certain Western donor agencies during the period which concerns us here generally served to cushion, to some extent, the impact of 'shocks' associated with international trade and finance. Countries like Vietnam, Cuba and Nicaragua were highly indebted at the time when reforms were introduced, but repayment of their debts did not generally constitute an overwhelming burden, given the fairly flexible terms granted by the socialist bloc countries and, in the case of Nicaragua, several Western European governments.

In several Eastern bloc countries, and to some extent in China, the crisis related more to a set of systemic constraints associated with centralized planning systems and the need to (a) achieve international industrial competitiveness; (b) develop alternative planning and management methods capable of dealing with the complex resource flows which characterize more developed economies; and (c) meet popular demands associated with *non-essential* consumption (consumer durables, improved housing, better quality and variety of food, and so on) (Fitzgerald and Wuyts, 1988b).

In countries such as Mozambique, Vietnam and Nicaragua the reform process was characterized by a very different rationale, related essentially to (a) a crisis of basic-needs provisioning, that is, to problems of *essential* consumption where the food problem loomed particularly large; (b) the need to develop a survival economy capable of withstanding internal destabilization and external aggression; and (c) the need to deal with a variety of chronic economic distortions and disequilibria – in relative prices, the proliferation of black-market activities, high levels of inflation, fiscal and balance-of-trade deficits, and so on.

In the case of the dependent transitional economies analyzed in this study, the crisis has been conceptualized in terms of the incapacity of the state to mobilize and appropriate surplus for basic needs provisioning and accumulation, as well as to direct the evolution of the economy. This latter aspect in turn relates to a crisis of orthodox models of planning and of 'hegemony', understood in the Gramscian sense of the capacity to exercise leadership on the basis of consensus and not coercion.

As indicated in Part IV, a number of important variations emerge in the nature of the reforms in the four countries, with Cuba representing a sort of half-way point between the Third World and Eastern Europe.

I have argued throughout this study that the content of the policy changes was determined as much by ideological considerations and the way in which political leaders and planners interpreted and analyzed the crisis as on the precise nature of the crisis, the type of social structure and the nature of demands and pressures brought to bear by different social groups. We have seen how changes in social structure and at the level of civil society, as well as in institutionalized forms of participation, considerably altered the balance of social forces during the period leading up to the reforms.

The capacity of certain social groups to obtain a greater share of the social product and to influence the process of policy design clearly increased. The role of the rich peasantry, in this respect, has been noted in all four of the country studies. In the case of Cuba, particular attention was focused on the increasing strength of urban middle-class interests. We have also noted certain changes occurring in the social composition of the central state apparatus or public sector itself, notably the rise of a technical/professional stratum with training in economics and management. This latter group not only defended certain material interests associated with middle-class consumer demands, but also upheld new ideas about economic development which contradicted more orthodox approaches.

Meanwhile the organizational strength and influence of other social groups declined. This was brought out clearly in the case of Nicaragua, where we saw that the shift towards a more pro-peasant strategy was tied up also with the situation regarding organizations of urban-based groups. The once powerful mass organization representing urban *barrio* residents had lost considerable base support. Other organizations representing industrial workers and women had also been weakened as a result of the leadership putting the party line before the immediate interests of rank-and-file members.

From the perspective of the post-revolutionary state in countries such as Mozambique, Vietnam and Nicaragua, the transition from orthodoxy to reform may be said to have both an economic and a political logic. The former expresses itself in the contrast between a 'dualist' strategy and one of 'articulation' (Fitzgerald, 1988a, p. 20).

The dualist approach which characterized orthodox socialist development strategy prioritized the modern state or socialized sector of the economy and attempted either to absorb (through employment in state enterprises), suppress (prohibition of private trade), rapidly transform (collectivization), or restrict/stifle (adverse terms of trade) the 'traditional' sector composed mainly of peasants. In the case of Nicaragua, where a fairly large capitalist sector continued to exist following the revolution, state regulations and controls over input supply, access to investment goods, the labour process and the realization of surplus had the effect of assigning much of this group the role of enterprise 'administrators' – a situation which did little to stimulate production or investment.

In contrast to this approach, articulation admits the longer-term coexistence of different forms of production and the need to create conditions conducive to the extended reproduction of petty-commodity or capitalist forms so as to stimulate production, private 'productive' investment, and the flow of goods and services.

This implies a reduction in the degree of direct state or collective control over production and exchange, but does not necessarily mean the abandonment of social control over patterns of resource allocation and accumulation. Indeed, the reforms may be said to entail, also, an administrative logic which recognizes the illusory character of social control under systems of centralized planning. As we have seen, the constraints (soft-budget) and biases (state-centred accumulation) characteristic of orthodox socialist models generate distortions and disequilibria which prevent the state from effectively regulating patterns of resource flows. Moreover, the structural conditions within which socialism in underdeveloped transitional economies generally must develop – a large petty-commodity sector, external dependency and low levels of development of the productive forces – pose major obstacles to centralized planning (Fitzgerald, 1985b).

In all four countries, not only petty-commodity producers but also workers and bureaucrats were increasingly sucked into the parallel or informal economy in the search for goods and higher incomes. It can be argued, therefore, that the reforms did not introduce deregulation in any qualitative sense, for deregulation was already a fact of economic life.

From the point of view of the post-revolutionary state, the problem was not only that the private sector was expanding at the expense of the 'socialist' sector, but also that the state had no control over patterns of private accumulation (Bettelheim, 1988; Mackintosh and Wuyts, 1988). As such, the economic reforms constituted an attempt on the part of the state to manage patterns of private accumulation through greater reliance on macroeconomic policy instruments and material incentives. Particularly important here was the attempt to direct resource allocation away from speculative or commercial activities and into 'productive' sector activities, notably agriculture.

As Fitzgerald points out, given the types of structural conditions prevailing in Third-World countries, 'central aspects of economic strategy must therefore be the management of commercial relationships with the world economy. . .and with the small-producer sector. . . rather than the planning of production in the state sector itself' (Fitzgerald, 1985b, p. 11). This implies a greater emphasis on macroeconomic (price, credit, exchange rate, fiscal policy) as opposed to administrative controls for regulating the non-state sector. Managing the domestic terms of trade, however, involves not only getting the official price right or price deregulation, but, more importantly, measures to expand the availability of inputs and consumer goods required by petty-commodity producers. This, in turn, has implications for the sectoral allocation of resources in the economy and the accumulation–consumption balance. In the cases we have looked at, the policy reforms have generally involved a reduced investment ratio, restrictions on the initiation of large-scale projects, and increased emphasis on food and agro-export production, as well as light industry.

The political logic behind the reforms may be understood with reference to the Gramscian distinction between 'domination' and 'hegemony'. Whereas 'domination' implies the imposition of the ideology of the dominant class or ruling bloc on the rest of society, and exercising power by means of coercion, 'hegemony' implies the ability of the ruling group to make economic/corporate sacrifices and compromises in order to achieve consensus, cement alliances and create conditions which facilitate the 'development of all the "national" energies' (Gramsci, 1971, p. 182).

Such an approach is crucial for surplus mobilization/appropriation and planning: to encourage people to participate in mass or voluntary work campaigns; to respond positively to appeals for 'belt-tightening'; to work harder, produce and invest; to pay taxes and/or sell to state trading agencies; and refrain from engaging in illegal activities associated with the black market, pilfering and corruption. It is also crucial to achieve the national unity essential to withstand attempts from within and without to destabilize the economy and regime.

Within this context it would appear that the reforms did not imply the abandonment of one of the essential defining characteristics of socialist transition, namely social control, (that is, the attempt to shape patterns of resource allocation and accumulation according to socially-determined priorities), but rather the search for new ways of achieving it based on an alternative blend of 'plan' and 'market'. This, however, was to be no easy task.

In the case of all four countries, the reform process experienced an abrupt change in course during the second half of the 1980s. Hence we see in Mozambique in 1987, as well as in Vietnam and Nicaragua in 1988/89, the introduction of the type of stabilization and structural adjustment measures more commonly associated with dependent capitalist economies in Latin America and Africa. In Cuba, also, there was a radical shift in approach, though of a very different character, involving what might be described as a sort of 'neo-socialist orthodoxy'.

In the case of the former group of countries, the shift from 'reform' to 'adjustment' was not simply a question that 'the moderates' had won out and that a stronger medicine was needed to correct distortions and macroeconomic disequilibria. Neither was the 'rectification' drive in Cuba simply a case of Fidel and 'the ideologues' having reasserted their position. One important element in accounting for the shift in approach in the former group of countries (and which could well influence events in Cuba in the 1990s), related to developments in the Soviet Union and Eastern Europe during the second half of the 1980s. Clearly, the will and capacity of the governments of these countries to supply the goods needed to support dependent transitional economies and to operate what, in effect, was a soft-budget constraint on an international level, were on the wane. And closer ties were necessary with a Western-dominated international order, where the rules of the game demanded a greater emphasis on export-led growth, liberalization, privatization, a 'hard-budget' constraint, and competitiveness.

What should also be stressed, however, is the fact that the reforms themselves prompted modifications in relations with foreign powers and the world economy, generated new tensions and contradictions, and led to ongoing changes in the balance of social forces. As a result of these developments it was to be expected that the reform process would change direction within a relatively short time-span and continue to do so into the 1990s.

Notes

1. The term 'direction' as used here has (as in the Spanish *dirección* or the Italian *direzione*) the connotation of leadership or capacity to lead.
2. In this specific context the term 'hegemonic' implies, as in the original Greek meaning, the domination of one foreign power over another.

Bibliography

Acosta, J. (1973) 'Cuba: de la neo-colonia a la construcción del socialismo', *Economía y Desarrollo*, no. 19.

Aganbegyan, A. (1987) 'The New Economic Strategy of the USSR and its Social Dimensions', *International Labour Review*, vol. 126, no. 1, January/February, pp. 95–109.

—— (1988) 'Coming in from the Cold', *New Socialist*, May/June, pp. 6–9.

Arana, M. (1988) 'Reforma Económica 1988: Notas Comparativas con Paquetes de "Choque Heterodoxo" – Tensiones y Disyuntivas', *Boletín Socio-Económico* no. 7, Managua: INIES.

—— (1990) 'Nicaragua: Estabilización, Ajuste y Estrategia Económica, 1988–89', in Arana *et al.* (eds), *Políticas de Ajuste en Nicaragua: Reflexiones sobre sus Implicaciones Estratégicas*, Managua, CRIES.

Arana, M., Stahler-Sholk, R. and Vilas, C. (1990), *Políticas de Ajuste en Nicaragua: Reflexiones sobre sus Implicaciones Estratégicas*, Cuadernos de Pensamiento Propio no. 18, Managua, CRIES.

Arguello, A., Croes, E., Kleiterp, N. (1987) *Nicaragua: Accumulación y Transformación 1979–1985*, Managua, UNDP.

Avendaño, N. (1988) 'Caracterización General de las Políticas Económicas en Nicaragua en el Período 1980–1987', in CIERA, (1988).

Bahro, R. (1978) *The Alternative in Eastern Europe*, London, New Left Books.

Barker, J. (1985) 'Gaps in the Debates about Agriculture in Senegal, Tanzania and Mozambique', *World Development*, vol. 13, no. 1, pp. 59–76.

Barone, E. (1935) 'The Ministry of Production in a Collectivist State', in F. Hayek (ed.).

Barraclough, S. (1991) *An End to Hunger? The Social Origins of Food Strategies*, London, Zed Press.

—— (1984) *Un Análisis Preliminar del Sistema Alimentario Nicaragüense*, Geneva, UNRISD.

—— and Scott, M. (1987) *The Rich Have Already Eaten: Roots of Catastrophe in Central America*, Amsterdam, Transnational Institute/Third World Publications.

—— van Buren, A., Gariazzo, A., Sundaram, A. and Utting, P. (1988) *Aid That Counts: The Western Contribution to Development and Survival in Nicaragua*, Amsterdam, Transnational Institute.

Baumeister, E. (1988a) 'Comentarios', in CIERA (ed.) (1988).

—— (1988b) 'Tres Condicionantes Político-Ideológicos en la Formulación de las Políticas Agrarias en Nicaragua', *Boletín Socio-Económico*, no. 7, Managua, INIES.

—— and Neira, O. (1986) 'The Making of a Mixed Economy: Class Struggle and State Policy in the Nicaragua Transition', in R. Fagen *et al.* (eds).

Bengelsdorf, C. (1986) 'State and Society in the Transition to Socialism: The Theoretical Legacy', in R. Fagen *et al.* (eds).

Benjamin, M., Collins, J. and Scott, M. (1984) *No Free Lunch: Food and Revolution in Cuba Today*, San Francisco, Institute for Food and Development Policy.

—— and Danaher, K. (1988) 'Mozambican Women Make the "Green Zones" Bloom,' mimeo, San Francisco, Institute for Food and Development Policy.

Bernales Alvarado, M. (1985) 'La Transformación del Estado: problemas y perspectivas', in R. Harris and C. Vilas (eds).

Bernstein, H. (1977) 'Notes on Capital and the Peasantry', *Review of African Political Economy*, no. 10, pp. 50–73.

—— (1986) *Capitalism and Petty Commodity Production*, Development Policy and Practice Working Paper no. 3, Milton Keynes, The Open University.

Bettelheim, C. (1975) *The Transition to Socialist Economy*, Sussex, Harvester Press.

—— (1976) *Economic Calculation and Forms of Property*, London, Routledge & Kegan Paul.

—— (1977) *Class Struggles in the USSR. First period: 1917–1923*, Sussex, Harvester Press.

—— (1978a) *Class Struggles in the USSR, Second period: 1923–1930*, New York, Monthly Review Press.

—— (1978b) 'The Great Leap Backward', in Burton, N. G. and Bettelheim, C., *China Since Mao*, New York, Monthly Review Press.

—— (1988) 'Economic Reform in China', (mimeo) in E. V. K. Fitzgerald and M. Wuyts (eds).

Bhaduri, A. and Rahman, M. (1982) 'Agricultural Cooperatives and Peasant Participation in the Socialist Republic of Viet Nam', in A. Bhaduri and M. Rhaman (eds), *Studies in Rural Participation*, New Delhi, Oxford Publications.

Binkert, G. (1983) *Agricultural Production and Economic Incentives: Food Policy in Mozambique*, Development Discussion Paper no. 154, Harvard Institute for International Development, Harvard University.

Biondi-Morra B. (1988) *Managing Food Policy Implementation in Developing Countries: The Case of the Nicaraguan State-owned Agribusiness Enterprises 1979–1985*, PhD thesis, Harvard University.

Brundenius, C. (1984) *Revolutionary Cuba: The Challenge of Economic Growth with Equity*, Boulder, Col. Westview Press.

—— (1987) 'Development and Prospects of Capital Goods Production in Revolutionary Cuba', *World Development*, vol. 15, no. 1.

Brus, W. (1972) *The Market in a Socialist Economy*, London, Routledge & Kegan Paul.

—— (1985) 'Socialism – Feasible and Viable', *New Left Review*, no. 153, September/October, pp. 43–62.

—— (1987) 'Experience of the Socialist Countries', in L. Emmerij (ed.).

Cabezas, O. (1989) 'The Communal Leader is the Fundamental Driving Force of our CDS Movement', Speech reported in *Barricada*, Managua, 20 March.

Cabrales, R. (1987) 'El Abastecimiento en Ocho Años de Revolucion',

Revista Nicaragüense de Ciencias Sociales, vol. 2, no. 3, December, pp. 41–7.

Carr, E. H. (1952) *The Bolshevik Revolution 1917–1923*, vol. 2, London, Macmillan.

Castro, F. (1986a) Speech at Second National Meeting of Agricultural Production Cooperatives, *Granma Weekly Review*, 1 June, pp. 3–4.

—— (1986b) Speech at meeting to analyze enterprise management in City of Havana, *Granma Weekly Review*, 6 July, pp. 2–3.

—— (1986c) Speech at Third Congress of the Committees for the Defense of the Revolution, *Granma Weekly Review*, 12 October, pp. 2–5.

—— (1987a) Speech at Opening of 11th Session of National Assembly, *Granma Weekly Review*, 11 January, pp. 2–5.

—— (1987b) Speech at meeting of the Provincial Committee of the Party in City of Havana, *Granma Weekly Review*, 25 January, pp. 2–4.

—— (1987c) Speech published in *Granma Weekly Review*, 29 November.

—— (1987d) Speech at meeting of the City of Havana Provincial Party, *Granma Weekly Review*, 27 December.

Chamorro, A. (1983) *Algunos Rasgos Hegemónicos del Somocismo y la Revolución Sandinista*, Managua, INIES/CRIES.

Chanda, N. (1984) 'Vietnam in 1983: Keeping Ideology Alive', *Asian Survey*, vol. XXIV, no. 1.

Chernenko, K. (1985) 'The Food Programme in Progress', *Socialism: Theory and Practice*, 2, 139, pp. 5–8.

CIERA (Centre for Research and Studies of the Agrarian Reform), (1980) *Encuesta de Trabajadores del Campo*, (all Managua, CIERA).

—— (1981a) *Las Clases Sociales en el Agro*, CIERA Archive.

—— (1981b) *La Reforma Agraria y el Desarrollo Económico Nacional en la Revolución Popular Sandinista*, mimeo.

—— (1984a) *Directorio de Políticas Alimentarias*, Tomo III del Informe Final del Proyecto Estrategia Alimentaria (CIERA–CIDA–PAN).

—— (1984b) *El ABC del Abastecimiento*, CIERA Archive, vol. 60.

—— (1984c) *La Problemática de la Producción del Maíz y el Frijol y el Problema Campesino: Conclusiones y Sugerencias*, CIERA Archive, vol. 43.

—— (1984d) *Participatory Democracy in Nicaragua*.

—— (1984e) *Managua es Nicaragua: El Impacto de la Capital en el Sistema Alimentario Nacional*.

—— (1985a) *La Capacidad de Gestión del Estado en la Ejecución de Proyectos y Programas Alimentarios-Nutricionales*, CIERA Archive, vol. 61.

—— (1985b) *Nicaragua: El Campesinado Pobre*, CIERA Archive, vol. 63.

—— (1985c) *Estudio de las Cooperativas de Producción*, CIERA Archive, vol. 72.

—— (1986) *Alimentos, Desarrollo y Transición*, draft document prepared for UNRISD's Food Systems and Society Programme.

—— (1987a) *Evaluación del Acceso de los Diferentes Grupos Socio-económicos a los Programas Sociales y Bienes de Consumo Básico en 1986*, CIERA Archive, vol. 78.

—— (1987b) *Evaluación del Efecto de la Liberación del Mercado del Maíz y Frijol en la Siembra de Primera*, CIERA Archive, vol. 78.

—— (1987c) *La Problemática de la Comercialización en Nicaragua*, CIERA Archive, vol. 82.

—— (ed.) (1988) *El Debate Sobre La Reforma Económica*,

—— (1989a) *La Reforma Agraria en Nicaragua, 1979–1989: Economía Campesina*, vol. IV.

—— (1989b) *Evaluación sobre el Sector Agropecuario*, mimeo.

—— (1989c) *La Reforma Agraria en Nicaragua, 1979–1989: Organización y Participación Popular en el Campo*, vol. VI.

—— (1989d) *La Reforma Agraria en Nicaragua, 1979–1989: Cifras y Referencias Documentales*, vol. IX.

—— and DGRA, 1987, *Balance de la Política de Acopio, Precios y Libre Comercio de Maíz y Frijol: primera y postrera, 1986/87*, CIERA Archive, vol. 78.

Cima, R. (1990) 'Vietnam in 1989: Initiating the Post-Cambodia Period', *Asian Survey*, vol. XXX, no. 1., January.

Cliff, J., Kanji, N. and Muller, M. (1986) 'Mozambique Health Holding the Line', *Review of African Political Economy*, no. 36, pp. 7–23.

Colburn, F. D. and de Franco, S. (1985) 'Privilege, Production, and Revolution: The Case of Nicaragua', *Comparative Politics*, vol. 17, no. 3, April, pp. 277–90.

Collins, J. (1985) *Nicaragua: What Difference Could a Revolution Make?*, San Francisco, Institute for Food and Development Policy.

Cook, E. C. (1987) 'Soviet Food Markets: Will the Situation Improve under Gorbachev?', *Comparative Economic Studies*, vol. XXIX, no. 1, Spring, pp. 1–36.

Coraggio, J. L. (1985) *Política Económica y Revolución Popular en Nicaragua: Los Costos Políticos de la Política Económica*, paper presented at IV Nicaraguan Congress of the Social Sciences, Managua, 30–31 August.

—— (1986) 'Economics and Politics in the Transition to Socialism: Reflections on the Nicaraguan Experience', in R. Fagen *et al.* (eds).

Cornia, G. A. and Jespersen, E. (1989) *Crisis, Adjustment and Human Conditions: The Case of Latin America in the 1980s*, paper presented at ISER/UNRISD Seminar on Economic Crisis and the Third World: Impact and Response, Kingston, Jamaica, 3–6 April.

Croll, E. (1982) *The Family Rice Bowl: Food and Domestic Economy in China*, Geneva, UNRISD.

Day, R. (1975) 'Preobrazhensky and the Theory of the Transition Period', *Soviet Studies*, vol. XXVII, no. 2, April, pp. 196–219.

Deere, C. D. (1986) 'Agrarian Reform, Peasant and Rural Production, and the Organization of Production in the Transition to Socialism', in R. Fagen *et al.*, (eds).

—— (1986) *The Peasantry in Political Economy: Trends of the 1980s*, Paper presented at LASA Congress, Boston, 23–25 October.

—— Marchetti, P. and Reinhardt, N. (1985) 'The Peasantry and the Development of Sandinista Agrarian Policy 1979–1984', *Latin American Research Review*, vol. 20, no. 3.

Delgado, R. (1986) *Nicaragua: Los Costos Económicos de la Agresion del*

Gobierno de los Estados Unidos de Norte America, paper presented at V Nicaraguan Congress of the Social Sciences, held Managua 9–12 October.

Deng Xiaoping (1985) *Beijing Review*, no. 39.

Deutscher, I. (1966) *Stalin*, Harmondsworth, Penguin.

Deve, F. and Grenier, P. (1984) *Precios y Subsidios de los Granos Básicos en Nicaragua*, Managua, PAN-MIDINRA.

Díaz, E. (1990) *Cuba: El Socialismo de los Años 90*, Centro de Estudios Sobre el Desarrollo, University of Havana, mimeo.

DGFCDC (Dirección General de Fomento Campesino y Desarrollo Cooperativo), (1988a) *Situación Actual del Abastecimiento Campesino*, Managua, mimeo.

—— (1988b) *Programa Nacional de Fomento a la Producción de Granos Básicos*, Managua, mimeo.

—— (1988c) *La Red de Distribucion en el Campo: Regiones I, V, VI*, Managua, mimeo.

Djilas, M. (1966) *The New Class*, London, Allen and Unwin.

Dolny, H. (1985) 'The Challenge of Agriculture', in J. Saul (ed.).

Dore, E. (1988) *Nicaraguan Agrarian and Commercial Policy 1979–1988: Its Effect on the Peasantry*, paper presented at Symposium on The Nicaraguan Agrarian Reform, Amsterdam, Netherlands, 4–8 July 1988.

Duiker, W. (1985) 'Vietnam in 1984: Between Ideology and Pragmatism', *Asian Survey*, vol. XXV, no. 1, pp. 97–105.

—— (1986) 'Vietnam in 1985: Searching for Solutions', *Asian Survey*, vol. XXVI, no. 1, pp. 107–11.

Dumont, R. (1970) *Cuba: Socialism and Development*, New York, Grove Press.

ECLAC (Economic Commission for Latin America and the Caribbean) (1984) *Notas para el Estudio Económico de America Latina y el Caribe, 1983: Nicaragua*, Mexico City, ECLAC.

—— (1987) *Notas para el Estudio Económico de América Latina y el Caribe, 1986: Nicaragua*, Mexico City, ECLAC.

—— (1990) *Notas para el Estudio Económico de América Latina y el Caribe, 1989: Nicaragua*, Mexico City, ECLAC.

Egero, B. (1987) *Mozambique: A Dream Undone*, Uppsala, Scandinavian Institute of African Studies.

Ellman, M. (1978) 'On a Mistake of Preobrazhensky and Stalin', *Journal of Development Studies*, vol. 14, no. 3, April, pp. 353–6.

—— (1979) *Socialist Planning*, Cambridge University Press.

—— (1981) 'Agricultural Productivity under Socialism', in K. Jameson and C. Wilber (eds).

—— (1984) *Collectivisation, Convergence and Capitalism: Political Economy in a Divided World*, London, Academic Press.

Emmerij, L. (ed.) (1987) *Development Policies and the Crisis of the 1980s*, Paris, OECD Development Centre.

ENABAS, (1984) *Informe Anual 1983*, Managua, ENABAS.

—— (1985) *Informe Anual 1984*, Managua, ENABAS.

Engels, F. (1975) *Anti-Dühring*, Moscow, Progress.

Enriquez, L. (1985) *Social Transformation in Latin America: Tensions between Agro-Export Production and Agrarian Reform in Revolutionary*

Nicaragua, PhD dissertation, University of California, Santa Cruz.
—— and Spalding, R., 1987, 'Banking Systems and Revolutionary Change', in R. Spalding (ed.).
Esterline, J. (1987) 'Vietnam in 1986: An Uncertain Tiger', *Asian Survey*, vol. XXVII, no. 1, pp. 92–103.
—— (1988) 'Vietnam in 1987: Steps Toward Rejuvenation', *Asian Survey*, vol. XXVIII, no. 1, pp. 86–95.
Evans, P., Rueschemeyer, D. and Skocpol, T. (eds) (1985) *Bringing the State Back In*, Cambridge University Press.
Fagen, R., Deere, C. D. and Coraggio, J. L. (eds) (1986) *Transition and Development: Problems of Third World Socialism*, New York, Monthly Review Press/Center for the Study of the Americas.
FAO (Food and Agriculture Organisation (of United Nations)) (1986) *1985 FAO Production Yearbook*, vol. 39, Rome, FAO.
Faune, A. (1986) *Resistencia Campesina a la Agresión Imperialista: Clave de la Derrota Estratégica*, paper presented at V Nicaraguan Congress of the Social Sciences, Managua 9–12 October.
Fforde, A. (1984) *Coping with the State: Peasant Strategies in North Vietnam*, London, Birkbeck College Discussion Paper no. 155.
—— (1985) *Reflections of the 'Vietnamese Socialist Revolution'*, London, Birkbeck College Discussion Paper no. 168.
—— and Paine, S. H. (1987) *The Limits of National Liberation*, London, Croom Helm.
Fine, B. (1985) 'On the Political Economy of Socialism: Theoretical Considerations with Reference to Non-European and European Experience', in D. Banerjee (ed.) *Marxian Theory and the Third World*, New Delhi, Sage Publications.
Fitzgerald, E. V. K. (1985a) 'Agrarian Reform as a Model of Accumulation: the Case of Nicaragua since 1979', *Journal of Development Studies*, vol. 22, no. 1.
—— (1985b) 'The Problem of Balance in the Peripheral Socialist Economy: A Conceptual Note', in G. White and E. Croll (eds), *World Development*, vol. 13, no. 1, January.
—— (1985c) *La Economía Nacional en 1985*, paper presented at the IV Nicaraguan Congress of the Social Sciences, held Managua, August.
—— (1986) 'Notes on the Analysis of the Small Underdeveloped Economy in Transition', in R. Fagen *et al.* (eds).
—— (1987a) 'An Evaluation of the Economic Costs to Nicaragua of U.S. Aggression', in R. Spalding (ed.) (1987).
—— (1987b) 'Notas sobre las fuerzas de trabajo y la estructura de clases en Nicaragua', *Revista Nicaragüense de Ciencias Sociales*, no. 2, March.
—— (1988a) 'State Accumulation and Market Equilibria: an Application of Kalecki–Kornai Analysis to Planned Economies in the Third World', mimeo, in E. V. K. Fitzgerald and M. Wuyts (eds) (1988a).
—— (1988b) 'Problems in Financing a Revolution: Accumulation, Defence and Income Distribution in Nicaragua 1979–86', in E. V. K. Fitzgerald and R. Vos (eds), *Financing Economic Development: a Structuralist Approach to Monetary Policy*, London, Gower.

—— (1988c) 'State and Economy in Nicaragua', *IDS Bulletin*, vol. 19, no. 3., July, pp. 17–23.

—— (1989) *Economic Crisis and Transition on the Periphery: The Case of Nicaragua*, paper presented at UNRISD/ISER seminar on Economic Crisis and Third World Countries: Impact and Response, Kingston, Jamaica, 3–6 April.

—— and Wuyts M. (eds) (1988a) *The Market within Planning: Socialist Economic Management in the Third World*, London, Frank Cass.

—— (1988b) 'The Debate on Economic Strategy in Third World Socialism', Editors' Introduction in E. V. K. Fitzgerald and M. Wuyts (eds).

Florez-Estrada, M. and Lobo, J. (1986) 'La Consigna es Sobrevivir', *Pensamiento Propio*, no. 33, June, pp. 25–9.

FRELIMO (1977) *Central Committee Report to the Third Congress of FRELIMO*, London; Mozambique, Angola, and Guine Information Centre.

—— (1983) *Draft Theses for the Fourth Congress of the FRELIMO Party*, Maputo, Agencia de Informacao de Mozambique.

Frente Estudiantíl Revolucionario (FER) (1972) *El Programa Histórico del FSLN*, Managua.

Friedmann, H. (1980) 'Household Production and the National Economy: Concepts for the Analysis of Agrarian Formations', *Journal of Peasant Studies*, vol. 7, no. 2, January, pp. 158–83.

Friedrich, C. J. and Brzezinski, Z. K. (1956) *Totalitarian Dictatorship and Autocracy*, Cambridge, Harvard University Press.

Gao Shangquan (1987) 'Progress in Economic Reform (1979–86)', *Beijing Review*, vol. 30, no. 27, 6 July.

Ghai, D., Kay, C. and Peek, P. (1986) *Labour and Development in Rural Cuba*, Geneva, ILO.

Ghose, A. K. (1984) 'The New Development Strategy and Rural Reforms in Post-Mao China', in K. Griffin, (ed.), *Institutional Reform and Economic Development in the Chinese Countryside*, London, Macmillan.

Glazunov, Y. (1987) 'Vietnam at the Stage of Innovation', *Socialism: Theory and Practice*, no. 7, pp. 58–65.

Goldin, I. and Pizarro, R. (1988) 'Perspectives on Nicaragua's Foreign Trade', *IDS Bulletin*, vol. 19, no. 3, July, pp. 24–31.

Goodman, D. and Redclift, M. (1981) *From Peasant to Proletarian: Capitalist Development and Agrarian Transitions*, Oxford, Basil Blackwell.

Gordon, A. (1978) 'The Role of Class Struggle in Rural Vietnam', *Monthly Review*, vol. 29, no. 8, pp. 22–34.

—— (1982) *The 'End' of Class Struggle in Rural Vietnam Since 1975: Some Implications in the Light of Contemporary Practice and Forms of Rural Property*, paper presented at the Third TNI Seminar on Transition to Socialism 'A Critical Examination of the Vietnamese Experience since 1975', Amsterdam, Transnational Institute.

Granma Weekly Review (GWR) 1981: 31 May; 1986: 11 January, 18 May, 29 June, 6 July, 14 September; 5 October; 1987: 11 January, 24 May; 1988: 10 January.

Gramsci, A. (1971) *Selections from the Prison Notebooks*, edited and translated by Q. Hoare and G. N. Smith, London, Lawrence and Wishart.

Gray, J. (1982) 'Conclusion', in J. Gray and G. White (eds), *China's New Development Strategy*, London, Academic Press.

Griffin, K. and James, J. (1981) *The Transition to Egalitarian Development: Economic Policies for Structural Change in the Third World*, London, Macmillan.

Guardian Weekly (1988) 'Soviet Farmers Struggle with a Failed System', 23 October, p. 18.

Gutiérrez, R. (1989) 'La Política Económica de la Revolución (1979–1989)', *Revolución y Desarrollo* no. 5, Managua, CIERA.

Hanlon, J. (1984) *Mozambique: The Revolution under Fire*, London, Zed Books.

Harris, R. and Vilas, C. (eds) (1985) *La Revolución en Nicaragua*, Mexico City, Ediciones Era.

Harriss, J. (ed.) (1982) *Rural Development: Theories of Peasant Economy and Agrarian Change*, London, Hutchinson.

Hayek, F. (ed.) (1935) *Collectivist Economic Planning*, London, Routledge.

—— (1949) *Individualism and Economic Order*, London, Routledge & Kegan Paul.

Hindess, B. (1976) 'Introduction', in C. Bettelheim.

Holmes, L. (1986) *Politics in the Communist World*, Oxford, Clarendon Press.

Hopkins, M. and Van Der Hoeven, R. (1983) *Basic Needs in Development Planning*, Aldershot, Hants, Gower Publishing House.

Hough, J. (1972) 'The Soviet System: Petrification or Pluralism?', *Problems of Communism*, vol. XXI, no. 2, pp. 25–45.

IFAD (1980) *Informe de la Mision, Especial de Programacion a Nicaragua*, Rome.

IHCA (Instituto Historico Centroamericano) (1985) 'The Nicaraguan Peasantry Gives A New Direction to Agrarian Reform', *ENVIO*, no. 51, September, pp. 1c–19c.

—— (1986a) 'Slow Motion Toward a Survival Economy', *ENVIO*, no. 63, pp. 13–38.

—— (1986b) 'Crisis Economica: Como Sobrevive Managua', *ENVIO*, no. 66, December, pp. 21–41.

—— (1987a) 'Rural Workers Confront the Economic Crisis', *ENVIO*, no. 71, May, pp. 24–33.

—— (1987b) 'Cooperativas: un nuevo giro', *ENVIO*, no. 72, June, pp. 13–38.

—— (1987c) 'Mas Cerca de la Paz: 3 Mil Días de Revolución', *ENVIO*, no. 73, July, pp. 16–45.

—— (1988) 'Sandinista Unions Take Stock', *ENVIO*, no. 79, January, pp. 27–37.

—— (1989a) 'La Organización Campesina', *ENVIO*, no. 93, May, pp. 30–43.

—— (1989b) 'From a Mixed Up Economy Toward a Socialist Mixed Economy', *ENVIO*, no. 94, May, pp. 33–54.

INEC (Instituto Nicaragüense de Estadísticas y Censos) (1989) *Nicaragua: 10 Años en Cifras*, Managua, INEC.

INIES (Instituto Nicaragüense de Investigaciones Económicas y Sociales)/

SPP (Secretaría de Planificación y Presupuesto) (1987) *Plan Económico 1987*, Managua, INIES.

Invernizzi, G., Pisani, F. and Ceberio, J. (1986) *Sandinistas*, Managua, Editorial Vanguardia.

Irvin, G. (1983) 'Nicaragua: Establishing the State as the Centre of Accumulation', *Cambridge Journal of Economics*, no. 7, pp. 125–39.

—— and Croes, E. (1988) 'Nicaragua: The Accumulation Trap', *IDS Bulletin*, vol. 19, no. 3, July, pp. 32–9.

Isaacman, A. and Isaacman, B. (1983) *Mozambique: From Colonialism to Revolution, 1900–82*, Boulder.

Jameson, K. and Wilber, C. (eds) (1978) *Directions in Economic Development*, Notre Dame, University of Notre Dame Press.

—— (eds) (1981) Socialist Models of Development, Special Issue of *World Development*, vol. 9, nos. 9/10.

Jessop, B. (1982) *The Capitalist State*, Oxford, Martin Robertson.

Jiménez, A. C. (1987) 'Worker Incentives in Cuba', *World Development*, vol. 15, no. 1.

JUCEPLAN (1975) *Anuario Estadístico de Cuba*, Havana, JUCEPLAN.

Kaimowitz, D. (1986a) 'Nicaraguan Debates on Agrarian Structure and their Implications for Agricultural Policy and the Rural Poor', *The Journal of Peasant Studies*, vol. 14, no. 1, October.

—— (1986b) *Agrarian Structure in Nicaragua and its Implications for Policies Towards the Rural Poor*, PhD dissertation, University of Wisconsin, Madison.

—— (1988) 'Agricultural Cooperatives in Nicaragua: A New Flexibility', *IDS Bulletin*, vol. 19, no. 3, July, pp. 47–52.

Kalecki, M. (1986) *Selected Essays on Economic Planning*, Cambridge University Press.

Kleiterp, N. (1988) *Implementing a New Model of Accumulation: The Case of Nicaragua*, Working Paper – Sub-series on Money, Finance and Development – no. 22, Institute of Social Studies, The Hague.

Kornai, J. (1980) *The Economics of Shortage*, Amsterdam, North Holland.

—— (1986) *Contradictions and Dilemmas*, Cambridge, Mass., MIT.

Kornbluh, P. (1987) *Nicaragua: The Price of Intervention*, Washington DC, Institute for Policy Studies.

Laclau, E. and Mouffe, C. (1985) *Hegemony and Socialist Strategy: Towards a Radical Democratic Politics*, London, Verso.

Lawson, C. (1988) 'Soviet Economic Aid to Africa', *African Affairs*, vol. 87, no. 349, pp. 501–18.

Lehmann, D. (1985) 'Smallholding Agriculture in Revolutionary Cuba: A Case of Under-Exploitation?', *Development and Change*, vol. 16, no. 2, pp. 251–70.

Lenin, V. I. (1965) 'Report on the Substitution of a Tax in Kind for the Surplus-Grain Appropriation System', *Collected Works*, vol. 32, Progress Publishers, Moscow.

—— (1965/66) *Collected Works*, vols. 29, 32, 33, Moscow, Progress Publishers.

LeoGrande, W. (1981) 'Two Decades of Socialism in Cuba', *Latin American Research Review*, vol. XVI, no. 1, pp. 187–206.

Le Hong Tam (1984) 'Vietnam: Building Industrial–Agricultural Complexes', in Ngo Manh-Lan (ed.), *Unreal Growth: Critical Studies on Asian Development*, vol. 1, Delhi, Hindustan Publishing Corp.

Limqueco, P. and McFarlane, B. (1979) 'Problems of Economic Planning for Underdeveloped Socialist Countries', *Journal of Contemporary Asia*, vol. 9, no. 1, pp. 5–26.

Littlejohn, G. (1979) 'State, plan and market in the transition to socialism: the legacy of Bukharin', *Economy and Society*, vol. 8, no. 2, May, pp. 206–39.

—— (1988) 'Central Planning and Market Relations in Socialist Societies', mimeo, in E. V. K. Fitzgerald and M. Wuyts (eds).

Lowy, M. (1986) 'Mass Organization, Party and State: Democracy in its Transition to Socialism', in Fagen *et al.*

Luciak, I. (1987) 'Popular Democracy in the New Nicaragua: The Case of a Rural Mass Organization', *Comparative Politics*, vol. 20, no. 1, October.

Luxmoore, J. (1983) 'Vietnam: The Dilemmas of Reconstruction', *Conflict Studies*, no. 147, pp. 1–26.

MacEwan, A. (1981) *Revolution and Economic Development*, London, Macmillan.

Mackintosh, M. (1985) 'Economic Tactics: Commercial Policy and the Socialization of African Agriculture', *World Development*, vol. 13, no. 1.

—— (1986) 'Economic Policy Context and Adjustment Options in Mozambique', *Development and Change*, vol. 17, pp. 557–81.

—— 1987, *Agricultural Marketing and Socialist Accumulation: A Case Study of Maize Marketing in Mozambique*, Development Policy and Practice Working Paper no. 1, Milton Keynes, Open University.

—— and Wuyts, M. (1988) 'Accumulation, Social Services and Socialist Transition in the Third World: Reflections on Decentralised Planning based on the Mozambican Experience', mimeo, in E. V. K. Fitzgerald and M. Wuyts (eds).

McWilliams, E. (1983) 'Vietnam in 1982: Onward into the Quagmire', *Asian Survey*, vol. XXIII, no. 1, pp. 62–72.

Mandel, D. (1988) 'Economic Reform and Democracy in the Soviet Union', *The Socialist Register 1988*, pp. 132–53.

Mandel, E. (1986) 'In Defence of Socialist Planning', *New Left Review*, no. 159, September/October, pp. 5–37.

Marchetti, P. and Jerez, C. (1988) 'Democracy and Militarisation: War and Development', *IDS Bulletin*, vol. 19, no. 3, pp. 1–11.

Marx, K. and Engels, F. (1940) *The Civil War in France: The Paris Commune*, New York, International Publishers.

—— (1984) 'Critique of the Gotha Programme', in *Basic Writings on Politics and Philosophy*, London, Fontana/Collins.

—— (1984) 'The Eighteenth Brumaire of Louis Bonaparte', Ibid.

Massey, D. (1987) *Nicaragua*, Milton Keynes, Open University Press.

MED (Ministerio de Educacion) (1987) *Documento Nacional Sobre la Educacion en Nicaragua en el Marco del Proyecto Principal de Educacion*, 1980–86, Managua, MED.

Medal, J. L. (1985) *La Revolucion Nicaraguense: Balance Economico y Alternativas Futuras*, Managua, CINASE.

—— (1988) *Nicaragua: Crisis, Cambio Social y Política Económica*, Managua, CINASE.

Mesa Lago, C. (1971) 'Economic Policies and Growth', in C. Mesa Lago (ed.), *Revolutionary Change in Cuba*, Pittsburgh.

—— (1978) *Cuba in the 1970s: Pragmatism and Institutionalization*, Albuquerque, University of New Mexico Press.

—— (1981) *The Economy of Socialist Cuba: A Two Decade Appraisal*, Albuquerque, Universtiy of New Mexico Press.

—— (1989) 'Cuba's Economic Counter-Reform (Rectificación): Causes, Policies and Effects', *Journal of Communist Studies*, vol. 5, no. 4. December, pp. 98–139.

Meszaros, I. (1979) 'Political Power and Dissent in Post-revolutionary Societies', in Ink Links Ltd (ed.), *Power and Opposition in Postrevolutionary Societies*, London, Ink Links Ltd.

Meyer, A. (1967) 'The Comparative Study of Communist Political Systems', *Slavic Review*, vol. XXVI, no. 1, pp. 3–12.

MICOIN (Ministerio de Comercio Interior) (1983) *Sistemas de Comercialización: Aspectos Globales*, vol. I, Managua, MICOIN.

—— (1987) *Evaluación de las Políticas de Abastecimiento Nacional de 1986*, Managua, MICOIN.

MIDINRA (Ministerio de Desarrollo Agropecuario y Reforma Agraria) (1983) *Marco Estratégico de Desarrollo Agropecuario*, Managua, MIDINRA.

—— (1984) 'Problemas y Perspectivas de la Migración Campo-Ciudad', *Revolución y Desarrollo*, no. 3, pp. 19–23.

—— (1986) *Organización Territorial de la Producción*, vol. 80, Managua, CIERA Archive.

—— (1987) *Plan de Trabajo 1987: Balance y Perspectivas*, Managua, MIDINRA.

—— (1990) 'Plan de Emergencia y Reactivación del Sector Agropecuario: Programa de Seguridad Alimentaria', mimeo.

Millar, J. R. (1978) 'A Note on Primitive Accumulation in Marx and Preobrazhensky', *Soviet Studies*, vol. XXX, no. 3, July, pp. 384–93.

—— and Nove, A. (1976) 'A Debate on Collectivization: Was Stalin Really Necessary?', *Problems of Communism*, vol. XXV, July/August, pp. 49–62.

MIPLAN (Ministerio de Planificación) (1980) *Programa de Reactivación Económica en Beneficio del Pueblo*, Managua, MIPLAN.

—— (1981) *Programa Económico de Austeridad y Eficiencia*, Managua, MIPLAN.

Mises L. von (1935) 'Economic Calculation in the Socialist Commonwealth', in Hayek (ed.).

Mkandawire, T. (1989) *Crisis and Adjustment in Sub-Saharan Africa*, paper presented at ISER/UNRISD Seminar on Economic Crisis and Third World Countries: Impact and Response, Kingston, Jamaica, 3–6 April.

Molina, C., Morales, O. and Neira, O. (1985) *Los Terminos Económicos de la Alianza Obrera-Campesina: El Caso de los Precios Relativos*, paper presented at IV Nicaraguan Congress of the Social Sciences, Managua, 30–31 August.

Moore Lappe, F. and Beccar-Varela, A. (1980) *Mozambique and Tanzania:*

Asking the Big Questions, San Francisco, Institute for Food and Development Policy.

Morawetz, D. (1980) 'Economic Lessons from Some Small Socialist Developing Countries, *World Development*, vol. 8, nos. 5/6, May/June, pp. 337–69.

Mouffe, C. (ed.) (1979) *Gramsci and Marxist Theory*, London, Routledge & Kegan Paul.

Munslow, B. (1984) 'State Intervention in Agriculture: the Mozambican Experience', *Journal of Modern African Studies*, vol. 22, no. 2, pp. 199–221.

New Internationalist, (1989) *'Mozambique: The Right to Survive'*, no. 192, February.

Ngo Vinh Long (1989) 'Vietnam: The Real Enemy', *Bulletin of Concerned Asian Scholars*, vol. 21, nos. 2–4, pp. 6–34.

Nguyen Huu Dong (1982) 'Collective and Family Agriculture in Socialist Economies', *IDS Bulletin*, vol. 13, no. 4, pp. 23–8.

Nguyen Tien Hung (1977) *Economic Development of Socialist Vietnam, 1955–80*, New York, Praeger.

Nove, A. (1969) *An Economic History of the U.S.S.R.*, London, Allen Lane.

—— (1972) 'Market Socialism and its Critics', *Soviet Studies*, vol. XXIV, July, pp. 120–38.

—— (1983) *The Economics of Feasible Socialism*, London, Allen & Unwin.

—— (1988) 'The Muscovite Marketeers', *New Socialist*, May/June pp. 11–13.

Nuñez, D. (1987) 'Intervención de Daniel Nuñez', *Economía y Revolución*, no. 1, October, pp. 42–6.

—— (1989) 'A 8 Años la Union Nacional de Agricultores y Ganaderos', *Cuadernos de Sociología*, Managua, no. 9–10, January–June, pp. 95–105.

Nuñez, O. (1980) *El Somocismo y el Modelo Capitalista Agroexportador*, Managua, UNAN.

—— (1987) *Transición y Lucha de Clases en Nicaragua 1979–1986*, Mexico, CRIES/Siglo XXI.

—— (1989) 'Reforma Económica y Orientación Socialista de la Revolución', *Revolución Desarrollo*, no. 4, January–March, pp. 5–16, Managua.

Nuti, D. M. (1981) 'Socialism on Earth', *Cambridge Journal of Economics*, vol. 5, pp. 391–403.

OECD (1987) *Geographical Distribution of Financial Flows to Developing Countries 1982–85*, Paris, OECD.

O'Laughlin, B. (1981) 'A Questão Agraria em Moçambique', *Estudos Mocambicanos*, no. 3, pp. 9–32.

Ortega, D. (1986) *Liñeas Del Plan Técnico Económico 1986*, Managua, Dirección de Información y Prensa de la Presidencia de la República de Nicaragua.

Ottaway, M. (1988) 'Mozambique: From Symbolic Socialism to Symbolic Reform', *Journal of Modern African Studies*, vol. 26, no. 2, pp. 211–26.

Perry, E. J. (1985) 'Rural Violence in Socialist China', *China Quarterly*, 103, September, pp. 393–413.

—— and Wong, C. (eds) (1985) *The Political Economy of Reform in Post-Mao China*, London, Harvard University Press.

Petras, J. and Selden, M. (1981) 'Social Classes, the State and the World

System in the Transition to Socialism, *Journal of Contemporary Asia*, vol. 11, pp. 189–207.

Phipps, M. (1989) *State–Trade Union Interrelations in Nicaragua 1979–86*, Ph D dissertation, University of Essex, Colchester.

Pinsky, B. (1985) 'Territorial Dilemmas: Changing Urban Life', in J. Saul (ed.).

Pizarro, R., (1987) 'The New Economic Policy: A Necessary Readjustment', in R. Spalding (ed.).

Post, K. (1982) *The Trajectory and Contradictions of the Vietnamese Revolution*, paper presented at the Third TNI Seminar, Transnational Institute, Amsterdam.

Poulantzas, N. (1978) *State, Power, Socialism*, London, New Left Books.

Preobrazhensky, E. (1965) *The New Economics*, Oxford University Press.

Raikes, P. (1984) 'Food Policy and Production in Mozambique since Independence', *Review of African Political Economy*, no. 29., pp. 95–107.

Ramirez Cruz, J. (1984) 'El sector cooperativo en la agricultura cubana', *Cuba Socialista*, vol. IV, no. 2, pp. 1–24.

Recarte, A. (1980) *Cuba: economia y poder (1959–1980)*, Madrid, Alianza Editorial.

Riskin, C. (1987) 'A Comment on Professor Brus' Paper', in L. Emmerij (ed.).

Ritter, A. (1974) *The Economic Development of Revolutionary Cuba*, New York, Praeger.

Rodriguez, J. L. (1987) 'Agricultural Policy and Development in Cuba', *World Development*, vol. 15, no. 1.

Roesch, O. (1984) 'Peasants and Collective Agriculture in Mozambique', in Barker, J. (ed.), *The Politics of Agriculture in Tropical Africa*, Beverly Hills, Sage Publications.

Ruccio, D. (1987) 'The State and Planning in Nicaragua', in R. Spalding (ed.).

Ruchwarger, G. (1987) *People in Power: Forging a Grassroots Democracy in Nicaragua*, South Hadley, Mass., Bergin and Harvey.

—— (1988) 'The Campesion Road to Socialism? The Sandinistas and Rural Cooperatives', *The Socialist Register 1988*, pp. 220–43.

Rutland, P. (1985) *The Myth of the Plan: Lessons of Soviet Planning Experience*, London, Hutchinson.

Saith, A. (1985) '"Primitive Accumulation", Agrarian Reform and Socialist Transitions: An Argument', in A. Saith (ed.), *The Agrarian Question in Socialist Transitions*, London, Frank Cass.

Sandbrook, R. (1989) *Economic Crisis, Structural Adjustment and the State in Sub-Saharan Africa*, paper presented at ISER/UNRISD Seminar on Economic Crisis and Third World Countries: Impact and Response, Kingston, Jamaica, 3–6 April.

Saul, J. (ed.) (1985) *A Difficult Road: The Transition to Socialism in Mozambique*, New York, Monthly Review Press.

Saulniers, A. (1986) *State Trading Organizations in Expansion: A Case Study of ENABAS in Nicaragua*, paper prepared for XIII International Congress of the Latin American Studies Association, Boston, 23–25 October.

Schejtman, A. (1983) *Lineamientos para el Analisis Integral de los Problemas*

Alimentarios Nacionales, paper presented at First (Nicaraguan) Food Strategy Seminar, Managua, February.

Schnytzer, A. (1982), 'The Socialist Republic of Vietnam', in P. Wiles (ed.).

Schroeder, G. E. (1988) 'Property Rights Issues in Economic Reforms in Socialist Countries', *Studies in Comparative Communism*, vol. XXI, no. 2, Summer, pp. 175–88.

Schvarzer, J. (1989) *The Inescapable Interrelationship between Crisis, Debt and the Opening up of the Economy*, paper presented at ISER/UNRISD Seminar on Economic Crisis and Third World Countries: Impact and Response, Kingston, Jamaica, 3–6 April.

Schulz, D. E. (1981) 'Political Participation in Communist Systems: The Conceptual Frontier', in D. E. Schulz and J. E. Adams (eds.).

—— and Adams, J. S. (eds) (1981) *Political Participation in Communist Systems*, New York, Pergamon Press.

Scott, C. (1988) 'Socialism and the "Soft State" in Africa: an Analysis of Angola and Mozambique', *Journal of Modern African Studies*, vol. 26, no. 1, pp. 23–36.

Serra, L. (1988) 'Un Proyecto Impulsado Desde la Base, *Pensamiento Propio*, no. 52, July/August, pp. 32–5.

Šik, O. (1981) *The Communist Power System*, New York, Praeger.

Simon, R. (1982) *Gramsci's Political Thought*, London, Lawrence and Wishart.

Skinner, G. W. (1985) 'Rural Marketing in China: Repression and Revival', *The China Quarterly*, no. 103, September, pp. 393–413.

Skocpol, T. (1987) *Explaining Social Provision in Western Nations: A Polity-Centred Approach*, The Fourth Fuller Bequest Lecture, University of Essex.

Spalding, R. (ed.) (1987) *The Political Economy of Revolutionary Nicaragua*, Boston, Mass., George Allen & Unwin.

Spoor, M. (1985) *The Economy of North Vietnam, The First Ten Years: 1955–1964*, MPhil. thesis, Institute of Social Studies, The Hague.

—— (1988) 'Reforming State Finance in Post-1975 Vietnam', mimeo, in V. K. Fitzgerald and M. Wuyts (eds.).

—— (1989) *Un Inventario de las Politicas Agrarias para los Granos Básicos en Nicaragua*, Managua, PAN.

Stahler-Sholk, R. (1985) *Politica Salarial en Nicaragua 1979–1985*, Managua, mimeo.

—— (1986) *La Normacion del Trabajo en Nicaragua 1983–1986*, paper presented at V Nicaraguan Congress of the Social Sciences, Managua, 9–12 October.

—— (1990) 'Ajuste y el Sector Agropecuario en Nicaragua en los 80: una Evaluación Preliminar' in M. Arana, *et al.* (eds).

—— and Spoor, M. (1989) *Nicaragua: Las Políticas Macroeconómicas y sus Efectos en la Agricultura y la Seguridad Alimentaria*, Managua, PAN/CADESCA.

State Department, United States' Government (1985) *Talking Points on Nicaragua's Economic Crisis*, Washington DC, mimeo.

Stern, L. (1987) 'The Scramble Toward Revitalization: The Vietnamese

Communist Party and the Economic Reform Program', *Asian Survey*, vol. XXVII, no. 4, pp. 477–93.

Streeten, P. (1979) 'From Growth to Basic Needs', in *Basic Needs Strategy as a Planning Parameter*, seminar proceedings, German Foundation for International Development, West Berlin.

Stubbs, J. (1989) *Cuba: The Test of Time*, London, Latin American Bureau.

Szajowski, B. (ed.) (1981) *Marxist Governments: A World Survey*, New York, St Martin's Press.

Timmer, P. C. (1980) 'Food Prices and Food Policy Analysis in LDCs', *Food Policy* vol. 5, no. 3, August, pp. 188–99.

—— Falcon, W. and Pearson, S. (1983) *Food Policy Analysis*, Baltimore, Md., Johns Hopkins University Press.

Timossi, G. (1989) *Centroamérica: Deuda Externa y Ajuste Estructural*, Havana, CRIES/CEA.

Torres, R. M. and Coraggio, J. L. (1987) *Transición y Crisis en Nicaragua*, San José, ICADIS.

Trotsky, L. (1967) *The Revolution Betrayed*, London, New Park.

Turits, R. (1987) 'Trade, Debt, and the Cuban Economy', *World Development*, vol. 15, no. 1, pp. 163–81.

UCA (Escuela de Sociología de la Universidad Centroamericana), (1986) 'La Estrategia de Sobrevivencia de los Sectores Populares de Managua y el Impacto del Mensaje Económico Gubernamental', *Encuentro*, no. 29, September–December, pp. 47–83.

UNAG (Union Nacional de Agricultores y Ganaderos) (1987) 'UNAG a 6 Años de su Fundación', *Productores*, no. 1, May/June, pp. 2–7.

Utting, P. (1983) *La Participación Popular en el Abastecimiento Urbano: El Caso de Managua*, Managua, mimeo.

—— (1985) *Limits to Change in a Post-Revolutionary Society: The Rise and Fall of Cheap Food Policy*, Managua, mimeo.

—— (1987) 'Domestic Supply and Food Shortages', in R. Spalding (ed.).

—— (1989) *The Political Economy of Food Pricing and Marketing Reforms in Nicaragua*, paper presented at UNRISD seminar on Food Pricing and Marketing Reforms, Geneva, 20–22 November.

—— (1990a) *Crisis, Reform and Participation in Nicaragua*, paper presented at UNRISD seminar on Social Participation in the Context of Restructuring and Liberalization in Eastern Europe and the Soviet Union, Geneva, 21–23 May.

—— (1990b) *Economic Adjustment and the Nicaraguan Food System*, UNRISD forthcoming.

Vergara, R., Castro, J. and Barry, D. (1986) *Nicaragua: país sitiado*, Managua, CRIES.

Vilas, C. (1984) *La Revolución Sandinista*, Buenos Aires, Legasa.

—— (1986a) *El Impacto de la Transición Revolucionaria en las Clases Populares: La Clase Obrera en la Revolución Sandinista*, paper presented at V Nicaraguan Congress of the Social Sciences, Managua, 9–12 October.

—— (1986b) 'The Mass Organizations in Nicaragua: The Current Problematic and Perspectives for the Future', *Monthly Review*, November.

—— (1986c) *La Construcción Popular del Estado Multiétnico*, paper presented at V Nicaraguan Congress of the Social Sciences, Managua, 9–12 October.

—— (1986d) 'Sobre la Estrategia Económica de la Revolución Sandinista', *Desarrollo Económico*, vol. 26, no. 101, April–June, pp. 121–42.

Weeks, J. (1988) *Private Entrepreneurship in a Revolutionary Context: A Case Study*, mimeo, Middlebury College, Vermont.

Werner, J. (1984) 'Socialist Development: The Political Economy of Agrarian Reform in Vietnam', *Bulletin of Concerned Asian Scholars*.

Wheelock, J. (1975) *Imperialismo y Dictadura*, Mexico City, Siglo XXI.

—— (1984) May Day Speech, printed in *Barricada*, 2 May.

—— (1985) *Entre la Crisis y la Agresión: La Reforma Agraria Sandinista*, Managua, Editorial Nueva Nicaragua.

—— (1986) 'Balance y Perspectivas de las Políticas de la Revolución en el Campo', in *Líneas para el Fortalecimiento de la Alianza con el Campesinado*, DAP/FSLN, Managua.

White, C. (1982a) *Debates in Vietnamese Development Policy*, Discussion Paper no. 171, University of Sussex, Institute of Development Studies.

—— (1982b) 'Socialist Transformation of Agriculture and Gender Relations: the Vietnamese Case', *IDS Bulletin*, vol. 13, no. 4, pp. 44–51.

—— (1983) 'Recent Debates in Vietnamese Development Policy', in G. White *et al.* (eds).

—— (1985) 'Agricultural Planning, Pricing Policy and Co-operatives in Vietnam', *World Development*, vol. 13, no. 1, pp. 97–114.

White, G. (1983a) 'Chinese Development Strategy After Mao', in G. White *et al.* (eds).

—— (1983b) 'Revolutionary Socialist Development in the Third World: An Overview', in G. White *et al.* (eds), ibid.

—— (1985a) 'The Impact of Economic Reforms in the Chinese Countryside: Towards the Politics of Social Capitalism?', mimeo.

—— (1985b) *Cuban Planning in the Mid 1980s: centralisation, decentralisation and participation*, University of Sussex, Institute of Development Studies, Discussion Paper 209.

—— Murray, R. and White, C. (eds) (1983) *Revolutionary Socialist Development in the Third World*, Brighton Sussex, Harvester Press.

Wilczynski, J. (1981) *An Encyclopedic Dictionary of Marxism, Socialism and Communism*, London, Macmillan.

Wiles, P. (ed.) (1982) *The New Communist Third World*, New York, St Martin's Press.

Wilson, P. (1987) 'Regionalization and Decentralization in Nicaragua', *Latin American Perspectives*, Issue 53, vol. 14, no. 2, Spring, pp. 237–54.

World Bank (1986a) *Poverty and Hunger: Issues and Options for Food Security in Developing Countries*, Washington DC, The World Bank.

—— (1986b) *World Development Report 1986*, Oxford University Press.

—— (1987) *World Development Report 1987*, Oxford University Press.

Wuyts, M. (1985) 'Money, Planning and Rural Transformation in Mozambique', in A. Saith (ed.).

—— (1989) *Economic Management and Adjustment Policies in Mozambique*, paper presented at ISER/UNRISD seminar.

Xue Muqiao (1987) 'Socialism and Planned Commodity Economy', *Beijing Review*, vol. 30, no. 33, August 17.

Zalkin, M. (1985) *Peasant Response to State Intervention in the Production of Basic Grains in Nicaragua: 1979–1984*, PhD dissertation, University of Massachusetts, Amherst.

—— (1987) 'Food Policy and Class Transformation in Revolutionary Nicaragua, 1979–1986', *World Development*, vol. 15, no. 7.

—— (1988a) *Estructura de Clases y el Campesinado Nicaraguense: 1980 Una Nueva Interpretacion*, Managua, CIERA.

—— (1988b) 'Campesinado Medio: Los Olvidados', *Pensamiento Propio*, no. 55, November, pp. 8–14.

Zamora, C. (1987) 'El Campesino es el Sujeto Principal', *Pensamiento Propio*, no. 42, May, pp. 37–41.

Zimbalist, A. (1989) 'Incentives and Planning in Cuba', *Latin American Research Review*, vol. XXIV, no. 1, pp. 65–93.

—— and Eckstein, S. (1987) 'Patterns of Cuban Development: The First Twenty-five Years', *World Development*, vol. 15, no. 1.

Other Sources

Africa South, AED, *Beijing Review*, *Far Eastern Economic Review* (FEER), *The Economist*, *Financial Times* (FT), *Granma*, *New African*, *Vietnam Courier*, *Yearbook on International Communist Affairs* (YICA).

Nicaragua:

Barricada; *Pensamiento Propio*; statistical bulletins of the Nicaraguan Institute for Statistics and Censuses (INEC), the Ministry of Foreign Trade and the Ministry of Agricultural Development and Agrarian Reform; data bank of the Centre for Research and Studies of the Agrarian Reform (CIERA).

Index